ROUTLEDGE LIBRARY EDITIONS:
EARLY WESTERN RESPONSES
TO SOVIET RUSSIA

Volume 12

NEW RUSSIA

NEW RUSSIA

ANATOLE DE MONZIE

Routledge
Taylor & Francis Group
LONDON AND NEW YORK

First published in French in 1931 under the title 'Petit Manuel de la Russie Nouvelle'
First published in Great Britain in 1932 by George Allen & Unwin Ltd

This edition first published in 2018
by Routledge
2 Park Square, Milton Park, Abingdon, Oxon OX14 4RN

and by Routledge
605 Third Avenue, New York, NY 10017

Routledge is an imprint of the Taylor & Francis Group, an informa business

British Library Cataloguing in Publication Data
A catalogue record for this book is available from the British Library

ISBN: 978-1-138-04993-2 (Set)
ISBN: 978-1-315-11072-1 (Set) (ebk)
ISBN: 978-1-138-08488-9 (Volume 12) (hbk)
ISBN: 978-1-315-11161-2 (Volume 12) (ebk)

Publisher's Note
The publisher has gone to great lengths to ensure the quality of this reprint but points out that some imperfections in the original copies may be apparent.

Disclaimer
The publisher has made every effort to trace copyright holders and would welcome correspondence from those they have been unable to trace.

Due to modern production methods, it has not been possible to reproduce the fold-out maps within the book. Please visit www.routledge.com to view them.

NEW RUSSIA

by

ANATOLE DE MONZIE

Translated by

R. J. S. CURTIS

LONDON
GEORGE ALLEN & UNWIN LTD
MUSEUM STREET

The French original, "Petit Manuel de la Russie Nouvelle," was published in Paris in 1931.

FIRST PUBLISHED IN ENGLISH IN 1932

PRINTED IN GREAT BRITAIN BY
UNWIN BROTHERS LTD., WOKING

DEDICATED TO

MONSIEUR EDOUARD HERRIOT

IN MEMORY OF THE TELEGRAM OF OCTOBER, 1924, IN WHICH FRANCE OFFICIALLY RECOGNISED THE U.S.S.R., AND ALSO IN TOKEN OF A FRIENDSHIP WHICH HAD ITS ORIGIN IN THE BITTER SORROWS OF THE YEARS 1925–1926

TRANSLATOR'S NOTE

The translation of Chapter IX has been carried out by Mr. John Peile. The translator is indebted to Mr. N. Scarlyn-Wilson, author of *The French Classic Age*, etc., and to Dr. H. B. Vaughan-Evans, Barrister-at-Law, for their valuable aid on technical points.

PREFACE

"There is only one possible position from which a picture can be judged correctly. From any other viewpoint it will be inevitably either too close, too far away or will be seen from a wrong angle. In the arts of drawing and painting, perspective settles the question. But who will settle what is the proper viewpoint to adopt towards matters pertaining to truth and morals?"

PASCAL

I do not believe in peace begotten of ignorance. If the world is some day to enjoy an era of tranquillity, it will only be after a period of mutual understanding. Goodwill may perhaps suffice to keep men in a state of brotherly love, according to Our Lord's promise; but strife between nations will only be prevented by the growth of knowledge.

The League of Nations can never hope to be anything but a league of intellects. Before it takes up its functions as world arbiter, as in due course it surely will, it must exercise a universal, magisterial sway and put the teaching of history in the forefront of its programme.

For countries which owe their origin to the War, or which bear its scars, now need to identify their interests, to reveal themselves under hitherto hidden aspects, to disclose the conditions of their new existence, together with the peculiar difficulties which hamper them: to co-operate in examining the universal conscience, to weigh accumulated bitternesses, consider treasured aspirations: to appraise anew their individual strengths, resources and possibilities. It would seem that an up-to-date Baedeker, which treats fully of European revolutions, is now an indispensable aid to the performance of civic duties; or, more particularly, there is a real need for a series of handbooks or guides to national psychology to which people anxious to find a way to truth through the tangle of personal recollections may have reference.

I had hoped that handbooks of this type would have been written and published under the direction of the Institute of Intellectual Co-operation, or even by that body itself. I imagined that the Institute would in this manner have found a way to carry out one of its main objects and to fulfil the definite wish expressed on this question in the French Chambers, which in 1925 gave the Genevan scheme its full protection. But our great men are distrustful of undertaking the building of cathedrals or the compilation of encyclopaedias; the taste for synthesis conforms ill with our critical mentalities.

I have therefore, with the slender means at my disposal, attempted to write a fragment of this general handbook of contemporary history, which I judged a worthy task for the combined labours of our greatest men; and I have chosen as my theme the explanation of revolutionary Russia, which is the most urgent problem of modern times, if not the most difficult, since the scope of our interests must embrace the sum total of human experience if we are to understand it.

"*The frontier of the realm of Law,*" said Michelet, "*remains where it was in the Middle Ages—on the Vistula and on the Danube.*" But beyond this frontier of conformity live 160 million beings trembling with impatience or moaning in anguish. The moral obligation to seek after knowledge does not end where the power of the Law—our Western Law—stops short. Whether "Russian youths" are "squinting, greedy-eyed Asiatics" or not, whether Russia seeks her destiny in Asia to overcome Europe by way of the East or follows some other plan, that cannot alter the logical fact that Europe is forced in her own interests and for reasons of self-preservation to gain an understanding of the present regime in that one-time empire of the Tsars, now the abode of permanent revolution. In his *Instructions sur la paix,* Bourdaloue, speaking of peace towards one's neighbour, recommended that "*not too much importance should be attached to the literal meaning of the phrase.*" Translated into secular terms, this advice is good for Europe.

Bolshevism has been the inspiration of passionate speeches, bitter indictments; of tales of travel *ad limina apostolorum*; of refugees' memoirs which are stamped with so great tragedy and sorrow that it would be almost improper to discuss the conclusions that can be drawn from them: but it has inspired few profound studies. A school of literature which can be relied upon for the accuracy of its information is now arising. It is not complete enough to absolve me from making a personal effort, but it is already of such proportions that I have been able to substantiate my statements with the documentary evidence furnished in its publications.

I apologise, in advance, for the omissions and imperfections of a work which perhaps has been prematurely written, in any case too hastily issued, but which is published to meet the demand of a public opinion that is weary of uncertainty.

DE MONZIE

CONTENTS

PART ONE

CHAPTER I

THE ANTECEDENTS OF THE REVOLUTION

Prophecies of some French thinkers—The remote causes of the Revolution—The December Revolt—Nicholas I (1825–1855)—Alexander II and the abolition of serfdom—Revolutionary organisations and their instigators: Herzen, Chernyshevsky, Lavrov—The call to the People—Economic evolution under Alexander III and Nicholas II—Introduction of Marxism and the formation of the Bolshevik Party—The 1905 Revolution, its causes and rival parties—Inter-revolutionary period—Picture of the social classes on the eve of the Russian Revolution.

The Russian Revolution has lasted longer than any other in history, but the period during which it was in the process of elaboration was also of unequalled duration. From the reign of Catherine II onwards appeared the signs that proclaimed its coming, and they were to recur again and again throughout the nineteenth century.

PROPHECIES OF SOME FRENCH THINKERS

Diderot foresaw the ruin of Russia at a time when she was all-powerful, in the reign of Catherine II. During his sojourn at St. Petersburg, he proposed vast political and legislative reforms to the Empress. She replied that his great principles would make fine reading but have bad practical results. Mortified at being thus repulsed, Diderot summed up his pessimistic opinion of Russia in these words: "It is a colossus with feet of clay" (Comte de Ségur's *Mémoires*, Volume III, p. 214).

Rousseau, who had "a strong leaning to sorcery," wrote in his *Contrat Social*: "*The Russians will never be policed because they have been prematurely policed. Peter had an imitative genius, not the true creative genius which can make everything out of nothing. While some of his acts were wise, the majority were misplaced. He saw that his people were barbarous, but failed to perceive that they were not ripe for police methods, and he was anxious to civilise them when the only thing essential was to train them for war. He wished to turn his subjects first into Germans or Englishmen when he should have begun by making Russians of them. The Russian Empire aspires to conquest but will itself be vanquished. The Tartars, the subject States of Russia or its neighbours will become its masters and ours. That appears to me to be the unavoidable conclusion."*

Voltaire, shocked that his hero should have been attacked (he had written a panegyric on Peter the Great), rebuked Jean-Jacques in these terms: *"Court jesters were very wise; they only insulted the weak with their buffooneries; they respected the powerful. Village clowns of to-day are more impudent . . ."* (*Dictionnaire Philosophique*).

But it was Condillac who, in the eighteenth century, showed the keenest insight into Russian affairs. He expressed his views in a work which to-day is too often forgotten: *Étude de l'histoire* (Part III, chapter iii). Condillac was very intimate with Rousseau, who introduced him to Diderot. These three men used to meet once a week at the Palais Royal and dine together at the Hôtel du Panier-Fleuri. There it was that they discussed Russian matters, and, under the impression that they were dogmatising, made their prophecies as to her future.

"Is it certain," wrote Condillac in his book, addressing himself to Peter the Great, "that you have begun your reforms by applying them to matters which are most in need of reform? If you have not done so, surely the defects which you have allowed to remain untouched will destroy all that you have built up? You have created soldiers, sailors, shopkeepers, builders and artists, but if you have not first taught them to be citizens, what permanent advantages will Russia reap from your labours, your talents and their knowledge? Holland is not admired for her shipyards, canals or sea-dykes, but for the spirit which has fashioned her, for the laws which have established her liberty. Russia was not in need of a carpenter, she awaited a law-giver.

"In States which enjoy free government, ordinary discussions, far from being a disruptive force, tend to strengthen the constitution. They are the proof of liberty in a country and, if I may say so, a sure sign of the strength of its national character. Profound calm is, on the contrary, the precursor of decadence. That was also the opinion of Tacitus: a too extensive power is always tottering.

" . . . All is lost if your subjects need Tsars resembling you. Legislators must take such measures that Governments can dispense with the services of abnormal men and need not fear mediocrity, not even the shortcomings of their rulers."

Napoleon went further along this line of reasoning, and showed even a greater understanding of Russia when he said: *"In fifty years, Europe will be either republican or Cossack."*

But undoubtedly the greatest of all experts in Russian affairs was Joseph de Maistre, who was well qualified by his mystical temperament to make the boldest of prophecies. At the beginning of the nineteenth century this perspicacious defender of absolutism deplored the negative side of the Russian character, which he stigmatised by calling "*rienisme*," and which caused him to prophesy violent, tempestuous times for the country. "If some academic Pugachef," he wrote in his *Lettres et opuscules*, "were to put himself at the head of a party, if the people were once stirred into action and were to set in motion a revolution on European lines, I have no expression strong enough to impress upon you what there would be to fear." And this theme was later taken up by a succession of French Liberals and Democrats for whom Russia represented the traditional enemy of modern Society.

"In Russia," wrote Madame de Staël, "the Government is a despotism, mitigated by strangulation."

But, above all, it is well to listen to Michelet's imprecations: "What is it [Tsarism] productive of? Who does not perceive that Russia is obliterated by it, that the country is sterile, apparently lifeless?" (*Les Martyrs de la Russie*, p. 240.) And again: "An admirably sound definition of Russia has been given, a definition of that dissolvent force, that cold poison which she gradually disseminates everywhere; which snaps life's sinews, demoralises its future victims and delivers them defenceless into its power: 'Cholera, that describes Russia!' " (*Pologne et Russie*, p. 45.)

And yet again: "The Russian is a figure of deceit, of falsehood. The peasant in his commune (which is no true commune) personifies deception. Noble, priest and Tsar, all are likewise figures of deception. A crescendo of falsehoods, misrepresentations and illusions. . . . Russia counts for nothing in Russia. A nation does not exist, only an office and a whip; the office is German, the whip Cossack." And Michelet, pouring curses upon this Tsarism which "maintained complete separation from Europe and established a kind of *cordon sanitaire* between the Russian peoples and the rest of the world," cried: "Who will save Russia from this infernal perdition and Europe the trouble of having to exterminate this raving, drunken monster ?" (*Pologne et Russie*, p. 105.)

As the Revolution drew nearer, however, it became increasingly rare to hear its advent prophesied by French critics. Official historians affected not to believe in it.

Anatole Leroy-Beaulieu wrote: "Happily for civilisation, there are few countries where even the temporary triumph of revolutionaries is so improbable. The vastness of the Empire, the scattered state of its population, the absence of big towns, all these are serious obstacles which militate against the success of those sudden uprisings which elsewhere overthrow a Government in a few days. There is no Paris to force a revolution upon the country, and in the capital there are no people to set one in motion. . . . For a long time to come, the only revolutions possible in Russia will be palace revolutions" (*Revue des Deux Mondes*, 15 February, 1880).

French public opinion, hypnotised by the Franco-Russian alliance, refused to perceive the imminence of the Russian Revolution, just as later it declined to grasp the reality of the situation when the storm broke. From a collection of articles published on Russia during twenty years, we will take this one sentence, written in February, 1905, by the anarchist Elisée Reclus: "We prophesy that for the Slav Revolution will be reserved the supreme joy of accomplishing the greatest deed in history: the reconciliation of the races of the world in a federation of equity."

THE REMOTE CAUSES OF THE REVOLUTION

The causes of the Revolution are multiple and deep-rooted in the past. This applies to the Russian Revolution more than to any others. Those primarily responsible for it would appear to be Peter the Great and Catherine II, because they instituted autocracy, aristocracy and serfdom.

"Peter the Great accustomed his nobles to feel that they were Europeans and free men by subjecting them to blows from his cane" (Rambaud, *Histoire de la Russie*).

He thus abolished the ancient Muscovite hierarchy, to replace it by a system of social grades which included the whole Russian official circle. Following the German example, titles were purely honorary and did not denote the real functions of the appointments; office-rank was entirely dependent on the *tchin*. As in France under Louis XIV, the nobility left their country estates to flock to Court and into the towns. During this period, on the domains abandoned by their masters merciless intendants bled the peasant.

Bureaucracy supplanted the boyars and raised up the cardboard wall of officialdom between the nation and supreme authority. At the beginning of the nineteenth century, Speransky created his administrative system, taking the work of Napoleon I as his model. The system became rigid. Under Nicholas I and his successors bureaucracy governed Russia but did not lead it.

Serfdom was sanctioned in Russia by a series of Governmental measures. It was first introduced during the period when, under the Mongol yoke, Russian society was being transformed into a hierarchy. The nobles found themselves forbidden to leave their lands; vassals and colons no longer able at will to flee their lords' domains. From one end of Russia to the other stretched an immense feudal chain: for the first time in history a whole people found itself bound to the soil.

Then, because of the State's ever-growing needs, the nobles became tax-collectors, and the revenues from the land went to maintain the increasing pomp and ostentation of their mode of living.

The necessity for the State to watch over the prosperity of landholders soon arose from the simple fact that it was in its own interests to do so. In order that the system of military service might be safeguarded and that there should be no falling off in revenues, the peasant was forbidden to emigrate. This was done, not only in the interests of the State and nobility, but also because it was beneficial to the peasant communes. These reached the height of their power in the sixteenth century. It was the commune or *mir* which owned the land, not the individuals, and was itself responsible for the payment of revenues to the lord of the manor. This responsibility conferred upon the commune a vast power over all its members. The "elders," who enjoyed supreme authority in its affairs, were chosen according to hereditary right, by election or by right of seniority, and were responsible to the State for the collection of taxes. Their disappearance was, for the communes, the prelude to bankruptcy. The policy of the Tsars of Moscow was to consolidate the *mir* as a fiscal unit, in order to ensure, by the joint responsibility of all its members, the prompt payment of taxes (Klyutchevsky, *Cours d'histoire Russe*). These two forces —the State and the commune—both working towards the same end, secured the permanent establishment of the "elders," following the ukase of 1568. Boris Godunov and Alexis Michaïlovitch, who bound the peasant to the soil by legislative measures passed between 1597 and 1649, did no more than legalise a custom, long practised by landowners.

The edifice raised by Peter the Great relied entirely upon serfdom as its foundation. The State granted the nobles power over the persons as well as control over the labours of the serfs. In return, it demanded that the noble should collect the taxes, and appointed him its police and fiscal agent. Serfdom provided the necessary funds for the upkeep of the nobility. According to the first census carried out by order of Peter the Great, there were 5,570,000 peasants in Russia; more than one million were the property of the State, and nearly four-and-a-half millions were serfs.

A series of ukases aggravated the peasants' lot. Peter the Great allowed them to be sold like goods, apart from the land, to factory-owners in order to encourage industry, then in the early stages of development.

Just as the peasant was bound to the landowner, so Peter the Great bound the landowner to the State. Further, he resolved to re-create a hereditary rural nobility and to re-establish the private ownership of land, which his predecessors had experienced so much difficulty in destroying. With the purpose of forming this noble class which was to be the main support of the autocracy, Peter handed over to the officers and employees of the State the lands which up to that time they had only held in exchange for a lifetime of service. The domains in which formerly the nobles had had but a life-interest, and from which they had been liable to instant dismissal, now, thanks to Peter's action, belonged to them by hereditary right, though they were obliged to serve the State throughout their lives from the age of twenty-one onwards. Distributed among the fourteen classes of the *tchin,* this newly created nobility soon took as watchword the phrase: "Let thy domain support thee, there take thy fill."

But these nobles, bound as they were to serve the State, grew impatient at having to carry out their obligations, and Peter III, on his accession, issued the manifesto of 1762 which "restored full liberty to the nobility." He did not consider that the old coercive law need be maintained, for "love of the sovereign and zeal in his service were everywhere widespread." He released the nobility from compulsory service, and yet left them their lands. To this the natural corollary should have been the abolition of serfdom and the cancellation of feudal dues, now robbed of their *raison d'être*. But this was not to be. The peasants had long been the slaves of their lords, and their obligation to serve them had ceased to bear any relation to the nobles' duty towards the Tsar. Peasant insurrections, which broke out following upon rumours of early legislative changes, were mercilessly put down in Catherine II's reign.

Catherine II (1762–1796) proclaimed herself to have leanings towards Liberalism. She summoned an assembly which was to examine the question of legislative reforms and the drawing-up of a new Code of Laws. Having purloined the ideas of Western philosophers, she prepared a "Paper of Instructions," full of axioms "forceful enough to knock down walls." But they were in reality nothing more than a collection of aphorisms, without any practical value.

The Tsarina decreed that a noble was at liberty to condemn a serf to serve a life-sentence in the Siberian mines, and that a peasant, imprudent enough to lodge a complaint against his lord, might be flogged with the knout. Comte de Ségur relates in his *Mémoires* how on feast days Catherine II used to make gifts of thousands of peasants to her favourites.

Then from the Volga province, a country still haunted by the century-old memories of Stenka Razin (1670), deserter and liberator, rose Pugachev. Like his predecessor, Pugachev was a Cossack ataman, and so brave, so inspiring a leader, that for one whole year (1773–1774) he was able to offer a successful resistance to the best generals in Russia, to hang at his leisure all the nobles he came across and to seize vast tracts of land between Orenburg and Kazan. Thanks to his courage and enthusiasm, he succeeded in stirring up the masses with whom he came in contact, and they even believed him to be Peter III himself. He freed them, mobilised them, infused them with energy, until the day came when, surprised and taken prisoner in battle, this hero suffered the punishment of a common criminal. His death ended the first epopee of Russian revolt.

After his execution, despotism tightened its grip upon the land. The Ukraine had hitherto been free from the bonds of serfdom: Catherine introduced the system into that country in 1783.

"By 1789 her genius was at its height. Russia never had had a sovereign so completely Russian as was this German. . . . The French Revolution upset her calculations and she detested it" (Albert Sorel, *L'Europe et la Revolution Française*). This hatred took the form of increased severity towards all liberal ideas, and of cruel punishment of any daring statements made by the people's writers. Radistchev suffered sentence of death (afterwards commuted, as an act of grace, to one of deportation for life) for having described the peasants' poverty and demanded reforms in his book, *From St. Petersburg to Moscow* (1790). "Nowhere in the world," was the reply of the sexagenarian Tsarina, "can peasants be better situated than those in our midst who live on the estates of a good *pomietschik* (landowner)."

That was not the opinion of the inarticulate peasant, if we are to believe the criticism of both Joseph de Maistre and Napoleon I. "I could have armed the greater part of the population against itself by proclaiming the liberty of the slaves," Napoleon declared before the Senate, on his return from Russia. "A great number of villages asked me to do so. . . ."

Napoleon had not lied. There had been no change, in spite of the mystical enthusiasm of Alexander I, the Blessed, the pupil of that virtuous person Laharpe, whom Herzen called "a crowned Hamlet."

THE DECEMBER PARTY

On their return from Paris, several officers of noble birth—the majority hailing from the Baltic provinces—imbued with French ideas, formed secret organisations, taking the Carbonari of the West as their model; whilst Aratchev, the founder of the military colonies, took the place of Speransky, the legislator and admirer of Napoleon I, at the Court of Alexander I. On the Tsar's death and during the troublous times that marked the accession of the late sovereign's brother, Nicholas I, who supplanted Constantine contrary to the troops' expectations, a revolt broke out amongst the Guards and the officers of the Southern army. These tidings reached the newly crowned Tsar on 14 December, 1825. Nicholas saw clearly that the situation did not permit of compromise, nor of a sentimental attitude. "The Guards had become accustomed to make as free with crowns as they did with balls" (Tchulkov).

"You want me to shed the blood of my subjects on the first day of my reign?" the Tsar asked. "Yes," replied his aide-de-camp, "in order to save your Empire."

The safety of his Empire was already in jeopardy; already the cannon were to be prepared and loaded.

The poet Ryleyev, who was one of the leaders of the plot, gave utterance to a phrase which was to be re-echoed throughout the length and breadth of Russia: "First and foremost, I am a citizen." When, on 25 July, 1825, the conspirators were executed, Ryleyev did not succumb to his hanging; as preparations were being made for the second attempt, he reproached destiny in these words: "It was said that I should be successful in nothing, not even in death."

Pestel, another leader in the conspiracy, said on the eve of his arrest: "Be sure to save one thing of mine—my Russian Code of Laws."

Pushkin, the greatest of all Russian poets, who was the contemporary and friend of the December Party, wrote these lines in their honour:

> "The heavy chains from off your limbs will fall,
> Destroyed will be th'encircling prison-wall.
> Release will bring the welcome of sweet liberty,
> Your swords by brothers' hands restored will be."

Michelet said of them: "That day, you were the conscience of Russia, her prophetic conscience. In Pestel's genius and Ryleyev's heart dwelt the thoughts that will be hers . . . when she begins to think" (*Les Martyrs de la Russie*).

NICHOLAS I

This attempted revolution which, in Herzen's judgment, was the first in the history of Russia, had been the work of young aristocrats. Consequently, Nicholas I considered that the nobility had ceased to be a reliable mainstay of the throne; he looked to bureaucracy for the necessary support. During his reign it was forbidden to leave Russia without the Emperor's permission, to receive foreign books and newspapers or to abjure the orthodox religion, under penalty of penal servitude. The Government's fear that the universities might become hot-beds of revolutionary ideas provoked restrictive measures. Science and letters suffered under a pestering and malevolent administration. The most rigorous measures of censorship were employed. An individual had only to be suspected of cherishing "subversive" ideas to be forthwith disgraced and to suffer "disciplinary" punishment. La Ferronays, the French Ambassador, once told Nicholas I that, as he understood the situation, all the upper grades of Russian society belonged to the opposition. "The greatest misfortune of all," he wrote, "lies in the fact that even very reasonable people, who remember with horror and disgust the events of

14 December, are of the opinion that reforms are necessary and cry out for them. They feel that a Code of Laws must be drawn up, that the basis and forms of justice must be entirely altered and that peasants need protection against the intolerable, arbitrary treatment of landowners; that it is dangerous to remain inactive, and that it is necessary to keep in touch with the spirit of the present century, even though so close a contact as is desirable cannot be effected: and to prepare without delay reforms of a very positive order."

In 1832 Speransky gave the regime "an appearance of legality" when he completed the publication of the forty-seven volumes which constituted the Code of Russian Laws passed since 1649. The police system was perfected: "the Third Department of His Majesty's Personal Chancery" was created, with Benkendorf at its head. Punishments were summary, though the sentences were ostensibly humane. "Cause the guilty to pass twelve times under a thousand rods," the Tsar wrote in a report, and he added: "Thank God! we have never had the death-penalty, and it is not for me to introduce it."

Beyond the frontiers of the Empire, the Holy Alliance no longer existed, but the fundamental principle of Nicholas I's policy remained the struggle against the spirit of revolution which, according to Nesselrode's formula, "was forcing Russia to maintain authority wherever it existed, to strengthen it where it was weakening, to defend it where openly attacked." In spite of the remonstrances of Nesselrode, who held that Russia had no right to meddle with Belgian affairs, Nicholas I commanded preparations to be made for a campaign against France and Belgium so that the disorders which were the outcome of the Revolution of 1830 might be suppressed. But the Polish insurrection, which lasted more than nine months, prevented the proposed intervention.

Russia desired to exercise an unlimited influence and to be all-dominant. The Grand Duke Michael, visiting St. Peter's on a day when the Pope happened to be the celebrant, cried: "That is beautiful, wonderful, but how much more beautiful it will be when we conduct the services here!"

Having crushed the Polish insurrection of 1830 and withdrawn from Poland its Constitution, in 1833 Nicholas I concluded an agreement with Austria and Prussia by which the Allied sovereigns promised mutual assistance in troublous times. The Tsar haughtily proclaimed Russia's right to intervene in European affairs. One of the diplomats of the regime, Tyutchev, who was also a poet, expressed the official view as follows: "For a long time now there have been only two real forces in Europe: Revolution and Russia. These two powers are now face to face, and to-morrow may be grappling with each other. Between them no truce, no compromise is possible. Life for one will spell death for the other. On the result of the struggle in which they will be engaged—the greatest struggle that the world has ever witnessed—will depend the whole political and religious future of humanity."

Nicholas I therefore made his principal and most urgent task the suppression of the spirit of revolution. In 1847, at the time of the constitutional movement in Italy, Nicholas put Russian funds at Austria's disposal and promised the co-operation of the entire Russian military forces against Piedmont and France. In 1849, when "the wave of revolution swept over Europe," Nicholas proclaimed the necessity of putting down the Hungarian insurrection by force of arms, and issued his famous manifesto: "Russia will fulfil her sacred mission. . . ."

This policy of interference, these violent, quarrelsome methods in diplomacy, having first aroused universal hatred, caused the formation of a coalition against Russia. From such beginnings sprang the Crimean War (1854–1856), which revealed the whole background of bureaucratic anarchy, of bribery and chaos that lay behind the imposing façade of the Tsarist edifice.

If Nicholas I suppressed Liberal movements and crushed revolutions outside Russia, he did so all the more within its confines.

Russian society of the period was divided into two camps: the Westernisers and the Slavophils. The Westernisers, full of admiration for European culture, disapproved of conditions in Russia and desired drastic reforms. But the Slavophils were likewise in opposition to the Tsar. Nicholas I had declared that "Orthodoxy, autocracy, nationality" was his motto. The Slavophils were in favour of developing and pushing to the furthest possible extent the traditional principles so closely united to Russian soil and to the Russian character, and which governed political and social life in that country. The Slavophils took the "Muscovite era" as their ideal of autocratic, orthodox rule, for during that period the Church, independent of the State, had represented the principle of universality, whereas the State represented the principle of nationality. The Slavophils saw in Nicholas I's system a distortion of the Muscovite regime, resulting from the close hold obtained by the bureaucratic elements over religious and political life. As for Russian "nationality," it had, in their opinion, been thrust back by Peter the Great and concealed under a heavy coat of European varnish.

Thus, in Nicholas I's reign, the best representatives of Russian thought were suspected if not persecuted.

The author Tchaadaev wrote in a letter published in 1836: "Russia's past is empty, her present state unbearable, her future barred."

Alexander Herzen (1812–1870) left Russia on 30 January, 1831, to escape the attentions of the police and Nicholas I's censorship. He first lived in France, the promised Land of Liberty, and later (August, 1852) in London, where he founded (July, 1857) the monthly pamphlet *Kolokol* (*The Bell*), which for ten years never ceased to stir the imaginations of Russians, to unsettle their views and prepare their minds for the reception of all revolutionary ideals.

THE TRIAL OF THE PETRACHEVSKY PARTY

In 1849, when the Russian army was engaged in crushing the revolution in Hungary, certain intellectuals and writers were accused at St. Petersburg of having met at the house of Petrachevsky, one of their number, and of having held discussions of a Socialist and Fourierist nature. Seven of them were condemned to death, Dostoyevsky being among them. He was not yet thirty, and had only recently published *Poor People*; his masterpieces all appeared subsequently. The condemned men were led to the gallows, where the preliminaries of execution were being carried out, when a messenger arrived with the news that their sentence had been commuted to one of hard labour. In a poem in which he describes this tragic scene, Stefan Zweig depicts Dostoyevsky as having his first attack of epilepsy on hearing this sentence. He went off to the Siberian mines, and from there brought back his terrifying *Memories of the House of the Dead.*

ALEXANDER II AND THE ABOLITION OF SERFDOM

The Crimean War had revealed the urgency of the need for reform. There was one matter, however, which required attention before all others: the abolition of serfdom.

All Russian writers had written and protested against serfdom, Gogol in *Dead Souls* and Turgueniev in *Tales of a Hunter*, in particular. Public opinion was unanimous in demanding a certain measure of freedom, which, moreover, was essential to the economic life of the country. As a result of the aggrandisement of the Empire, the conquests of the eighteenth century and of the growth of foreign trade, Russia had already left the system of natural economy far behind by the middle of the nineteenth century, and a regime was rapidly being introduced whose chief characteristics were the development of trade and of industrial production. The mines and factories worked by a certain number of landowning nobles could not compete with the establishments managed by merchants with large capital and provided with more up-to-date machinery. Slave-labour was clearly incapable of providing satisfactorily for the needs of intensified production in industry. According to a remark of an expert of the time (Vilkins), *corvée* was the name always given to anything done slowly, carelessly or grudgingly. Russia's fast-developing industry needed a supply of free, cheap labour, and this could only be found among the peasant masses.

Immediately after his accession to the throne, Alexander II invited the representatives of the nobility to "reflect" upon the ways and means by which reform might be effected. "It is better," he said, "to approach the matter of the abolition of slavery from above rather than to wait until it begins to break up from below."

After four years spent in preparation, slavery was abolished by the Imperial decree of 19 February, 1861. Prior to the emancipation, the unfreed population of Russia numbered 47,200,000 souls. This total was made up by 20,000,000 Crown peasants, 4,700,000 who lived on the nobles' domains, 21,000,000 who were in the service of landowners and 1,500,000 unattached serfs.

The manifesto of 1861 gave the peasants nothing save their personal freedom, without any right to the land. This remained the owners' property, and in return for the payment of farming rents, the peasants received only concessionary grants of land which, on the payment of redemption dues, might become their property. But the plots of land were not large enough, peasants being allotted on an average only three-and-a-half hectares (about nine acres) each. "Following upon the peasants' emancipation," wrote Chernyshevsky, "the process of ruining them was set in motion, and this has brought about the agrarian crisis."

Serfdom was no more, but feudal imposts still remained. Redemption payments took the place of feudal dues, and for the *corvée* was substituted the peasant's obligation to work off his debt to his lord by labouring on his domain. There had been a change in the legal relationship of noble and peasant; but the economic framework remained untouched. The liberation of the serfs in 1861 maintained the system of servitude—that "everlasting condition of peasants," as it was called in the eighteenth century—in its economic form. The ruling class had postponed the solution of the agrarian question, and made it more acute by the obvious inadequacy of the reform. By driving the peasantry into poverty, they were preparing the way for future risings and for the final overthrow of the whole governmental system.

Alexander II gained no advantage from this measure, which, moreover, removed the main prop of absolutist rule—the system of servitude. He felt "inferior to his works," and only to the moralists of the time did these labours of his appear in any way great. Two years later, in 1863, Alexander II allowed his hangman, Muraviev, to submerge the Polish revolution in a sea of blood. And Herzen, who had hailed him as "Tsar and liberator," on the morrow of 19 February cried: "Alexander Nicolaievitch, why did you not die that day? Your name would have been handed down to posterity as a hero's."

THE ZEMSTVOS

Only institutions controlled by one class—the nobility—and carried on to their profit, were formerly recognised in law. The year 1864, however, saw the creation of institutions in which all classes were to be represented. Landowners, shopkeepers and factory-owners who owned land above a certain value, together with rural communities, had the right to elect their own delegates, who sat for three years in the district assemblies. Once a year the delegates from all the district assemblies of a province met in the chief town. Under the presidency of the marshal of the provincial nobility, they formed the provincial assembly which controlled all economic interests. These institutions, as a body, formed the zemstvo.

The zemstvos helped to hasten the construction of railways, the foundation of banks and industrial and commercial undertakings. Once purely administrative centres, the towns now became centres of economic activity. The zemstvos were the organs through which the budding Russian bourgeoisie expressed its wishes.

ALEXANDER II'S JUDICIAL REFORMS AND HIS WORK REVIEWED

This was a great reform, or at least would have been considered great by the jurists of any Western State if it had been faithfully fulfilled. There was to be no more corporal punishment, and those found guilty of breaking the common law were no longer to be branded on the forehead (Ukase of 17 April, 1863). In the place of the tribunals, which dated from Catherine II's time (*soslovnie*) and which were caste-tribunals, in 1864 tribunals were set up in which—in theory—all classes had their share of duties and "all subjects received equal treatment." Cases were to be tried verbally, publicly and after the hearing of all parties.

Alexander II made a notable endeavour to aid academic and university establishments: the number of high schools increased rapidly from 88 to 280; universities were created at Odessa, Warsaw and Tomsk. Women were given free access to secondary and higher education. As a result of these reforms, appointments in the State Government and in local administration gradually ceased to be more or less the complete monopoly of the nobles (*dvorianin*), and there was a great influx of new men to fill the vacant posts.

"*The internal life of the country took on a classless, democratic character*" (Professor Platonov). In his work *Subterranean Russia*, the Socialist historian Stepniak described it as "a half-measure; hypocrisy full of contradictions. . . ." Reforms had indeed become ineffective: liberty alone was not enough.

As soon as the liberation of the serfs was an established fact, Herzen had published an article in his pamphlet *Kolokol* headed: "What are the People's Needs?" The writer's answer was: "Simply, land and liberty." These two words, "land and liberty" (*zemlia i volia*), were to be adopted as the name of the first Russian revolutionary party.

At the beginning of the year 1862, Chernyshevsky and several others founded a society in Russia for which the slogan of the exiled Herzen was taken. If the December Party is excepted, this was the first organisation which had a plan of action and a definite programme. With its foundation begins the true revolutionary period in Russian history.

KARAKASOV'S ATTEMPT ON THE TSAR'S LIFE

On the 4th of April, 1866, as Alexander II was leaving the Summer Garden and getting into his carriage, Karakasov, a man of the people, fired point-blank at him. A drunken peasant who happened to be passing by at the moment knocked up his arm and the bullet missed its mark.

This was the first time that an attempt had been made on the Tsar's life by one of the masses.

Alexander II told his courtiers who hastened up to congratulate him on his escape: "The saddest thing about it is that he should have been a Russian."

After having been tortured in prison (his warders made it impossible for him to gain an instant's repose), Karakasov was hanged.

The shot fired by Karakasov was the signal for the return to reactionary methods of extreme violence. At Moscow, university circles were broken up, and not only people who lay under the slightest suspicion were arrested, but also those who were found to have a portrait of Chernyshevsky in their homes.

CHERNYSHEVSKY (1823–1889)

Chernyshevsky was the chief of the revolutionary movement in the period 1860–1870, and one of the instigators of the same movement from 1870 to 1880. Writing as a political economist, he became known by his *Open Letters* and by his translation of Stuart Mill's *Principles of Political Economy*, to which he added notes written in a spirit of Utopian Socialism. He was also noted for a series of works devoted to the diffusion of

Socialist knowledge and to criticisms of the peasant reform of 1861. He believed that Russia would be able to avoid the Capitalist phase, and he considered the *mir* to be the embryo of Socialist society. The *Narodniki* (Populists) had the same ideas. As a literary critic, Chernyshevsky produced a series of brilliant articles (which were in reality political manifestoes) in the *Sovreymennik* (*Contemporary*), of which he was, with Dobroliubov, one of the editors.

Chernyshevsky is closely allied to the great French Utopians of the first half of the nineteenth century—Saint-Simon and Fourier. His novel, *What Can be Done?* was of the Fourierist type. In his study of sociology and his application of practical methods he resembles Karl Marx, who, moreover, learnt Russian so as to be able to read Chernyshevsky's work in the original.

MICHAEL BAKUNIN (1814–1876)

But the paladin of the pre-revolutionary period was really Bakunin. Saint-Simon's phrase suits him: "*He lived a life that others would scarcely dare to dream of.*" He was of high, noble birth, an ex-officer of artillery, a passionately enthusiastic disciple of Hegel and a friend of Turgueniev. He always kept in close touch with the spirit of the French capital through the works of Michelet, Lamennais and Proudhon. He took part in nearly every revolution in 1848–1849; he was arrested and condemned to death in Germany and Austria. Having been exiled to Siberia, he escaped, reaching Yokohama, to reappear later in Stockholm. When a revolution had been in progress two months, he invariably acted as if it had lasted nine; consequently, any movement in which he had a hand always proved a complete failure. In 1863 he assisted in the Polish insurrection; in 1864 he was haranguing Florence and Naples, and a little later French

Switzerland. He was accused of espionage by Liebnecht at the Basle Congress in 1869; in 1871 he was stirring up Lyons and Marseilles; in 1872 Marx excluded him from the Internationale. "A great nomad, a great vagabond, made of the stuff which produces agitators, tribunes, preachers, party-chiefs and soldiers. A man who kept religiously to all the customs of his native land—or rather to the customs he had acquired when a student at Moscow—who went marching on in his seven-leagued boots over the mountains, over the seas, through the years, through the centuries" (A. Herzen). He died in 1875 at Berne, after nearly succumbing at Locarno.

According to his doctrine, there was to be a wholesale destruction of the landed classes and the expropriation of the land and factories to the profit of voluntarily formed groups of the enfranchised. There was to be no revolutionary dictatorship, for "all power, however revolutionary it might be, would end by betraying the people and tend to become permanent."

Bakunin, a Bohemian in thought and in matters revolutionary, was the only Russian—with the exception of Lenin—who played a rôle in the history of European revolutions. In Russia, where he became known chiefly after the publication of his book, *The State and Anarchy* (1873), his ideas attracted attention in intellectual circles and enjoyed a short-lived vogue.

NETCHAYEV (1848–1882)

Following in Bakunin's train, Netchayev made his appearance. He had received his investiture as a revolutionary at Bakunin's hands in 1869, and Dostoyevsky later made him the hero of his novel, *The Maniacs*.

He was a fanatic who looked upon all men, even his friends, as pawns that could always be sacrificed. "Full steam ahead, whatever the going . . ." was his watchword.

In his *Catechism*, which was later to become famous, Netchayev wrote:

"The revolutionary is a man who lies condemned. He has nothing he can call his own; no interests, feelings, ties, property or name. He is swallowed up by one single thought, one single passion: and his interest is centred on this one thing alone —revolution. . . . He has wholeheartedly snapped the links that bound him to established order, to the civilised world with all its laws, proprieties, conventions and morals. This world is his pitiless enemy, and if he continues to live on in it, it is only with the object of being able more surely to destroy it. . . .

"The revolutionary can and even must live in society, hiding his real identity. He must go everywhere, into every kind of *milieu*, into shops as well as into nobles' mansions; he must meet with bureaucrats, army men, literary people, members of the Third Section [which later became the Ochrana] and even make his way into the Winter Palace itself."

Finally, paragraph 23 of Netchayev's *Catechism* stated:

"National revolution must not be taken as having anything in common with, or to be in any way modelled on, the movement which is common to class-warfare in Western Europe. This movement always stops short when property, tradition and so-called civilising, moral principles are in danger; and up to the present time its action has been confined to replacing one political system by another. The people's salvation must depend on setting in motion a revolution which will root out the State system in its entirety and completely destroy class and governmental traditions in Russia."

Netchayev divided society into six categories, and those who belonged to the first were to be immediately condemned to death and executed.

In order to obtain necessary funds, Netchayev called for free-will offerings, and forced rich merchants, who dared not refuse, to make their contributions. Finally, the revolutionaries expropriated sums of money, of which the most famous example was the theft from the Treasury of one million-and-a-half roubles.

In thirty-seven provinces Netchayev laid the foundations of a secret society which he called "Narodnaya Raspravta" (The People's Revenge). Following the execution of a supporter whom Netchayev accused of being a spy, arrests were made. Netchayev fled abroad, but the Swiss authorities handed him over as a common criminal. Condemned in 1873 to serve a sentence of twenty-five years' hard labour, he was incarcerated in the prison of Peter and Paul. From his cell he set to work to form conspiracies which had as their object the murder of Alexander II.

"Netchayev," wrote the historian Glinsky, "disappeared over the horizon, but for a long time afterwards his spirit still hovered over the Russian revolutionary cause, inspiring it with his example of fanatical energy and with his faith in the necessity for a bloody *dénouement* in the struggle between society and government."

Netchayev died in prison in 1883. He had exercised a profound influence upon young people still at school; he had given definite shape to the Nihilist type, and had stamped the revolutionary movement with the tragic, pitiless forces of his character.

LAVROV (1823–1900)

Bakunin considered that the Russian people were ripe for revolution. But in 1875, or about that date, the course of the movement was also being governed by influences that were not his: Lavrov's Socialism and Tkatchov's Jacobinism.

Born in 1823, a professor of mathematics at twenty-one, a poet, philosopher and sociologist, Lavrov joined the *Zemlia i Volia* Society in 1862. In 1866 he was arrested as the result of the attempt on Alexander II's life and condemned for having spread subversive ideas. He escaped in 1870, arrived in Paris, worked with Broca and the bookbinder Varlin, and became a member of the Internationale. He proposed a reform in education to the Government of the Commune, crossed the lines at Versailles in 1871, and went over to London, where he asked the Internationale to send aid to the stricken Commune. He then became acquainted with Marx and Engels, edited a revolutionary paper, *Vperiod* (*Forward*), and returned in 1877 to Paris, where he lived until his death.

Between 1861 and 1869 Lavrov published his *Historical Letters*, in which he exhorted the intellectuals "to turn to the people." "This means," he explained, "that all ties with the past must be broken, and parents, friends, studies and social position forsaken: a man's whole life must be given up to the service of the masses. You say that, as a revolutionary, you may be sentenced to hard labour? But have not the people to whom we are henceforth going to devote our lives been, in a sense, sentenced to hard labour? Have they not worked even harder than convicts for their miserable crusts of bread? You fear the prison-chains? But is the nation free, unfettered? No, it is enslaved by poverty just as we are enslaved by the most wretched of all tyrannies." It was essential to "turn to the people" so that by means of a protracted campaign of propaganda, the spirit of Socialism might once more be instilled in them.

Lavrov had in mind that such would be the possible trend of events in Russia, but he under-estimated the enthusiasm of those revolutionaries who preferred to hold fast to the doctrine of immediate action preached by Bakunin and Tkatchov.

TKATCHOV (1844–1885)

Tkatchov, the Jacobin, Blanquist and Babouvist, attracted the sympathies of youthful revolutionaries. It was he who propagated the idea of getting the supreme power into the hands of a revolutionary minority, now that a Socialist transformation was taking place in society.

In 1869 he was implicated in the Netchayev affair and sentenced; in 1873 he emigrated to Geneva, where he published a review, *Nabat* (*The Tocsin*).

Tkatchov's views differed from Bakunin's in that he insisted upon the necessity of establishing a central organisation and setting up a revolutionary dictatorship. Neither did he agree with Lavrov, who held that preparation for a revolution was the revolutionaries' chief task.

"Revolution," wrote Tkatchov, "is being prepared by the people's exploiters, by Capitalists, landowners, priests and the police; by the Conservative, Liberal and progressive parties, etc. The revolutionary does not prepare for revolution, he sets one in motion." The Revolution was to sweep away all institutions which prevented the establishment of equality and fraternity, and would set up others favourable to their development.

THE PEOPLE'S PARTY IN THE PERIOD 1870 TO 1880

Lavrov's *Historical Letters*, which reminded the educated classes of their duty towards the masses, Bakunin's and Netchayev's propaganda and their appeals and exhortations to youth to "turn to the people," the glorification of the masses by great Russian writers, Dostoyevsky, Turgueniev, Nekrassov, etc. . . ., all these influences combined in creating a secret current of enthusiasm which, among the intellectuals, had the effect of inspiring a veritable crusade on behalf of the common people. Just as the Slavophils had done, the "popular, progressive party" proclaimed what was to be the special destiny of the Russian people, but looked upon the Communist principles of the Russian peasant's life, and the *mir* in particular, as signs of what the people's future state would be.

The *Narodniki* (Populists), who carried on the struggle between 1870 and 1880, were educated men whose main object was to stir up the peasant masses. Their courage was boundless.

The beliefs of the propagandists of the period 1870–1880 were more religious than revolutionary. In spite of evidence to the contrary, they firmly believed that the Revolution would break out this day, that day or the next, just as men in the Middle Ages believed that the Day of Judgment was at hand.

The Populists of the period are remarkable for the originality of their opinions and for their youthful heroism. The popular movement reached its height towards 1875. The chief leader of the group was Tchaikovsky, who lived long enough to see the Bolshevist Revolution in progress and, moreover, to fight against it. Other members of this group were Sophia Perovskaya, the first woman ever hanged in Russia, and Prince Kropotkin (1842–1918), a descendant of the Ruriks, as highly born as any Romanov and a member of the *Corps des Pages,* who joined the anarchist party after making the acquaintance of Benoît Malon. Imprisoned in the Peter and Paul for two years and for another three at Clairvaux (which he left at the same time as Louis Michel, a friend of Jean Grave and Elisée Reclus), "he lived," Brandes wrote of him, "the life of a workman and of an aristocrat. Seldom has there been a revolutionary so gentle, so humane."

The movement begun on behalf of the people, apart from certain cases of individual violence, continued to be conducted on open, peaceful lines up to the year 1875, up to the beginning of the Terrorist period which coincided with the great series of famous revolutionary trials, in which members of secret committees and groups, driven from their often tomb-like hiding-places, were publicly exposed as the result of judicial proceedings.

THE TRIAL OF THE FIFTY AND THE HUNDRED AND NINETY-THREE

In February–March, 1877, came the trial of the Fifty. Alexeiev, a peasant from the Smolensk province, said: "We of the common people, we are still serfs. . . . The younger generation will guide us until the maddened, rebel people raises its powerful, muscular hand." This was new language indeed! The defence was conducted with unheard-of daring. Sophia Bardin, a woman of noble birth and the governor of Tambov's daughter, who sat next to the rebel peasant on the benches of the accused, defied the tribunal, supported by the public in court, whose hoots and boos caused the President, Peters, an expert in this type of trial, to fall back in astonishment. Between October, 1877, and January, 1878, another batch of one hundred and ninety-three prisoners, among whom were certain revolutionaries as yet unknown, but destined to become famous—Yeliabov and Catherine Breshko-Breshkovskaya (later to be called the "Grandmother of the Revolution") in particular—faced the charges preferred against them, in company with the most violent of all agitators, Michin. During the hearing blows and insults were exchanged by prisoners and police. The twenty-eight who were acquitted were placed under police supervision. But the sentences of hard labour and deportation meted out to the others increased the revolutionary fury which had already been kindled by a stream of publications of the most intense kind.

THE PERIOD OF TERRORISM

When the student Bogoliubov, who was confined in one of the St. Petersburg prisons, refused to salute Trepov, the Chief of Police, the latter ordered him to be beaten with rods.

Thereupon, Vera Zassulitch, a rich and beautiful young woman, who was not personally acquainted with the victim, fired a revolver at the astonished bully. Brought before the Assize Court, she was acquitted by the jury (31 March, 1876), and cheered by the crowds when she left at the close of the trial. Everywhere eyes filled with tears when people heard this story. This event, or rather this verdict, by acquitting Vera Zassulitch, condemned Trepov and one administrative or governmental system in particular. The *Neue Freie Presse* (Vienna) saw in this verdict "the Mene, Tekel, Upharsin of autocracy." A Polish newspaper prophesied a Russian version of the "Taking of the Bastille." "For several days Europe has called a truce to its perplexities, has ceased to wonder if the Congress will meet, if the honest broker will succeed in reconciling the rival pretentions of elephant and whale. For the space of forty-eight hours Europe has forgotten everything—peace, war, Herr Bismarck, Lord Beaconsfield, Prince Gorchakov, and can talk and think of nothing else but Vera Zassulitch" (*Revue des Deux Mondes*).

At any moment now the era of Terrorism would be beginning. Yeliabov, one of the Terrorist chiefs, said: "*History moves too slowly, it must be hustled.*" The party programme was still confused; the people were to have the land, the workmen the factories; a Constituent Assembly was to be formed and a Republic established. Terror was to be the weapon employed. "*Political assas-*

sination is one of our most effective weapons in the struggle against despotism," proclaimed *Land and Liberty*, the party organ. Outrages increased in number. The Chief of Police was stabbed in the street at St. Petersburg, the Governor of Kharkov hanged. In April, 1879, the student Soloviev fired five revolver-shots at Alexander II.

On the first day of December, 1879, there was an explosion near the lines over which the Imperial train was due to pass; the Tsar was saved by a sudden change in the schedule. On 17 February, another explosion destroyed the dining-hall in the Winter Palace: the Tsar owed his escape to the fact that the meal was served a few moments after the usual time. Several days later, a special Council was called by Alexander II, and, as outcome of its deliberations, Loris Melikov, the victorious army leader and conqueror of Kars, was given full authority to root out this Terrorism, or rather to round up the fifty Terrorists who were filling Russia with the sound of sudden reports and ear-splitting explosions. But Melikov did not succeed in bringing to book the Executive Committee of the *People's Will* Party, which, hidden in the shadowy background, continued to pass sentences of death upon its enemies and to inform its victims of the fate in store for them.

THE "NARODNAYA VOLIA" (THE PEOPLE'S WILL) 1879

On the morrow of the attempted murder of Alexander II and the execution of his assailant, Soloviev (28 May, 1879), the *Land and Liberty* revolutionary society decided to hold its annual congress at Voronezhd. There were many members of the People's Party who disapproved of political outrages. The Terrorist section, composed of seventeen youths, held a preliminary meeting at Lipetsk, formed themselves into a secret society under the leadership of Yeliabov, and took as their watchword: "A death for a death."

The congress at Voronezhd made apparent a divergence of views within the movement. Before it ended, a compromise was reached between the two main tendencies of the movement, but henceforth they were destined, nevertheless, to follow each its own course of development.

The centralising Terrorist section was led by Yeliabov, Mikhailov and Morosov, and had its own oıgan, the *Narodnaya Volia*, which appeared in 1879 and gave the party its name. The section which disapproved of Terrorist action also had its own organ, the *Tchorny Perediel* (*The Dark Lot*), which appeared in January, 1880. Its leaders were Plekhanov, Deutsch and Vera Zassulitch.

The student Phekhanov had appeared for the first time on the revolutionary stage when he displayed the red flag in the square in front of the Kazan Cathedral at St. Petersburg on 6 December, 1876.

The division which occurred within the party was to influence the whole subsequent course of the revolution in Russia. In later days, the *Narodnaya Volia* and the *Tchorny Perediel* produced two separate doctrines—revolutionary Socialism and Socialism proper. But the party which was soon to be divided by doctrinal differences was, in 1880, still united by one common object.

The Empress Maria Alexandrovna died during the summer of 1880, and the Tsar, though old in years, was still young enough to fall in love. He married (morganatically) the Princess Dolgoruki, Catherine Mikhailovna, who bore him three children. Loris Melikov tried to obtain his sovereign's signature to a proclamation summoning a meeting of certain men of high position whom he was anxious to see appointed to serve in the Government. The Tsar hesitated, and at times showed unmistakable signs of grief at his helplessness in face of the menace which continued to overshadow him. On the first day of May, 1881, Alexander II was blown to bits by bombs near the Palace Mikhailovsky. The Executive Committee of the *Narodnaya Volia* had at last succeeded in bringing to book him whom they called the "crowned wild beast."

As a result of this outrage, Yeliabov and Sophia Perovskaya were hanged, and the *Narodnaya Volia* Party lost the most daring of its combatants; but the struggle was carried on with other weapons and in other forms.

REIGN OF ALEXANDER III (1881–1894)

Just as Nicholas I had done, Alexander III began his reign with a batch of executions. Pobiedonostsev, the new Tsar's mentor, became the sovereign's chief source of inspiration and obtained the repudiation of Loris Melikov's liberal views. He demanded the hanging of the regicides for whom Vladimir Soloviov, a philosopher and opponent of the capital sentence, had implored pardon in a famous speech. Pobiedonostsev had dreamed of utilising Dostoyevsky's genius in its latest form as a means to revive orthodox and autocratic methods in Russia. By the death of Fedor Mikhaïlovitch Dostoyevsky (1881), Russia's rulers were deprived at the beginning of a new reign of the inspiration which his idealism, his dreams for the great "grey-smocked masses," would certainly have been to them. But suddenly the employment of forceful measures quickly terminated the period of inactivity. Alexander III proclaimed autocracy to be "unshakeable"; he founded the *Ochrana*, or political police (1881), and established a preventive censorship (1882). In the country districts, nobles chosen by the landowners were appointed heads of the rural communes (*zemskie natchalniki*) and given wide powers (1889). Students, now obliged to wear uniform, were placed under police supervision. A "Nobles' Real Estate Bank" provided assistance for poor, small landholders, while the "Peasants' Real Estate Bank" did the same for well-to-do peasants. The neighbouring countries—Poland, Finland, the Baltic Provinces, Caucasus—all experienced the rigours of a campaign set in motion to Russianise them. The Jews, who were obliged to take up their residence in the provinces of the south-west or in Poland, were forbidden, except in special cases, to enter the cities of St. Petersburg and Moscow. In 1883 nearly one million-and-a-half Jews drifted back into the countries of their birth, and this caused overcrowding and destitution in the ghettoes. Only a limited number of Jews were granted facilities to attend university courses, 10 per cent. in so-called Jewish territory, 2 per cent. in the capitals: and this was the "*numerus clausus.*" Anti-Semitic pogroms became a Government weapon, a means to side-track, to check the revolutionary movement. Rambaud declared that under Alexander III, "the Jews' situation somewhat resembled that in which the Huguenots found themselves as a result of the revocation of the Edict of Nantes." Only the Revolution of February, 1917, put an end to this practice of passing laws only applicable to certain communities.

In foreign affairs, Alexander III, dissatisfied with the policy followed by Germany at the Congress of Berlin, allowed the loosening of the ties which had always bound Hohenzollern to Romanov, and in 1891 entered into an alliance with France.

Alexander III looked upon education as the source of all evil. On his Minister's report he wrote: "The unfortunate thing is that the peasants send their children to school." And on another occasion: "Education must be abolished."

Prince Troubetzkoy, the sculptor, carved an equestrian

statue of Alexander III which was set up in a St. Petersburg square. The Tsar was represented as a massive figure pulling at his horse's reins. The people looked upon the statue as symbolic of a Russia recoiling under her master's uplifted hand.

ECONOMIC CHANGES

While revolutionary manifestations seemed entirely suppressed or doomed to utter failure, a twofold phenomenon made its appearance in Russian life: the rapid development of industry and the rise of a new class, the proletariat.

The tariff system, which was intended to benefit national production, sent up the price of manufactured articles—a very serious matter for the peasant. The lack of land and their poverty-stricken condition forced the peasants to leave the country and to seek work in the towns and factories. Therefore, in big towns and industrial centres a large artisan population grew up, adrift from the land and reduced to working with their hands for a living. The relations between workmen and employers became very strained, and finally scenes of violence took place between them.

The living conditions of the proletariat were unbelievably wretched. As a general rule, workmen even slept in the factories or in cellars. There was no limit to the length of the working day; the St. Petersburg weavers worked fourteen hours a day, and it was only in 1889, after they had come out on strike, that they obtained legislation for an eleven-and-a-half hour day. Night-work for women and children was permitted, and wages were irregularly paid.

Numerous strikes were a feature of Alexander III's reign, and they brought about the formation of Trades Union and Co-operative groups. The first strike to be successful occurred in the Morozov Mill at Orekhova-Zuef (1885). The Government—certainly without wishing to do so—aided in developing the political consciousness of the working class by making every strike a criminal offence and by showing the workman that he could not rely on the Government to treat his claims with justice—claims which, once purely professional, had now become political. The sufferings endured by the workmen and their fury at the treatment meted out to them caused many to become members of the partisan organisations.

In 1878 the carpenter Khalturin, working with Plekhanov, attempted to form the *Workers' Union of Northern Russia.* His plan failed, however, and, joining the ranks of the Terrorists, he perished on the scaffold in 1882.

But, having fled to Geneva, Plekhanov had founded in 1883 the "Emancipation of Labour Group" in that city, with the assistance of Vera Zassulitch and Axelrod. Unlike the Populists, he declared that no reliance could be placed on a purely peasant revolution, and that the principal force in the revolutionary movement in Russia would be the working class, which was rapidly developing and increasing in strength.

THE FIRST CLASH OF THE MARXISTS WITH THE POPULISTS

The Populists of the period 1880–1890 did not realise the deep-seated changes that were taking place in the Russian social structure. They held that the rural commune, the *mir,* whose disintegration was becoming more and more apparent, had nothing to do with Socialism. The very constitution of the Russian proletariat showed how mistaken were the Populists who had declared that Russia would follow an evolution *sui generis,* which would exempt it from passing through an industrial phase. Mikhailovsky, the Populists' idealist and theorist, declared: "In Russia, a workers' movement of the Western European type cannot come to pass, because, properly speaking, the working class is non-existent; the workman remains bound to his village, to which he can always return; he is a landowner and need never be afraid of unemployment."

In reply, the Emancipation of Labour Group prepared a plan which formed part of the Social-Democrats' programme. This was the first appearance of Marxism in Russian political life.

Immediately following the terrible famine of 1891–1892, which spread over an area of 475,000 square kilometres, causing suffering to close upon thirty millions of people, Plekhanov wrote in a pamphlet headed *The Socialists' Aims in the Fight Against Famine in Russia*:

> "The rôle of the proletariat in history is as revolutionary as the moujik's is conservative. For millions of years oriental despotism supported by the moujik has remained unshaken; in a relatively short space of time the proletariat has shaken the whole foundations of Western European society, and in Russia, its development and political education is proceeding far more rapidly than was the case in the West. In Russia, the proletariat, like the giant of the fairy-story, is literally growing larger and stronger every hour. In ten years or so it has been changed out of all recognition."

The Russian proletariat became particularly strong during Alexander III's reign, that is, during the period of the most violent reaction, when the disillusioned *intelligenzia* were losing faith in themselves and their ideals. In this country where education and all liberal ideas had been sentenced to extinction, where even those who held fast to these ideas began to think that nothing could stem this retrograde movement in this poor, oppressed land, the work of carrying out an internal renovation was, nevertheless, being faithfully pursued.

The working class was beginning to become interested in the Western proletarian movement, to read, to learn; to be imbued with a limitless hatred of despotism, to feel its own might, its dignity, and by these means to nullify the reactionary endeavours of the previous ten years. Russia in 1890 was much riper for revolution than in 1870, despite the country's apparently peaceful internal condition.

During this period the *Narodniki*, who were advocates of individual Terrorist methods, seemed more revolutionary than the Marxists, who were content to do no more than form workers' clubs.

Plekhanov was responsible for the idea which was to be the very root of Bolshevism—the hegemony of the proletariat and its rôle as leader of the coming revolution. At the first Congress of the Second Internationale in Paris in 1889 Plekhanov, who was the undisputed leader of the revolutionary Marxists, declared: "The Russian Revolution will either succeed as a workers' revolution, or it will not succeed at all."

It was between 1887 and 1895, with these underlying ideas, that the first Social-Democratic workers' clubs were formed at St. Petersburg, Moscow, Ivanovo-Voznesensk and Odessa. Among their members was Lenin (born 10 April, 1870), whose brother Alexander, implicated in one of the conspiracies organised by the *People's Will* Party, was hanged in 1887; Krupskaya (Lenin's future wife), the engineer Kryjanovsky (later head of the State Plan of the U.S.S.R.), Martov, Steklov, Ragnov and Trotsky.

NICHOLAS II (1894–1917)

Immediately upon his accession, Nicholas II made clear his intention of following his father's system of government and of upholding autocratic principles with the energy and firmness which Alexander III had shown. In the course of the celebrations which followed the coronation in the Khodinka plain, near Moscow, people in the crowds were crushed and stamped on in the rush to receive presents distributed by the Tsar. The nation saw in this a sinister omen.

At home, the Government's markedly conservative tendencies were so opposed to the most urgent needs of all classes that conflicts were inevitable. In proportion as the people's discontent increased, so repressive measures were intensified, and this only accentuated the feeling of general uneasiness.

In foreign affairs, Nicholas II's policy hinged on the Franco-Russian alliance (the Tsar visited Paris in October, 1896). In France this alliance was hailed with general rejoicing, though Jaurès protested against it and wrote: "The rulers have allowed a friendly relationship to degenerate into one of entire dependence, because by losing sight of what was the spirit of the Republic, they have failed to perceive what was the spirit of France herself."

At the invitation of Nicholas II, two "Peace Conferences" were held at The Hague, in 1899 and again in 1907, with the object of discovering a way to the peaceful settlement of international disputes and of securing a general limitation of armaments. These conferences proved powerless to prevent warfare; impotent to stop the race for armaments which was inevitably to lead to war.

BIRTH OF THE SOCIAL-DEMOCRATIC PARTY

Contemporaneously with the rise and growth of the proletariat, Marxism had penetrated into Russia. It was to spread and increase in strength in the course of its struggle against Populism.

The Marxists pointed out that Russia would inevitably

pass through the Capitalist phase, and for this reason disavowed the main thesis of Populism. But as regards their plan of action they were divided, some being inspired by the theories of Struve, who later developed into a monarchist of an extreme type, others accepting the leadership of Plekhanov and, already, of Lenin, whose personality was beginning to be recognised. Whilst the "legitimate" Marxists (Struve's followers) were satisfied with their formula: "Let us join the Capitalist school," the revolutionary Marxists were anxious to organise the rising working class and to form a workers' party.

The first Russian Social-Democratic Party was held at Minsk in 1898. Nine delegates were present. Struve drew up the party manifesto, in which it was stated: "The closer one draws to Eastern Europe, the more feeble, cowardly and vile does the bourgeoisie appear, and the greater become the political and cultural duties incumbent on the proletariat."

When, about the year 1895, the Social-Democrats began to substitute active work among the masses for their activities in the clubs, economic problems assumed a position of considerable importance. The "economic" tendencies which made their appearance deep down in the Social-Democratic movement, caused the limitation of its main purpose to the redress of economic grievances. This "economic theory" advocated the division of labour, by which the liberal bourgeoisie was to concentrate on politics and the workers on the struggle for the amelioration of economic conditions.

When Lenin had served his sentence in Siberia he emigrated, and began to publish a newspaper which was to serve as a rallying-point and kernel for the organisation of an illegal party. The *Iskra* (*Spark*), of which the first number appeared in December, 1900, at Munich, and which continued to appear in Switzerland, obstinately opposed the economists and the first Russian Social-Revolutionary organisations. It attempted to rally the students to the proletariat, for at this time they composed the advance-guard of the revolutionary movement; in particular, it struggled to form an entirely proletarian party and to create one centralised, political organisation for the whole Russian proletariat.

In 1902 appeared *What is to be Done?*, a title borrowed from one of Chernyshevsky's novels, but which here masked a work of doctrine whose influence was later to prove decisive. Lenin took up the question which the revolutionaries had been asking themselves for generations. But he answered it in his own way.

In his reply, Lenin strongly opposed "primitivism," by which he meant the mean practices carried on in isolated, self-sufficing clubs. He criticised and mocked at those revolutionaries who thought that the existence of one club in one town or of two in another was a matter for congratulation. What was required was a Pan-Russian revolutionary party composed of professional revolutionaries—that is to say, of people giving their whole time to the cause and who, thanks to a rational division of labour, would be able to manœuvre like highly-trained tacticians, when acting in defiance of the laws, under the most difficult conditions: and who could carry on the revolutionary movement against that colossus, autocracy, with its vast bureaucratic, military and police systems which had been moulded by an exercise of authority three centuries old.

THE SOCIAL-REVOLUTIONARY PARTY

The Social-Revolutionary Party came into being in 1901 as a result of the fusion of a multitude of groups in which the Populist traditions—those that Plekhanov and Lenin had striven to abolish—were still preserved. Unlike the Social-Democratic, or party of the proletariat, the Social-Revolutionary Party was intended to represent intellectuals, peasants and the proletariat alike. It was led by men of education who, imbued with the doctrines of Lavrov and Mikhailovsky, gave the individual and the hero a leading part. Rejecting the theory of class-war, the Social-Revolutionary group persisted in regarding the *mir* as the basis of Russian Socialism of the future, without paying any heed to its disintegration under the influence of the new-born Capitalist system which was gradually penetrating into the country districts. As their tactics, they instituted individual Terrorist methods which had been condemned by the Marxists in favour of united action on the part of the masses.

The Social-Revolutionary Party was composed of members of the educated classes and relied for its support on the humbler bourgeoisie and country people. Lenin, who opposed them, said that the Social-Revolutionary leaders were often nothing more than Liberals armed with bombs and Brownings. The Social-Revolutionaries showed themselves to be the fiercest of fighters, their exploits recalling the Terrorist period of 1879–1881. On 27 February, 1901, the student Karpovitch assassinated Bogolepov, Minister for Education. In 1902 a "pioneer group" was formed, which was roused to action by the fiery utterances of two passionate Jews, Gregory Gershuni and Michael Goltz. Acting on the orders of this group, another student, Stefan Balmachev—not a Jew, but descended from ancient Russian stock—killed Sipiagin, the Minister for the Interior. The hecatomb continued. But following an unsuccessful attempt at assassination, Gershuni was arrested, and soon afterwards Michael Goltz, the invalid millionaire and revolutionary, followed him to prison. The Terrorist dictatorship passed into the hands of a Jewish engineer, Evno

Azev (died 1918), the most extraordinary *agent provocateur* of modern times, who was responsible for the murder of Plehve, Sipiagin's successor, and the Grand Duke Serge; who organised attempts on Stolypin's life, tried to bring about the assassination of Lopukhin, Chief of Police, led to some extent a double life, living with his wife yet at the same time consorting with the most dissolute women of the town, and serving as an official in the Tsarist *Ochrana* while he remained paramount chief of the *Boeviki* (fighting organisations). Between 1902 and 1909 (the year in which "Azev with the golden hands" was unmasked, thanks to the tenacious efforts of the ex-revolutionary Brutzov), Terrorism was merely a game of a sadist type played to serve the ends of this man "who was both a defender and a destroyer of Tsarism, a revolutionary and a police-officer, all at one and the same time, and a remorseless, pitiless murderer of his human pawns—men scarcely worthy of the name" (Pierre Fervacque and Pierre Tugal). Boris Savinkov, whose bravery was later to cause such discomfiture to the Whites and Reds, worked out his strange destiny beside this illusive monster to whose evil influence he was also a victim. The statistics for the assassinations are as follows: 58 in 1905, 93 in 1906, 71 in 1907.

THE EVENTS LEADING UP TO AND THE CAUSES OF THE 1905 REVOLUTION

In 1902 there was a series of great manifestations by the workers at Nizhni-Novogorod and Rostov. In the place of economic claims, they began more and more to advance political claims. It was evident that Russia was moving towards revolution. Kautsky, one of the leaders of the German Social-Democrats, was able to write in the *Iskra*: "In 1848 the Slavs were, so to speak, the hard frost which destroyed the flowers of the people's springtime. Perhaps it will now be their lot to be the storm-wind which will break up the frozen rivers of reaction and, in irresistible fashion, carry with it a new-found, happy springtime for the peoples." The centre of revolution, which for so long had been in France, moved from the West to the East, and henceforth became established in Russia.

Having been inaugurated in Brussels and terminated in London, the Second Congress of the Social-Democratic Party brought about a division between Bolsheviks and Mensheviks. Among those belonging to the first group who desired to keep the party on a strictly proletarian basis, were Plekhanov and Lenin; among the adherents of the second were Axelrod and Martov. Both these two distinct currents of ideas were henceforth to remain deep-down within the Social-Democratic movement.

It has been said that the Revolution of 1905 was the dress-rehearsal to the Great Revolution.

Every class felt that great changes were needed.

Just previous to 1905, 10 million peasant families owned 73 million dessiatins (about 219 million acres) of land; 62 million dessiatins (186 million acres) were held by 27,000 landowners: one-third of this vast domain belonged to 699 nobles. Ten million wretched peasants were faced by 699 nobles: and this was, in short, the main feature of the agrarian situation in Russia.

As a result of the over-population of agricultural districts, the peasant literally "hungered for land"; he was overwhelmed with taxes, crushed by farm-rents, ruined by money-lenders. While the country was famine-stricken in 1895, 1896, 1897, 1898, 1901, the foreign export of wheat still continued. By 1902 agrarian troubles had broken out.

The condition of the proletariat was wretched in the extreme, and workmen possessed no rights. The working-day, which varied between ten and fourteen hours, was longer than anywhere else in Europe and wages were lower. Concentrated to a very large extent in a few big industrial towns, the proletariat would prove a very dreadful foe when it became imbued with revolutionary ideas.

The oppressed and cheated lower bourgeoisie could not become possessed of landed property; the educated and shopkeeping classes were victimised by the caste-rule and its arbitrary, autocratic methods, and there was serious interference in their interests.

Bourgeois and traders suffered from the stagnation of business, and found themselves out of touch with the drift of political opinion in the country. The country districts in their ruinous state provided but poor opportunities for trading. Impeded in every direction, Capitalism advanced only with difficulty in semi-feudal Russia, so that it could be justly said that Russia was suffering as much from Capitalism as from inadequate development.

The Government's rejoinder to these strikes, assassinations and popular movements was to raise anti-Semitic pogroms: the one which occurred at Kishinev, and was organised by Plehve's police detachments, was particularly bloody. As a means to trick the proletarian revolutionary movement, the police-officer Zubatov encouraged the foundation of workers' associations under the triple patronage of police, the Saints of the Church and the clergy. But this "police Socialism" did not succeed in putting an end to strikes.

With the exception of the great landowners, nobility and a section of the rich bourgeoisie, all classes of Russian society desired a revolution. Leo Tolstoy, whose theory of non-resistance to evil was not to influence the Russian Revolution to any real extent, but who played a very important part in its elaboration simply by voicing his opinions from far away in his retreat at Yasnaya Poliana —this Tolstoy, whom the Orthodox Church had excommunicated, wrote to the Emperor Nicholas II in these terms:

"Sire, no conspiracy has been formed by any party, revolutionary or otherwise; no plot has been laid against your person or against autocratic rule by any group whatsoever in the Socialist Party: it is Russian society as a whole which is conspiring to destroy the entire existing regime."

THE RUSSO-JAPANESE WAR (1904–1905)

Count Witte has related in his *Mémoires* (p. 222) how the Minister Plehve once said to General Kuropatkin, who reproached him for desiring war: "You have no idea of Russia's internal situation. We need a minor war in which we are victorious to stem the tide of revolution."

Continuing its policy of territorial expansion, though this time turning its attention to the Far East, the Tsarist Government had obtained the cession of Port Arthur on lease. Encouraged by this initial success, it had dreams of conquests in Manchuria and of penetrating into Korea. A private company, which had been formed to exploit the forests on the banks of the River Yalu (Korea), acted in such an outrageous manner and with such obvious official encouragement that Japan, already irritated at not having profited from her victory over China ten years before through the fault of Russia, decided to break off the negotiations which were dragging on with the *Pont-aux-Chantres* and, hastening the rupture, opened hostilities. "During the night of 4 February, 1904, the torpedo-boat flotillas attached to the main Japanese fleet penetrated into the Port Arthur roadstead and sank some Russian ships whose officers were absent at a ball given by the Governor of the Citadel" (N. Brian Chaninov). Things had indeed begun badly!

Instead of the victories that had been confidently expected came the depressing news of defeats on land and sea. The supreme command was split up between Admiral Alexeiev and General Kuropatkin. In August, 1904, the Russian army suffered a serious reverse at Liao-Yang, and was forced to beat a retreat. The whole situation was going from bad to worse, for the army's misfortunes were aggravated by the blunders of the fleet. There was the incident of the attack on the English trawlers (October, 1904), which was followed by the capitulation of Port Arthur (20 December, 1904), the disaster at Mukden and the annihilation of Rozdestsvensky's fleet near the Tsushima Archipelago.

Russian foreign policy was so much thrown out of gear that, in direct opposition to the Franco-Russian alliance, Nicholas signed the Treaty of Bjoerkoe with William II, an event which remained a secret until *Izvestia* published the facts on 29 December, 1917. On 5 September, 1905, the Treaty of Portsmouth was signed. Count Witte, who was responsible for its negotiations, brought the Russo-Japanese War to an end, at the same time sweeping away the prestige of the monarchy, or, at any rate, of Russian absolutist rule.

Such was the feeling in the country that the news of the Russian reverses on land and sea were hailed with unbounded joy by the parties of the advance-guard. Gershuni, the Social-Revolutionary, who was then imprisoned in the Peter and Paul, related how the whole prospect seemed to him to be miraculously brightened when he learnt of the disasters.

In October, the railwaymen's strike was the prelude to a general strike in all the big industrial centres. "It is no longer possible to communicate with St. Petersburg except by sea," the Tsar telegraphed to a Grand Duke in the Crimea. "It is shameful."

GROWTH OF THE LIBERAL MOVEMENT

During the Russo-Japanese War, to the disturbance caused by strikes and the students' movement was added the intense unrest in the zemstvos, or provincial assemblies, composed for the most part of Liberal bourgeois representatives. The Liberal bourgeoisie foresaw that the war would bring about the granting of the Constitution just as the Crimean War had led to the enfranchisement of the serfs in 1861. It increased the number of its meetings and banquets; it sent out a greater number of petitions demanding the establishment of public liberty in Russia.

At this juncture came about the formation of the Constitutional-Democrat (or Cadet) Party, a body of the *élite* made up of university men, barristers and big landowners. Among others, this *élite* included the celebrated historian Milukov, Rodishev—the Cadets' Mirabeau—Prince Paul Dolgoruki (shot in 1926), the barrister Nabokov (assassinated in Berlin by fanatics of the Extreme Right in 1924), Professor Kareev, the Jewish jurist Hessen and Count Orlov-Davidov, who owned vast estates in the Volga country. The ideas of all these men had been moulded by their close contact with the French school of thought; they were all Francophils, all in love with the theory of parliamentary government, with or without hereditary monarchy and, unconsciously, all haunted by memories of the Girondins, whose spirit of law and doctrine they altered to their own liking. They were all convinced that the example set by Western Europe ought to be followed in their country, that the traditional *mir* should be broken up and the moujik given facilities to become a smallholder (of the French pattern). Finally, they were all persuaded that Roman law should be introduced into the Slav civilisation, yet at the same time kept in mind the thousand-years-old ties with Byzantium.

In 1905 the Cadets seemed, in Parisian eyes, to be the very incarnation of the Russian Tiers-État. But this was a mirage. Russia possessed an *élite* split up into various classes or belonging to no class at all, but no bourgeoisie.

RED SUNDAY, 9 JANUARY, 1905

Since the beginning of January, 1905, the St. Petersburg factory strikes had degenerated into a political uprising. The monk Gapon, who was a mixture of a latter-day Savonarola and a police spy, stirred up the masses by his enthusiastic example and advocated the holding of a vast demonstration as a means to obtain liberty. Thus it came about that there were as many as 100,000 petitioners and strikers. On 9 January, carrying no arms but bearing with them ikons and portraits of the Tsar, thousands came running up from every quarter of the capital and made their way towards the Winter Palace. They were received with rifle-fire. The blood from hundreds of corpses stained the snow on this mournful Sunday. The Tsar noted in his private diary:

"9 January, Sunday. A very sad day. Serious disorders occurred at St. Petersburg owing to the desire of the workers to approach the Winter Palace. The troops were forced to fire at several points in the city, and a great number of people were killed and wounded. Oh God! how grievous and painful it all is! Mamma returned from the city at lunch-time. We lunched *en famille*. . . ."

THE ATTITUDE OF THE BOLSHEVIKS

Towards the middle of the year 1905 the Bolsheviks held their congress in London, while the Mensheviks summoned a conference in Geneva.

The Bolsheviks declared that armed insurrection was impossible, and drew up a detailed programme of the approaching revolution.

Lenin analysed the situation as follows:

(1) The Russian revolutionary movement, which was faced with carrying out tasks of a bourgeois and democratic order, found the bourgeoisie incapable of taking the lead. This bourgeois revolution, which from its inception had been forsaken by the bourgeoisie, would be enabled to attain its object thanks to the proletariat which would assume the leadership of the peasants in revolt against the feudal system.

(2) The main problem was the agrarian question.

(3) The peasant revolution, carried out under proletarian leadership, was to sweep away the remnants of feudalism and prepare the way for the class-struggle of the proletariat and peasantry against the bourgeoisie. What was required, therefore, was a *revolutionary, democratic dictatorship of the proletariat and peasantry* in order to root out completely all vestiges of feudal bondage.

The Mensheviks, who held a separate conference under the presidency of Martov (1873–1923), a personal friend of Lenin but an opponent of his ideas, disagreed with the watchword: "The dictatorship of the proletariat and peasantry," and were of the opinion that the working class should not consider seizing the supreme power but ought rather to support the Liberal zemstvos and set up a powerful opposition party in the midst of the bourgeois democrats.

Through Trotsky the third tendency of Russian social democracy found expression. Taking as his watchword: "Down with the Tsar! Long live the workers' Government!" he bound together the destinies of the Russian Revolution and the European workers' movement by his theory of revolution as a permanent State.

THE REVOLUTION OF 1905

On 15 June, 1905, there was a mutiny in the ironclad *Kniaz-Potemkin*. The fleet did not dare to attack the mutinous vessel, and the ship's company, having exhausted all supplies, took refuge in Roumania.

On 6 August the Empire Duma, which had been planned by Bulyguin, was created by Imperial Edict. This was to be a purely consultative assembly, elected by a strictly limited body of voters. Out of the million-and-a-half inhabitants in St. Petersburg, there were not more than ten thousand people who had the franchise. "Bulyguin's Duma" was destined never to meet.

At the beginning of October the general strike, which was political in character, entirely paralysed the life of the country. On 13 October was established the Soviet (Council) of workers living in the capital, composed of one member for every 100 workmen.

Under the pressure of circumstances, Nicholas II published on 17 October, 1905, a manifesto in which he guaranteed the liberty of his subjects and established the Duma as a legislative assembly.

In the meanwhile, revolutionary unrest did not subside. Mutinies occurred in the army, at Cronstadt, and in the Black Sea fleet under the leadership of Lieutenant Schmidt, who was afterwards executed. In November, Soviet Councils sprang suddenly into being at Moscow, Kiev, Odessa, Samara, Saratov, Rostov and Baku.

On 7 December a general strike was declared at Moscow. Under the leadership of the strike committee and the Soviet, it at once became insurrectionary in character. Barricades were set up. The whole of the Krasnaya Presniya quarter fell into the hands of the insurgents. As a result of violent fighting, the Moscow insurrection was deluged in blood.

In 1906 the revolutionary movement abated in the

towns, whilst the widespread peasant revolts were suppressed.

THE ST. PETERSBURG SOVIET

The St. Petersburg Soviet was under the leadership of a barrister, a man of the people, Krustalev-Mossar by name, who was soon arrested and replaced by Trotsky.

The idea of setting up Soviet Councils was not taken from an idealist's writings; its conception was spontaneous and the outcome of the desire for permanent councils, voiced by the strike committees and shown by the establishment of factory representatives or delegate bodies (Soviets). The first Soviet in Russia was elected during the strike in the summer of 1905, at Ivanovo-Voznesensk, the great centre of the textile industry and the Manchester of Russia.

The St. Petersburg Soviet was to a great extent Menshevist. On his return to Russia, Lenin attended two of its sittings as a spectator. From that moment onwards he saw in the Soviet "the political expression of the workers' power" and "the germ of the proletarian and peasant dictatorship."

The St. Petersburg Soviet was the embryo of a system of proletarian government. It must drive out the Tsarist Government or be driven out by it. The second of the alternatives came to pass. The Soviet attempted to force the authorities to accept the eight-hour working-day; it was broken up after having existed only a few weeks, its leaders arrested, condemned and deported to Siberia. Harassed by the twelve months' struggle, the St. Petersburg proletariat's only reaction to these repressive measures was to declare a partial strike which was, however, soon called off.

CAUSES OF THE FAILURE OF THE 1905 REVOLUTION

The failure of the Revolution of 1905 was due to several causes.

(1) The Liberal bourgeoisie were frightened by the people's entry into the political arena, just as were the later *Encyclopédistes* in France.

(2) The mass of peasants remained passive and only began to show signs of action after the workers' insurrection had been crushed.

(3) The Tsar's Government was able to rely upon the army, which remained loyal, and received great assistance from foreign countries in the shape of loans negotiated by Witte and Kokovtsev.

But none of the causes of the revolution was removed. Russia kept her semi-feudal system, the inequality of civil rights and a corrupt, incapable bureaucracy. The agrarian problem was left unsolved. The proletariat had, however, even in the process of being defeated, arrived at a very mature political state.

THE DUMAS

In fulfilment of the Imperial manifesto of 17 (30) October, 1905, which had been inspired by Count Witte, the last but one of the great Tsarist statesmen, who granted the subjects of the Empire "the unchangeable foundations of civil liberty," the first session of the first Duma opened on 10 May, 1906, at the Taurida Palace. Witte had retired after making all preparations for the assembly of the Duma and obtaining a loan of 2 milliards 250,000,000 francs, "the greatest loan ever floated by a single nation in foreign countries" (Witte's *Mémoires*). He felt that his prestige was weakening under the attacks made upon him by Trepov, the Tsar's councillor from the Right. Nicholas II sent for Goremykin, who could be produced—so it was said—"from naphtha" in case of need. Although he had the support of Stolypin, who saw that the monarchy could no longer be maintained on its ancient feudal basis, the aged Goremykin was hostile to the Duma; he was in no way anxious to collaborate with that body, and only tabled two legal measures, one of which was for the erection of a wash-house in the University of Dorpat. The franchise law then in force had been promulgated on 11 December, 1905, when the Moscow insurrection was at its height; the Duma election was carried out by guilds, landowners, town-dwellers, workmen and peasants, each voting as a separate body, but not returning the same number of representatives: the landowners and town-dwellers had two members, the workers three and peasants four. The Constitutional-Democratic Party had been returned in force, despite the pressure brought to bear on the electorate by the provincial Governors. Its leaders wished to carry out their liberal programme. But the cards fell badly for them. Just as the Duma was engaged in debating a new agrarian legislative system, Goremykin procured the Tsar's signature to a decree proclaiming early in July, 1906, the dissolution of the "People's Hope" Duma. He was commanded to surrender the power entrusted to Stolypin, but the struggle had already begun. The Cadets withdrew to make their protests at Vyborg. From there they issued an appeal to the country not to pay taxes nor to furnish recruits for the army.

When Stolypin had replaced Witte, who had fallen into disfavour, the Second Duma was summoned in February, 1907. A non-political programme, practical in its objects, had been prepared, a type of which only an exceptionally intelligent, determined Prime Minister could have been capable. But the Second Duma, which the Social-Democrats had not boycotted as they had done the first, proved to be, even on the opening day of the session, 20 February, 1907, more radical than its predecessor. Stolypin dissolved it on 3 June, 1907, and at once prepared a measure restricting the franchise, by which the election of a so-called representative Chamber —the Third Duma—was regulated. Fifty per cent. of the workers and 56 per cent. of the peasants lost their right to vote, while in contrast to this there was an increase of 33 per cent. in the number of landowners to whom the franchise had been granted. The new law deprived the greater part of Asiatic Russia of its right to representation. "Thank God we have no Parliament in Russia," said Kokovtsev, the Finance Minister.

The Second Duma was composed of 64 Social-Democrat deputies, the great majority being Mensheviks. The Third Duma was made up as follows: out of 437 deputies, there were 145 who belonged to the Right, 170 to the October Party (those who stood by the manifesto of October, 1905), as well as 78 Cadets, 14 Labour, 15 Independents and only 15 Social-Democrats.

THE BOLSHEVIK PARTY AFTER THE REVOLUTION OF 1905

Immediately following the failure of the Revolution of 1905, the Bolsheviks and Mensheviks met again and held their Fourth Congress in Stockholm (1906). Then the Mensheviks made the following declaration to the Bolsheviks: "You are Utopians, you will not recognise that we are now as in 1849, not as in 1847. We are beaten and the revolution is dead. Russia is entering upon a stage of Constitutional Monarchy."

The Bolsheviks replied that the Revolution of 1905 had been only a "dress-rehearsal," and that Russia was on the eve of the Revolution proper.

The Menshevist tendency proved the stronger.

While the Mensheviks deplored "the historical error" of the Moscow insurrection and Plekhanov cried: "There must be no resort to arms!" Lenin was learning the lessons of 1905 so as to be guided by them in the struggles of the future.

At the Fifth Congress of the Social-Democratic Party held in 1907 in London—the last before the War—the Bolsheviks gained a small majority, thanks to the votes of three new organisations: the Polish Social-Democratic group, of which Rosa Luxemburg was a delegate, the Lettish Social-Democratic Party and the Jewish Bund.

LENIN'S STRUGGLE AGAINST "OTZOVISM" AND "LIQUIDATIONISM"

Since the Third Duma could not, owing to the electoral law, be anything but a reactionary body, the Bolsheviks showed a definite inclination to boycott the Duma and, later, to recall the Social-Democrat members who had been elected. This was the policy of "Otzovism" (from the verb *Otzovat*, to recall). Lenin advocated the employment of all possible legal measures, and he was anxious that the Social-Democrats should not shut themselves up in small, exclusive clubs and thus become completely isolated from political life.

"Liquidationism" was a tendency which owed its inception to the Mensheviks. The liquidators maintained that clandestine action should be "wound up," by which they meant the abandonment of illegal organisations; that revolutionary policy should be adapted to the existing legal framework and the fact recognised that the revolution was at an end. Lenin strenuously opposed the liquidators.

STOLYPIN'S POLICY WITH REGARD TO THE PEASANTS

Stolypin, who had been Count Witte's mediate successor, was one of the most intelligent servants of autocracy. Though he hurled his famous insults at the revolutionaries: "You will not terrify me!" and "You need great upheavals and we need a great Russia," he certainly understood that the creation of a Conservative peasant class in Russia, as found in the countries of Western Europe, was urgently required. Such was the object of Stolypin's and Krivochein's agrarian reforms (1906–1910), and they were destined to increase the amount of property allotted to the peasants by granting them facilities for leaving the *mir* and for claiming the assignment of their holdings as private property. The Peasants' Bank, founded in 1882, was to advance loans to the peasants for the improvement and development of their properties. The Bank held real estate consisting of lots amounting to 2,000,000 dessiatins, and these were re-sold to the peasants who were allowed credit facilities.

According to Stolypin's plan, the creation of a class of well-to-do peasants, allied to the nobility and upper grades of the bourgeoisie, was to avert all danger of a revolution for at least twenty years.

This estimate could not be verified owing to succeeding events. On the other hand, the agrarian reforms, by freeing the richest peasants from the *mir* and increasing their land-holdings at the expense of the poorest, hastened the process of concentration and proletarisation which had been foretold by the Marxists.

THE AWAKENING OF THE REVOLUTIONARY MOVEMENT

After Stolypin's assassination at Kiev on the 1st of September, 1911, the Government showed reactionary tendencies and a rupture occurred between the supreme authorities and the Duma.

The Fourth Duma, which met in 1912, although moderate in tone, nevertheless blamed the attitude of the Government. The Tsar suppressed with increasing vigour the liberties that had been granted to the people, and the national representative body was nothing more than an ornament, an illusion.

In May, 1912, workmen employed in gold-placers on the Lena in Siberia came out on strike; the company ordered the crowds to be fired on, with the result that 270 people were killed. As a sign of protest, great strikes broke out at St. Petersburg and Moscow, indicating that the spirit of revolution had been re-awakened.

Numerous Social-Democratic newspapers made their appearance throughout Russia at this time, *Izvestia* (*Star*) and, later, *Pravda* (*Truth*) being among the foremost.

At the very beginning of 1914 strikes broke out in St. Petersburg. In July, when President Poincaré came to visit the Tsar Nicholas II, barricades were set up in the working-class districts of the capital.

The Great War, which checked the revolutionary movement and temporarily thrust it back, eventually infected it with a spirit of irresistible violence, provided it with great opportunities, and brought about a condition which was exceptionally favourable to its success.

THE PRICE OF AUTOCRACY

Tsarism did not rely for support only on the nobility. The moujiks worshipped the Tsar mystically, religiously. It was this attitude of the masses that gave the principle of absolutist rule in Russia its limitless, unconditional character. When the people's faith in their Tsar was shaken, the principle of absolutism was swept away.

Tsarist Russia reached the zenith of its power under

Catherine II and the zenith of its culture under Alexander I. Russia of the Tsars could give no more than that. Owing to its unprogressive, bureaucratic structure, it was doomed to destruction. With the exception of the war against Turkey, Russia was not again victorious in the field. Her power continued to expand in Asia, where no resistance was encountered, but the Crimean and Manchurian Wars resulted in her defeat, and even the Russo-Turkish War of 1877–1878 culminated in a political reverse. In unprogressive, agricultural Russia, ideas had not advanced beyond the pastoral-idyllic stage of Gogol's time, whereas the whole of the rest of Europe was hurling itself madly into the industrial age. A political and economic ditch divided Russia from the rest of the world, a ditch which Tsarism was powerless to fill.

Imperialist Russia of the last two centuries was the outcome of Peter the Great's revolutionary changes. In order to put fresh life into the tottering Muscovite State, he inoculated it with strong doses of Western culture. Pugachev's revolt, together with Novikov's and Radistchev's Liberal policy, brought the era of enlightened absolutism to an end. From the close of the nineteenth century right up to its downfall, Tsarism took up a defensive attitude. It endeavoured to preserve, not the national life of the Russian people, but the achievement of one particular period of its destructive rule—the mummified work of Peter the Great. In that work the whole weakness of Russian Conservatism is discernible; what it feared most was education—books written for the people. In the words of Leontiev, the theorist of Russian Conservatism: "Russia must be chilled"; her decaying body must be frozen and her decomposition and death delayed as long as possible.

THE NOBILITY

In the eighteenth century only the nobility had any standing at Court, having a very marked precedence over the clergy and merchants. Peter the Great had bound the noble class to the service of the State. Peter III restored its liberty. Henceforth, released from State service, free, owning serfs that worked for them, the nobles could savour the treasures of culture and consequently gave Russia her great writers and poets.

The Decembrists, who were nobles, did not represent the true current of thought in Russia: they were imbued with Western Liberal ideas. In Prussia, with Stein as their leader, they might have built up a national State: in Russia they showed themselves to be a "useless" body. After the rising of the Decembrists, autocracy lost confidence in the nobility, and the nobles withdrew to their domains. From the time when the boyar whom Ivan the Terrible impaled upon a stake cried: "My God, save the Tsar!" throughout his two days' ghastly agony, right up to the December rising, can be traced the gradual process by which the nobility became disowned.

The nineteenth century screened the anguish of the nobility. Turgueniev and Gontcharov have described the life in these "nests of gentlefolk" and the debilitated state of a workless Oblomov. No longer called upon to serve the State, the noble class could not even conduct its own affairs: there was a falling-off in the cultivation of its lands, and the liberation of the serfs in 1861 dealt a final blow at its prosperity. When Tolstoy depicted its condition in his life-like sketches, he thereby pronounced even sentence of death upon it.

THE BUREAUCRACY

Bureaucracy, in the form given it by Nicholas I, shut down like a lid upon Russia. It was machine-like, incapable, corrupt. It ignored public opinion and gave the Government of autocracy but unreliable support. It carried out the functions of a ruling body, but was the plaything of Court favourites. A dissolute staretz, Rasputin, one of the Tsar's councillors, nominated and dismissed ministers between two drunken orgies, and ruled the Empire.

THE INTELLECTUALS

Educated persons in Russia were viewed with suspicion by her rulers. Since the time of Alexander I and the French Revolution, Tsarist rule had been obscurantist through fear and in principle. The shadow of Metternich hovered over Russia. "The red ink used in Nicholas I's campaign of censorship was drawn from the blood of the writers" (Nekrassov).

The more elevated Russian thought became, the farther it became estranged from the existing ruling system.

The intellectuals of Western Europe, since they were drawn from the people, shared in the triumph of the middle class when it succeeded in setting revolutions in motion. Russian intellectuals were sprung from every class, and owing to the peculiar conditions of Tsarist rule —and even on account of their culture alone—rapidly became social outcasts.

They were passionately eager to serve the national welfare, they threw themselves enthusiastically into politics; they wished to save Russia. What attitude would they ordinarily adopt? Liberalism of the French type, with its representative institutions, had no place in Russia, where it degenerated into a kind of booby-trap. They were out-and-out Socialists, shown by their programme and tactics ready to be content only with the maximum of success; they were plunged from the giddy heights of pure theory into the maelstrom of events. They detested monarchy and even Russia herself as moulded by Tsarism. They were internationalists and defeatists.

THE MIDDLE CLASS

There is one remarkable fact in the history of Russia—an incomprehensible fact, if the course of development of Western European countries is examined. The middle class took no part in the revolutionary movement. "Kulak," "hundred per cent. black," all the names which branded the counter-revolutionaries, were habitually applied to the merchants. It was to the merchant-class that the Tsarist Government appealed for help against the intellectuals, and it was this class also which it hurled into the anti-Semitic pogroms. The middle class showed itself incapable of setting a democratic revolution in motion.

In the West, agrarian revolutions witnessed the revolt of the peasant masses under middle-class leadership against the feudal system. In Russia the interests of the middle class were closely allied to the State's, and the Government put the police system at its service and at the disposal of property owners.

The Russian middle class welcomed the War with enthusiasm, since they were financially bound to Western Europe. European banking groups financed the Russian banks, which became agents for Parisian and London bankers and the manufacturers of Sormovo and Ivanovo-Voznesensk. Foreign capital rapidly obtained a firm hold over Russian industry. On the eve of the War, French banks controlled 67·5 and 75 per cent. of the capital invested in the metallurgical industries and in coal-mines respectively; English banks controlled 40 per cent. of the naphtha output, 57 per cent. of the production of copper and 51 per cent. of the gold and platinum yield. German Capitalists had only managed to obtain a monopoly of the electro-technical industry.

THE PEASANTRY

Despite Stolypin's reforms, the condition of the peasantry had undergone an almost negligible improvement. More than ever before, the peasants "hungered for land." They had lost faith in the Tsar, and their age-long hatred for the landowners, which had been inflamed by the punitive measures of 1906, was only kept within bounds by their sense of prudence.

The War ruined the peasant; it robbed him of his son and his horse. The male population in the country districts fell by 20 per cent.; two million horses were requisitioned. In exchange for his animals the peasant received bad paper money which rapidly depreciated in value. He lost courage, sowed less land, and became more wretched than ever. The War hastened the rise of class differences in the village as well as the proletarisation and pauperisation of the masses.

But at the same time, it put an end to the break-up and the whittling away of the peasant holdings; it transformed the peasantry into a compact, armed and organised mass.

THE PROLETARIAT

The wretched proletariat, worn out by long working-hours and living often in dreadful surroundings, was not numerous (in 1917, it only represented 7 to 8 per cent. of the total population), but its specific weight was tremendous.

The influx of foreign capital made possible the establishment of great factories in which thousands of workmen were concentrated. On the eve of the War there were 902,000 working in concerns employing more than 1,000 men; in Germany, where the proletariat was considerably more numerous, 880,000 workmen were employed in similar establishments. The centralisation of industry in America was highly developed; in 1914, however, only 32·5 per cent. worked in factories employing 5,000 hands; in Russia, the proportion was 54 per cent. The average number of workmen employed in big factories was, in Russia 1,400, in the United States 1,100 and in Germany 900.

Sprung from agricultural stock, the Russian proletariat had not broken its ties with the country. The workman and the peasant were not strangers to each other.

The Russian Revolution was to bring about the combination which Marx had considered as early as 1856 to be the most favourable to success: proletarian revolution carried on in conjunction with a universal peasant uprising.

CHAPTER II

FROM THE FALL OF TSARISM TO THE COMING OF THE SOVIETS

The War—Rasputin's death—Sir George Buchanan's warnings—The Allied Conference at Petrograd—The February Revolution—Improvised dual Government—Nicholas II's abdication—Provisional Government—Prikaz No. 1—Revolution in the balance—Lenin's advent—The Insurrectionary attempts of 20–21 April, 1917—From one crisis to another—The outbreaks of 3–5 July, 1917—The Moscow Conference—Kornilov's sedition—Spread of Bolshevism—The Revolution of 25 October—The Great Decrees—Kerensky's end—Situation in Moscow—The resistance of the Head-quarter Staff—France's amazement—The Higher Command of the victorious Bolshevist Party.

THE WAR

"The Russian people looked upon the War as an unforeseen *corvée* similar to their daily tasks of drudgery and one which must be carried through to the end" (Alexis Tolstoy). Such was the people's attitude to the War when it answered, "without knowing why," the call to arms. The mass power and passivity of the Russian people had been over-estimated by the Allies. In 1915 "the Entente were still anxious to win the War through Russia's efforts" (General Ludendorf). In the imagination of the French, the Russian army still remained the "steam-roller," by which the might of Germany would be finally crushed.

Until the spring of 1916, despite the many disappointments, defeats and the confusion reigning in higher command circles, "the Russian troops marched to the attack manifesting a truly fanatical spirit of sacrifice" (von Richter). At this period, 37 per cent. of the German forces were retained on the Russian frontier.

Losses sustained in the field mounted rapidly to an excessive figure owing to the lack of munitions and to totally inefficient staff work. In 1917, when Russia withdrew from the struggle, she had paid the price of her disasters in the field by the loss of 2,500,000 of her soldiers. "The treachery and venality of some, the selfishness and indifference of others, general ignorance and amazing thoughtlessness—to this the destruction of the Empire of the Tsars was due" (Brian Chaninov). Treachery lurked at the War Ministry, where Sukomlinov was in command; the Court, swayed by Rasputin, who was always ready to sell his influence or favours, was the home of venality and intrigue. "In so far as it is possible to compare the twentieth century with the seventeenth, the anæmic rule of one of Michael Romanov's successors reduced Russia to a depressed and anarchical state similar to that from which, three hundred years before, the founder of the dynasty had raised her up" (Jacques Bainville). Moreover, "the Empress is mad and the Emperor blind," said the Grand Duchess Maria Pavlovna to M. Maurice Paléologue, the French Ambassador.

On more than one occasion the Duma—a predominantly liberal and national body—drew the Government's attention to the necessity for making alterations in the administration by the appointment to ministerial office of men enjoying the confidence of the country, and by the dismissal of intriguers and incompetent persons exercising an occult influence over the Court. "As a result of the military disasters and the internal situation created by the War," wrote Milukov, "the likelihood of a revolution gradually changed into certainty and became unavoidable, inevitable. The lessons of the 1905 Revolution should have been a serious warning as to what lay in store. But those lessons were not understood."

RASPUTIN'S DEATH

The extraordinary power which that hideous monk, Grigori Rasputin, had exercised in Russia for the last twelve years, caused violent individual attacks to be made upon him; in 1912 the fiancé of a woman whom he had outraged made a vain attempt to liberate Holy Russia from this human horror. It seems that in February, 1915, a conspiracy was formed against Rasputin in which the Minister for the Interior, M. Khvostov, had a share. But the monk continued to bear an enchanted life and emerged scathless from every attempt to murder him.

The day came, however, when the Grand Dukes and certain of the higher aristocracy saw that it was imperative that he should be removed in order to safeguard their rights, dignity and even the throne itself. The young man who was to carry the plan into execution was Prince Yussupov, Count Sumarokov-Elston, who belonged to one of the most illustrious among Russian families. Since hired assassins were not forthcoming, and in view of the urgency of the matter, Prince Yussupov determined to do the deed himself. The murder was carried out in the Sokolniki Palace, where the Tsar Ivan the Terrible had played chess, and which belonged to Peter the Great before becoming part of the patrimony of the Yussupov family. Everything was ready for the 17th of December. A fashionable gathering, which was attended amongst others by the Grand Duke Dmitri Pavlovitch, Purichkevitch, a deputy from the Extreme Right, and an army officer, provided the opportunity. Lured into a trap by an appeal to his lustful nature, Grigori was given poisoned cakes and wine, and when his robust body struggled obstinately against death, was killed by two shots from Yussupov's and Purichkevitch's revolvers. His body was thrown into the Neva and afterwards recovered on a sandbank near the Petrovsky Island. It was taken to hospital in an official's car and buried by night somewhere in Tsarskoie Selo. Later, as if Russia at last rid of the man wished to be free from any survival of his witchcraft, his body was exhumed, thrown on to a woodstack, quicklimed and burnt to a cinder.

But immediately following the murder, the Empress Feodorovna not only demanded that the Tsar should pronounce immediate sentence of death upon the Grand Duke Dmitri Pavlovitch and Prince Yussupov, without holding an enquiry, but that the Grand Duke Mikhaïlovitch's children should suffer the same penalty, simply on account of their friendship with Dmitri Pavlovitch. Only with the greatest difficulty was she mollified. The Grand Duke Dmitri Pavlovitch was sent to Persia to join General Baratov's detachment—an extremely severe punishment in view of the Grand Duke's feeble state of health and the dreadful conditions with which the army, decimated by epidemics, had to contend.

The Imperial family were indignant at the punishment inflicted on their favourite, all the more as the Grand Duke vehemently protested his innocence. The Emperor's relations were quite ready to look upon the Grand Duke's banishment as an act of personal vengeance on the part of Nicholas II. In fact, it was said that two weeks before Rasputin's murder, the Grand Duke, who had thought seriously of marrying Olga, one of the Tsar's daughters, had definitely given up all idea of the match.

All the members of the Imperial family, having met at the Grand Duke Kyril's palace, wrote the following letter to the Tsar:

"SIRE

"We, whose signatures appear at the foot of this letter, one and all beg you in all earnestness and sincerity to soften the severe decision you have taken concerning Dmitri Pavlovitch. We know how ill he is, how broken is his spirit. As his guardian, you know with what great love for you and for our fatherland his heart was filled. We beseech Your Majesty, in consideration of the Grand Duke's age and feeble state of health, to permit him to choose either Curussovo or Villenskoie as his place of residence.

"Your Majesty knows the difficult situation in which the troops in Persia are placed, owing to the lack of cantonments and the frequency of epidemics. To send the Grand Duke to that country will be tantamount to signing his death-warrant, and Your Majesty's heart will be softened towards the young man you once loved, who from his youth up has experienced the happiness of being often in your company and always found in you a good father.

"May God inspire you with the desire to change your decision and allow clemency, not anger, to guide you in your deliberations.

"Your Majesty's devoted servants:

OLGA CONSTANTINOVNA, Queen of the Hellenes.
MARIA PAVLOVNA, the Elder.
ANDREI VLADIMIROVITCH.
MARIA PAVLOVNA, the younger.
IVAN CONSTANTINOVITCH and his wife, Helen.
GAVRIL CONSTANTINOVITCH.
SERGE MIKHAÏLOVITCH.
KYRIL VLADIMIROVITCH.
PAUL ALEXANDROVITCH.
ELIZABETH MARIKIEVNA.
NICOLAI MIKHAÏLOVITCH."

A few days later the Grand Duke Paul Alexandrovitch received this letter back, bearing, however, the following note in the Emperor's handwriting:

"No one has the right to commit murders. I know that the consciences of several people allow them no peace, because Dmitri Pavlovitch was not the only one implicated in this affair. I am astonished at the appeal you have addressed to me.

NICHOLAS."

"From this moment onwards until the end of the reign, no Grand Duke appeared at Court" (Bienstock).

SIR GEORGE BUCHANAN'S WARNING

The Tsar had not lacked warnings. In February, 1916, Sir George Buchanan, the English Ambassador at Petrograd, begged the Tsar to institute a liberal policy in view of "the increasing discontent among all classes of society." On 18 August, 1916, Buchanan wrote to his Government as follows: "If in the future the Tsar retains his reactionary councillors, I very much fear that the revolution is inevitable." On 18 October of the same year, Buchanan told Nicholas II at General Headquarters that the peasants "were beginning to lose faith in the infallibility of the Tsar and that the autocratic regime was discredited." Finally, on 12 January, 1917, Buchanan sought an audience of the Tsar and was received by him in the great drawing-room of the palace. "I told him," wrote Buchanan, "that he had created an unbridgeable gulf between his people and himself and that if Russia was to-day united it was only because she was in opposition to his present policy. Rising to his feet and looking severely at me, the Emperor said: 'Do you think that I merit my people's confidence, or that they deserve to be trusted by me once again?' " And henceforth the English Ambassador was looked upon as an ally of the Liberal parties, their mainstay if not their counsellor. A legendary version of these events soon spread, and it resembled to some extent the story which had been woven round the name of one of his predecessors, Lord Whitworth, who had been accused of being in part morally responsible for the Emperor Paul I's assassination in 1801. History recommenced with a new edition of this legend.

THE ALLIED CONFERENCES AT PETROGRAD

On the 1st of February, 1917, a Conference of the Allies was opened at Petrograd, to which France sent as her delegate M. Gaston Doumergue, a Senator and formerly

Minister for Foreign Affairs, who was elected President of the Republic in 1924. General de Castelnau was M. Doumergue's assistant, and his presence removed all doubts concerning the object of this journey. Lord Milner and M. Scialoja—both ministers without portfolio—represented England and Italy respectively at this conference; and its object, though ill-defined in the instructions issued by the various Governments, was undoubtedly to co-ordinate the common effort in view of the uncertainty attaching to victory. There was a series of receptions, conversations and congratulatory speeches. An undercurrent of anxiety concerning the internal crisis was discernible during the official festivities. Maklakov, the deputy for Moscow, a man of pure Muscovite origin, whose speeches were full of Western reminiscences, warned the French statesman in a paraphrase of Mirabeau's remark: "Beware of asking for time to act! Misfortune never grants it." But a certain forced optimism, which seemed consistent with the terms of the protocol, damped the enthusiasm of the speeches and robbed ideas of all their force. The foreign delegates could only carry away with them a feeling of apprehension produced by their impressions of the situation. The Chancelleries of the Allies were still kept in complete ignorance of the real situation in Russia, of the storm that was about to burst and sweep away the existing Governmental system in that country.

The Duma of the Empire was to resume its labours on 27 February; excitement became intense as that day approached. Nothing definite appeared on the horizon, beyond the Neva; but General Khabalov, Governor of the capital, took certain precautions which revealed his anxious state of mind.

THE REVOLUTION
(27 FEBRUARY–12 MARCH, 1917)

On 14 February the Duma reassembled. The measures which it was intended to pass were the same which had been placed before the States-General on the opening day of its session in 1789. But there was a general conviction that a sudden and violent change was to be expected. The administration seemed to have already lost its power; Prince N. D. Galitsin's Cabinet, which had been formed a month before, was but an arrogant pretence of government; the prohibition of congresses and meetings by Protopopov, Minister for the Interior, intimidated no one at this moment when latent revolt was widespread and had become aggravated by the chaotic conditions in transport and revictualling, by the scarcity of provisions and fuel and the sudden, mad rise in prices.

The Revolution could not be accomplished from above. It was to be accomplished from below. The people were suffering great hardships at Petrograd, where their misery was increased by the extreme cold—43 degrees below zero. Queues formed outside the shops and it was found increasingly difficult to obtain food-stocks; 57,000 railway-trucks were either held up on the systems or damaged.

The Tsar was alone, far away in the old Mohilev prefectoral palace, at General Headquarters. News reached him from Protopopov and from General Khabalov commanding the Petrograd zone. Khabalov had been taken quite unawares by the course of events and showed, moreover, a marked pusillanimity of character. At the first alarm, Khabalov was given the support of an old, worn-out soldier, General Ivanov, who had suppressed the rising at Cronstadt in 1906—a senile, anachronistic figure. On 26 February, Rodzianko, president of the Duma, telephoned to the Emperor: "The situation is serious. Anarchy reigns in the capital. The

Government of the country is paralysed. Transport, food and fuel supplies are totally disorganised. The general discontent is increasing. There is intermittent firing in the streets. Parties of soldiers are firing at each other. The constitution of a new Government must be entrusted to someone enjoying the country's confidence. There can be no delay. Any delay means death."

It was too late. It was too late for Rodzianko's and General Alekseev's combined appeal to be properly heard. The Revolution had begun on 27 February in the barracks of the Volynsky and Litovsky regiments and among factory workers.

IMPROVISED DUAL GOVERNMENT

On 27 February (12 March) the news spread that the Duma was dissolved. Following its dissolution as a regular assembly, it became all-powerful as a revolutionary body. But it hesitated, it was afraid of its own sovereignty. Nevertheless, it decided to sit as an unofficial body. By this decision it put itself on the same plane as other organisations which had not been given the popular mandate. From this day onwards, a dual system of rule was in operation; on the one hand the Duma, shorn of its prerogatives but retained to supply the needs of the Revolution and represented by its temporary committee, and on the other the Council or Soviet of workers and soldiers raised by its audacity to a position of *de facto* collaboration and represented by its executive committee —something similar to the Paris Commune after 1792.

The Provisional Committee, invested with the powers of the Committee of Public Safety, whose memory was henceforth to haunt all Russian revolutionaries, included leaders of all parties, except the Extreme Right and the Governmental Nationalists. Rodzianko, Shulgin, Milukov and Sheidzy were the chiefs of the Provisional Committee.

Kerensky hastened to find accommodation in the Taurida Palace for the Soviet of workers' and soldiers' representatives which had just been formed, and in which he was orator, hero and idol. "Why are you laughing, Alexander Feodorovitch?" a reporter asked him. "Don't you know that you are all-powerful in Russia at the present moment?"

Kerensky, an eloquent barrister, a tribune beloved of the people, belonged to a Labour group in the Fourth Duma and found himself placed in a position of highest responsibility in circumstances somewhat similar to those in which, after 1870, Gambetta started upon his political career.

When the Duma and the Soviet had got in touch and combined their efforts, a programme was immediately drawn up, of which the most important point was the question of the Emperor's abdication. Reservations were made as to the succession; the Tsarevitch was to rule in his father's stead, the Grand Duke Michael, the Tsar's brother, was to be regent, a responsible ministry formed, a Constituent Assembly elected and equality in law granted to all races.

NICHOLAS II'S ABDICATION (FROM THE NIGHT OF 2 TO 15 MARCH, 1917)

The Tsarist regime was plainly incapable of resisting this attack launched by the masses. The Tsar understood what fate had decreed for him before Gutchkov and Shulgin brought the news to him in the station at Pskov, the headquarters of the Northern armies, where he had come to receive the opinions of General Roussky and the army commanders. When Gutchkov advised him on behalf of the Duma to abdicate, Nicholas II answered, "in the calmest of tones, as if only the most ordinary matter were under discussion" (Maurice Paléologue):

"Yesterday I decided to abdicate," and ten minutes later issued a typewritten document which put an end to his reign. This memorable proclamation was worded as follows:

> By the Grace of God, We, Nicholas II, Emperor of all the Russias, Tsar of Poland, Grand Duke of Finland, etc. . . . to all our faithful subjects, be it known:
>
> At this time when a vast struggle is taking place against a foreign enemy, who for the past three years has endeavoured to enslave our country, God has seen good to subject Russia to a new and terrible trial. Internal troubles threaten to have a fatal repercussion on the progress of this War. The destiny of Russia, the honour of our heroic army, the happiness of the people, the whole future of our dear country requires that the War be carried through at all cost to a victorious end.
>
> Our cruel enemy is making his final effort and the day approaches when our valiant army, acting in concert with our glorious allies, will finally overthrow him.
>
> In these times, when Russia's very existence is being decided, our conscience bids us to facilitate the close union of our people and the organisation of all its forces in order to bring about the rapid realisation of victory.
>
> That is why, in common with the Duma, we think that we are right to abdicate from the throne of the Russian State and lay down the supreme power.
>
> Unwilling to part from our well-loved son, we bequeath our heritage to our brother, Michael

> Alexandrovitch, and will give him our benediction when the time arrives for him to ascend the throne. We beseech him to rule in close union with the Nation's representatives who sit in the legislative assemblies, and to take an inviolable oath before them in the name of this beloved country.
>
> We appeal to all the loyal sons of Russia, we beg them to carry out their holy, patriotic duty by obeying the Tsar, and, together with the country's representatives, to lead the Russian State along the paths of prosperity and glory.
>
> May God help Russia!
>
> NICHOLAS.

Two days later, in the course of an interview with Prince Lvov, Rodzianko, Milukov, Nekrassov, Kerensky, Nabokov, Shingarev, Baron Nolde, Gutchkov and Shulgin, the Grand Duke Michael signed—if not spontaneously, at any rate voluntarily—an act of abdication which was styled provisional and conditional, the refusal to reign being revocable should the Russian people decide otherwise through the medium of a Constituent Assembly. What decorous reservations! What useless civility to the past! The coin had been spun and the Tsarist regime had lost.

THE PROVISIONAL GOVERNMENT

The day before Nicholas II signed his act of abdication the provisional executive committee of the Empire Duma had made way for a Provisional Government, in which Prince Lvov, who was given charge of the department of the Interior, was Prime Minister. He was a veteran among the leaders of the Reform Party, a representative of the zemstvos, and the gentlest and least decided of the theorists. The historian Milukov, chief of the Constitutional Democrats, Liberal and ardent patriot, had been entrusted with the portfolio of Foreign Affairs. M. Gutchkov, a member of the October or Conservative Party, who was the representative of the great factory-owners and traders, was made Minister for War and the Navy. M. Terestchenko, a provincial of note, singled out because of his wealth, his reputation as a philanthropist and his knowledge of the manufacture of war materials, was created Minister for Finance. Only one Socialist received an appointment: Kerensky was given the post of vice-president of the Council with the portfolio of Justice. Immediately following its constitution, the Provisional Government issued a manifesto: "The Provisional Government," this document declared, "will faithfully uphold its alliances and do all within its power to bring the War to a victorious conclusion."

Nothing more. There was no mention of agrarian reforms!

The French Socialists, however, gave an enthusiastic welcome to Kerensky, who, in their eyes, stood for "*the advent of the working class and of Russian Socialists to participate in the free government of their country.*" "Once more, like our ancestors of the Great Revolution, and with an effort similar to theirs," read a telegram from Jules Guesde, Sembat and Thomas (18 March, 1917),

"you must secure the people's independence and the defence of your country. By carrying the War through to the end, through the heroic discipline of our citizen-soldiers, to whom liberty is so dear, we shall now together cast down the last-remaining and most formidable citadel of absolutism—Prussian militarism."

Alexander Kerensky, Minister for Justice, vice-president of the Council of Workers' and Soldiers' Representatives, acknowledged this Socialist appeal to arms by sending

Jules Guesde a telegram couched in grandiloquent and reserved language:

"We have never entertained any doubts concerning the whole-hearted sympathy and moral support which has been offered us by French Socialism during our struggle. The Russian people is free. Thanks to the sacrifices made by the working class and the revolutionary army, Russian Tsarism, which in all ages was the rampart of universal reaction, has been destroyed. The people itself will henceforth arrange its own way of life. Saluting the heroic efforts of republican and democratic France in the defence of her native soil and unanimously resolved to carry the War through *to an end worthy of our democracy*, Russian Socialists trust in the internal solidarity of the working classes to triumph over violent and reactionary Imperialism and to procure the peace which is so vital for the development of the human personality."

The agreement to carry on the War still remained; but the fact that opinions were beginning to diverge was already evident in the dissimilar styles of these two pronouncements.

PRIKAZ NO. 1

The advent of the revolutionary regime caused no great stir among the regular troops. The collapse of an ancient dynasty had not led to a military rising of the Vendéan pattern. There were, it appears, only "three cases of vehement protest": the march of General Ivanov's detachment on Tsarskoie Selo—a manœuvre organised by General Headquarters during the first few days of the disorders, very clumsily carried out and soon suspended—and two telegrams sent to the Emperor by the commanders of the Third Cavalry Corps and the Guards regiment, Count Keller and the Khan of Nakhitchevan. They both put themselves with their men at the Emperor's service to suppress the mutiny . . ." (General Denikin). The remainder stayed loyal, for if the system of government was changed, the army remained the same. This was so despite the Prikaz or ordinance No. 1, which the Soviet workers and soldiers had issued on 14 March, with the purpose of bringing the influence of the Revolution to bear on army regulations; and this was what it accomplished later.

PRIKAZ No. 1.

1 March, 1917 (Old Style).

To the garrison of the Petrograd army zone, to all soldiers of the Guards, the artillery and to the men of the Fleet, this ordinance is addressed for immediate and punctual execution, and to the workers of Petrograd as information.

The Council of workers' and soldiers' representatives has decided:

1. In every company, battalion, regiment, artillery-park, battery, squadron and every kind of military administrative service, as well as in the ships of the fleet, elections will be immediately held to choose Committees composed of representatives elected by soldiers of the above-mentioned units.

2. In every military unit which has not yet elected its representative for the Council of workers' and soldiers' delegates, one representative per company will be elected, and these representatives must present themselves bearing a written warrant at the Palace of the Empire Duma on 2 March prox. at ten o'clock in the morning.

3. Military units will obey the Council of workers' and soldiers' representatives and its

committees in the matter of political manifestations.

4. The orders of the War Commission of the Empire Duma must only be executed as far as they are not in contradiction to the orders and decisions of the Council of workers' and soldiers' representatives.

5. Every species of arms, such as rifles, machine-guns, armoured-cars, etc., shall be at the disposal and under the control of the company and battalion committees and cannot under any circumstances be handed over to the officers even when they require that this shall be done.

6. In the ranks and while carrying out their military duties, soldiers must observe the strictest military discipline; but when off duty and not on parade, soldiers cannot be deprived of any of the rights enjoyed by all citizens, in politics, and in civil and private life.

In particular, the "attention" and the obligatory military salute are abolished outside duty-hours.

7. In the same way, titles given to officers, such as Your Excellency, Your Grace, etc., are replaced by the following modes of address: Mr. General, Mr. Colonel, etc.

Brutal treatment of soldiers of any rank and, in particular, the use of the second person singular in addressing them are forbidden, and any breach of this order as well as all misunderstandings arising between officers and soldiers must be brought by the latter to the knowledge of the company Committee.

THE PETROGRAD COUNCIL OF WORKERS'
AND SOLDIERS' REPRESENTATIVES.

Four days after the promulgation of Prikaz No. 1, Admiral Niepenin, commanding the Baltic Sea fleet, was assassinated at Helsingfors. And almost at the same time the spirit of the old army, the omnipotence of the Stavka (General Headquarters), the possibility of a successful counter-revolution, was to disappear. Any enthusiasm for the War that still remained was destroyed.

REVOLUTION IN THE BALANCE

The ideas of the Revolution were hastily carried into practice by measures initiated in a contradictory manner by the Provisional Government and by the Soviet alternatively.

On 19 March,[1] a general amnesty. The autonomy of Finland is proclaimed.

20 March: the Emperor and Empress are declared to be under arrest and are taken to Tsarskoie Selo. The Tsar is notified of this decision by four members of the Duma, the Tsarina by General Kornilov.

22 March: the United States, anticipating all other Governments, recognise *de jure* the Provisional Government in Russia.

24 March: the eight-hour day is applied to the workers of Petrograd and the death-penalty struck out of the Code of Laws. The Grand Duke Nicholas Nicholaievitch, who was appointed generalissimo by the Tsar when his downfall was imminent, is replaced by General Alekseev; Denikin becomes Chief of the General Staff. In making these appointments, Gutchkov, Minister for War, is anxious to straighten out the military situation: furthermore, he disclaims Prikaz No. 1.

On 27 March, as a set-off to this, the Soviet of Petrograd appeals to the peoples of the whole world to conclude a democratic peace.

[1] The following dates are given according to the old calendar, which remained in force till January, 1918; thirteen days must be added to obtain the correct date according to our calendar.

On the 29th, acting in the same spirit, the Provisional Government gives Poland her independence.

On the 31st, a special Committee is set up to study problems peculiar to the Ukraine. This is a concession to federalism.

On the 1st of April: a decree announces radical agrarian reforms for which a central standing-committee is to investigate ways and means.

2 April: the First Pan-Russian Congress of Trade and Industry is summoned by the Republic. The Provisional Government confers the franchise upon women and makes them eligible for election.

But on 3 April, the defeat of Russian troops on the River Stokhod inaugurates a series of reverses and setbacks.

On 6 April, the United States declares war on Germany. Milukov congratulates M. Maurice Paléologue, the French Ambassador, but the people have no longer any faith in war.

LENIN'S ADVENT

At this time, France sent Albert Thomas, Minister for Munitions, on a mission to Petrograd She viewed with much anxiety the disagreements which had arisen between the Provisional Government and the Soviet, between Milukov and Kerensky, concerning the aims of the War. The French Socialist Party, likewise a prey to anxiety, despatched three of its deputies, Marcel Cachin, Montet and Ernest Lafont, to Petrograd, where they arrived in company with two members of the British Labour Party, O'Grady and Thorne, and the great Swedish Socialist, Branting. But at the same time by a different route and with different objects in view, Lenin arrived in the capital.

At the beginning of 1914 the Bolshevist Party had been completely destroyed in Russia: the central Committee of the party had issued an appeal drawn up by Lenin, who made the transformation of the Imperialist war into civil war his watchword. The five Bolshevist delegates to the Duma were arrested, together with nearly all the members of the Central Committee, with the exception of Lenin and Zinoviev, who were abroad.

Lenin was at Cracow, near the Russian frontier, and was directing the revolutionary movement from that place. After being arrested by the Austrians and then set free, he reached Switzerland, where, having announced that the Second Internationale had failed, he advocated the creation of a Third which was to be entirely free from opportunism.

While the aged Plekhanov, who had introduced Marxism into Russia, showed himself to be in favour of national defence, Lenin and Zinoviev conducted a violent defeatist campaign and proclaimed the necessity for, and the imminence of, an international Socialist revolution.

From 5 to 8 September, 1915, a conference of Socialists who were opposed to war was held on the initiative of the Italians at Zimmerwald, in the Bernese Oberland. Among those present were Lenin, Zinoviev, Trotsky, Martov and Rakovsky. When Lenin saw his manifesto rejected, he put his signature to the manifesto adopted by the majority.

A conference, held at Kienthal, which was attended by three French Socialist representatives—Alexandre Blanc, Pierre Brizon and Raffin-Dugens—produced a more definite manifesto than that which had been issued from Zimmerwald: the necessity for engaging immediately in a struggle for the realization of Socialism was expressly mentioned.

Lenin was at Zurich when the news of the February Revolution reached him. He addressed his *Letters from Afar* to his comrades in Russia and in them appealed to the Russian proletariat to organise itself now that supreme power was in its hands.

But, first and foremost, Lenin must get back to Russia.

Through the mediation of the Swiss Socialists, Grimm and Fritz Platten, the German Government consented to let the Bolsheviks pass through its territory in a sealed carriage. Lenin and his wife, Zinoviev, Radek and Sokolnikov were thus able to return to Russia.

Krupskaya, Lenin's wife, described the journey as follows:

"Throughout the journey we did not say a word to a single German; outside Berlin some German Social-Democrats got into a neighbouring compartment, but none of us engaged them in conversation. . . . [In Finland] the platforms of the stations we went through were thronged with soldiers. Yussevitch leant out of the window. 'Long live world revolution,' he cried. The bewildered soldiery began to stare at the travellers. A pale-faced lieutenant passed several times up and down near us, and as Ilitch and I were in an almost empty compartment further up, he sat down beside my companion and opened the conversation. The lieutenant was a die-hard, and said so; Ilitch defended his point of view and was, like the German, very pale. The coach became gradually full of soldiers, who climbed on the seats to get a better view of what was going on and to get a clearer hearing of the man who was speaking against the War in language so easy to understand. Their attention became more and more wrapt and their expressions graver and graver. . . .

"We arrived at Petrograd. The working masses, soldiers and sailors flocked to meet their chief. How did they recognise him? I do not know. All around us was a seething mass of human beings.

". . . Red flags, a naval guard-of-honour from Cronstadt, the searchlights from the fortress of Peter and Paul lighting up the way from the Finland station to the Kechinskaya Palace; armoured cars, the road lined with workmen and workwomen. Ilitch was hoisted on to the top of an armoured car. He began to speak. He was surrounded by all those he held most dear in the world—the masses."

The first words that Lenin addressed to the workers and soldiers of Petrograd were the following: "No support for the Capitalists' Government! Down with Imperialist war! Long live the social revolution!"

INSURRECTIONARY ATTEMPTS OF 20–21 APRIL, 1917

The First Pan-Russian Conference of the Soviets had just come to an end. On 4 April the Bolshevist delegates to this conference met to hear Lenin. He read them his "theses." In them he advocated a policy of fraternisation, the establishment of a Soviet Republic, the confiscation of all property belonging to landowners and Soviet control of production.

Plekhanov, the old militant Marxist, dubbed Lenin's speech "a delirium." The majority of Bolsheviks themselves felt that it was "like a cold douche." Almost alone in his views, Lenin was looked upon as mad by the Social-Revolutionaries, and was represented by the middle classes as a traitor and as having sold himself to Germany.

Sukhanov, a Menshevik, who has left some interesting *Notes on the Revolution,* wrote on the subject of the "theses" which Lenin proclaimed in April:

"Never shall I forget Lenin's astounding speech, which not only shocked and bewildered me, a heretic who happened by the merest chance to be there, but even all orthodox Bolsheviks. I declare that no one expected anything like it. At one moment it seemed that the elements had been unchained, that the spirit of destruction, which allowed no obstacle, no doubts, no human design to stand in its way, passed like a squall through the conference chamber down on to the heads of the fascinated disciples. I went out feeling that someone had been hitting me all night on the head with iron clubs."

While Lenin was thundering out his watchwords: "Peace," "Supreme power for the Soviets," "The land for the peasants," the Provisional Government announced its intention of carrying on the War and postponing all attempts to solve the agrarian problem until the Constituent Assembly assembled. Paying no heed to the people's weariness and growing irritation, Milukov continued to speak of the Dardanelles as if there had been no change in Russia's war aims since the February Revolution. When Milukov announced that the Provisional Government's declaration concerning war aims did not tie his hands as Minister for Foreign Affairs, the Finnish regiment of the Guard and detachments of armed workers paraded the streets in Petrograd on 20 and 21 April, protesting against the War. "The outburst of hatred against Milukov in the Soviet as a result of this incident," wrote Kerensky, "revealed the profundity of the Government's psychological crisis and the catastrophic lack of confidence which had been developing since the Revolution began, and which was due to the discrepancies existing between the composition of the Cabinet and the grouping of political forces in the country." A few days later, Gutchkov left the War Ministry, to be replaced by Kerensky; Milukov resigned, while the people thronged the streets shouting and clamouring ceaselessly for peace, and while M. Maurice Paléologue, Ambassador of France and representative of a policy which henceforth was at an end, made his way back to Paris in company with some very disconcerted French Socialists.

FROM ONE CRISIS TO ANOTHER

The reform of the Provisional Government was accomplished with the introduction of certain new elements: Terestchenko, a bourgeois of some standing, was transferred from the Ministry for Finance to that for Foreign Affairs, but several members of the Soviet, invited by Prince Lvov to participate in the Government, readily accepted in spite of their guarded attitude to certain points of doctrine. Skobelev went to the Ministry for

Labour, Chernov to Agriculture, Pechekhonov to Food, and Tseretelli to Posts and Telegraphs. To meet the requirements of the military situation, Kerensky was forced to take up the rôle of army organiser and to curtail the liberties granted by his predecessor Gutchkov and by General Polivanov, who had been specially entrusted with the task of turning, at whatever cost, officers and men of the Tsarist army into democrats. Unable to take an authoritative stand, he employed persuasive measures, of which a campaign of speeches conducted among the troops—it has no parallel in history—was the outcome. It was in the course of this campaign, conducted in concert with General Brussilov, that Kerensky came to a decision to launch the offensive and, first of all, to nominate Brussilov generalissimo.

Anti-war propaganda became intensified while these sermons were being preached at the front. The Allies would not consent to a revision of war aims. In France, Renaudel vainly requested that his Socialist comrades should be allowed to confer with neutrals on the problems which this revision would present. M. Ribot, president of the French Council, refused to grant Renaudel and his comrades the passports which would have enabled them to go to Stockholm where Branting hoped to bring about this meeting. From the 1st to the 5th of June, meeting first in secret committee then in public, and after hearing the reports of Montet and Cachin—just returned from Russia—the Chamber of Deputies extolled its warlike wishes and its inability to understand the new Russia. M. Briand, Minister for Foreign Affairs, whose speech had a highly spirited and figurative ending, was received with cheers:

"France will carry on the War until victory is hers. But Russia, standing by her signature and carrying out her obligations, must have the honour of being able to tell the Russian people in later days: 'The cause of liberty in the world has triumphed through the efforts of France, but Russia was with her in the struggle.' " (Loud and prolonged applause on the Left, Centre, the Right and on several Socialist Party benches.)

On returning to his place the speaker received the congratulations of his colleagues. (Secret meeting in committee, the 1st of June, 1917, and the session of Friday, 2 June.)

M. Terestchenko's note proposing the convocation of an Inter-Allied Conference was answered by definite *non possumus.*[1] The last chance of foreign support which Kerensky could rely upon was therefore finally removed. Mutinies in the Black Sea fleet, the resignation of Admiral Koltchak, disunion in the army, marked this setback of which the Allies did not realise the gravity.

Treachery or the fear of treachery filled everyone's thoughts at this time. The Provisional Government struggled against the Rada which had been arbitrarily set up in the Ukraine, and with the *Union for the Liberation of the Ukraine,* which was suspected of having pro-German leanings or sympathies. In France at the same moment, M. Clemenceau was calling upon M. Maloy to answer publicly to the charges brought against him; Italy was floundering amid the horrors which preceded the grievous disaster of Caporetto.

The way was open for a Bolshevist advance on Petrograd. Launched on 18 June, on the Galician front, the offensive which the Allies were accused of having forced on Russia produced only minor successes followed by a *débâcle* at Tarnopol: the humbling of the national pride, useless bloodshed, the mutinous attitude of the troops towards their leaders, created an atmosphere favourable to any audacious move.

[1] Against which the author recalls with pride that he protested at the tribune of the Chamber, 2 June.

THE OUTBREAKS OF 3–5 JULY, 1917

Bolshevism gained a unique recruit: Trotsky joined Lenin. Born in 1879, a revolutionary from the age of seventeen, president of the first St. Petersburg Soviet, deported to Siberia, whence he escaped, expelled from Austria in 1914, from France in 1916, and later from Spain, he was at New York when he learnt of the Revolution. He embarked on a Norwegian ship, but was arrested by the British authorities and interned in a concentration camp at Halifax (Canada). Released at the express demand of Milukov, Minister for Foreign Affairs, Trotsky arrived at Petrograd towards the middle of May.

Since 1903 he had taken up a peculiar position midway between the Bolsheviks and Mensheviks. But on his return he joined the Bolshevist Party and was henceforth, with Lenin, leader of the Revolution.

On 3 and 4 July, a mutinous soldiery surrounded the Taurida Palace. Thousands of armed sailors and workmen disembarked from Cronstadt. But Lenin considered that it was too soon to act, that the situation was not ripe and that they must still hold their hand. At the last minute the Central Committee, converted to the opinion of its chief, launched through *Pravda* an appeal inviting the masses to overthrow the Provisional Government. Deprived of central organisation, the rising was suppressed. The day following the outbreak the Minister for Justice published certain documents which purported to convict Lenin of being in league with the enemy. The Kechinskaya Hotel, where every day in the late afternoon Lenin's appeals to the rebels were heard ringing out from a balcony, was seized by Government troops. Trotsky, Lunacharsky and Krylenko were arrested; Lenin and Zinoviev managed to reach Finland and hid near the frontier in a thatched cottage belonging to a peasant.

On the morrow of the rising Prince Lvov withdrew, leaving Kerensky as leader of the Government.

THE MOSCOW CONFERENCE (11–15 AUGUST, 1917)

Kerensky, who on 20 July became Prime Minister and leader of a Government which the Soviet Pan-Russian Committee called the "Government of the Revolution and the Country's Salvation," held, in fact, the power in his own hands, since in the new coalition Cabinet—formed after endless negotiations—the old political parties, as regards voting power and the part they played in its deliberations, were now only in a minority. It was the culminating period of the regime. The Moscow Conference which met between 11 and 15 August, 1917, proposed the consolidation of political institutions in democratic Russia.

Then came the scene when the drama of Lamourette's kiss was re-enacted in a Slav setting. The Georgian, Tseretelli, from the Extreme Left, clasped the hand of Bublikov, the protagonist of Capitalist finance and industry, in a theatrical scene depicting national union. General Kornilov, the symbol of order, received a welcome which betrayed the hidden thoughts of patriots: he made a speech in which he prophesied that a catastrophe was at hand; he denounced "the atmosphere of suicide" which must be cleared with all possible despatch. Some hailed him as a saviour.

Kerensky, Terestchenko and Nekrassov were the only ministers who had remained in office since February. That did not prevent them, however, from congratulating themselves on the increased power and stability of rule that had been acquired. Three months after the election of the Constituent Assembly the system of parliamentary rule was established on Russian soil, still strewn with the debris of the past. The Moscow Conference was the crowning-point of a policy of optimism which has no equal in history, unless, perhaps, it is the blindness of the Girondins.

KORNILOV'S SEDITION

Kornilov, the son of a Cossack and a Uzbek woman, was a brave army officer who had won promotion in the Russo-Japanese War and made his reputation in the Austro-Russian War, in the course of which he was made prisoner, afterwards escaping out of Hungary. A just man, beloved of his men for his honesty and sincerity, he was, unlike Brussilov, incapable of dissimulation and unversed in diplomacy; he could be, however, harsh and brutal when he imagined that he was being fooled by a politician. The February Revolution had seen him entrusted with the military government of Petrograd, which meant the command of the revolutionary regiments from which the Soviet was unwilling ever to sever its connection. In June, 1917, having been appointed general in command of the Eighth Army, he victoriously broke through the Austrian line and occupied Kaluktsch and Halitch. Appointed Commander-in-Chief on the south-west front the day of the Tarnopol disaster, he appeared the man best qualified to restore to the Russian army its fighting power. His appointment was one of the consequences of the brief outburst of patriotic feeling which followed the Bolshevist insurrections in July.

Before Kornilov's arrival at Mohilev, the General Headquarters Staff was in a ferment, hoping, longing for a counter-revolution. There is no evidence to show that the Commander-in-Chief had any political designs. But, having first appealed for help, it was not long before he demanded full powers. Kerensky negotiated, was evasive, and gave the impression of having agreed to the re-establishment of the death-penalty; the troops became unnerved, exasperated and went as far as to present an ultimatum. This was the result of crazy ambition—a move suggested by people about them. Kerensky's attitude changed without warning from one of extreme indulgence to one of extreme severity; he recalled Kornilov and invited him to return to Petrograd.

Beside himself with rage and mad boaster that he was, Kornilov refused to obey. The rebellion had begun and panic was widespread. General Krasnov marched on Petrograd at the head of the *Savage Division*. But the Cossacks believed that he was coming to support and not to overthrow the Provisional Government. As soon as the fraud had been discovered, and without there being any occasion to denounce it, General Krasnov found himself without an army and doomed to die by his own hand. Kornilov's attack had already lost its fire before it developed, and it abated like a bad fever (13 September, 1917).

But the people were once again mobilised in defence of the new system of rule; they stood by armed, ready for the alarm to be raised. A series of murderous attacks indicated a recrudescence of hatred for the War and still more for the officers. Methods of mob-justice were to a certain extent generally employed by the soldiers and sailors. The whole situation was going from bad to worse; the elections had been postponed, the agrarian question evaded. The Germans, with Riga in their hands, now threatened to attack Petrograd. The Republic was actually proclaimed in Russia on 17 September, 1917; this constitutional formality had been omitted.

GROWTH OF BOLSHEVISM

At the beginning of October the revolutionary movement increased in its intensity throughout the country.

At the front the troops were making friendly overtures to the enemy and threatened to leave the trenches. At the end of August the peasants rose, seized the crops belonging to landowners, burnt their estates and divided the live-stock among themselves. The provinces of Tula, Tambov, Riazan and Kaluga were in a state of insurrection. A peasants' revolt of enormous proportions swept over the country districts, where the peasants divided up among themselves the lands seized from the landowners.

In the towns the Soviets underwent a transformation. Composed at the outset of the Revolution of Mensheviks and Social-Revolutionaries, they now fell under Bolshevist influence. On 31 August, for the first time, Bolshevist motions obtained a majority. On 19 September President Wilson cabled his congratulations to Catherine Breskovskaya, the "grandmother of the Revolution." On 25 September Trotsky was elected president of the Petrograd Soviet. In the municipal elections Mensheviks and Social-Revolutionaries sustained an overwhelming defeat; at Moscow, out of the 710 municipal councillors re-elected, 350 were Bolsheviks, 184 Cadets, 104 Social-Revolutionaries and 31 Mensheviks.

During the second half of September onwards, the Bolshevist Party definitely set about the task of organising the revolt in prospect. The democratic conference which established the preliminary Parliament met between 14 and 22 September at Petrograd. Lenin, back from his retirement in Finland, demanded the withdrawal of the Bolshevist faction in the preliminary Parliament, after issuing a declaration of war against the Provisional Government and the ruling class. "The fiery words of Trotsky, who had just experienced the sweetness of prison-life under the bourgeois and Menshevist regime," said someone present at the sitting, "cut to pieces the plots hatched by various orators from the Centre as if he had used a sword. In language that was clear and definite he declared that it was now impossible for us to retreat; that the workers had not envisaged such a course, and that their eyes were only fixed on the path leading towards the new revolution. A death-like silence had fallen upon the assembly; a flutter of uneasiness was seen to pass over the chairs and benches occupied by the bourgeois leaders. . . . Applause thundered out from the tribunes and filled the hall. . . ."

Proletarian dictatorship or the Generals' dictatorship—Russia was now betwixt these two. Every chance of success was on Lenin's side. He, who up to this time had temporised, felt that the hour had come. On 10 October the Central Committee of the Bolshevist Party passed by ten votes against two the proposal to make immediate preparations for the insurrection. (Present: Lenin, Zinoviev, Kamenev, Stalin, Trotsky, Sverdlov, Uritsky, Dzerjinski, Kollontai, Bulnov, Sokolnikov and Lomov.) A political committee composed of Lenin, Trotsky, Zinoviev and Stalin was entrusted with carrying out these preparations.

The Second Soviet Pan-Russian Congress, which was to have been held at Petrograd on 15 October, had been postponed till the 25 October on the insistence of the Mensheviks. It was clear that the Bolsheviks would have a majority at the Congress, at which general opinion would favour the immediate seizure of the supreme power. Trotsky wanted to keep the insurrection under Congress control, but Lenin considered that the insurrection should anticipate Congress action, and that body would only have to sanction it as a *fait accompli*.

In giving his last words of advice on the eve of action, Lenin recalled Marx's phrase: "Like war, armed insurrection is an art." An insurrection never was to be played with, and once it was begun it was vital to seize upon the idea of carrying it through to the end. "The triumph of the Russian Revolution as well as of world revolution," he wrote, "will depend on two or three days' struggle."

Preparations for the rising were being conducted methodically and quite openly. It was to break out on the date arranged beforehand.

THE REVOLUTION OF 25 OCTOBER–7 NOVEMBER

On 12 October the Petrograd Soviet decided to set up a revolutionary Military Committee. The garrison of the capital had been won over to Bolshevism. The Provisional Government, on the pretext that a German offensive was imminent, decided to send the least trustworthy regiments to the front. The revolutionary Military Committee opposed this plan and enjoined the troops to obey no orders issued by the local authorities. The two powers which claimed authority over the army now confronted each other; insurrection was latent.

While Kerensky was busy discoursing and making pretentious remarks such as: "All Russia is with us! We have nothing to fear!" on 24 October the Red Guard and some revolutionary regiments seized the central telegraphic office, the bridges, the State Bank and the stations. Reinforcements arrived from Finland for the rebels; the cruiser *Aurora* lay broadside on in the Neva covering the Winter Palace, where the Provisional Government was sitting, with her guns.

In the morning of 25 October, revolutionary workers, soldiers and sailors, who had come from Cronstadt, surrounded the Winter Palace.

There were scenes of amazing agitation at the Smolny Institute where the Second Soviet Pan-Russian Congress was in session.

While the *coup d'état* was being carried out, Lenin "remained aloof in one of the rooms of the Institute, which, if I remember rightly, was almost empty of furniture, or nearly so. Someone came later to cover the floor with rugs and threw down a couple of pillows. We rested there, Vladimir Ilitch and I, side by side. Every five or ten minutes someone ran out from the assembly-hall to tell us what was going on . . ." (Trotsky).

John Reed, who was an eyewitness of these events, has left us a portrait of the Bolshevist leader as he came out into the light of day:

"A short, dark, dumpy silhouette, a huge, round, bald head sunken between his shoulders, little eyes, a flat nose and an unpronounced chin. . . . His suit was shabby, his trousers much too long. Not, physically, the kind of man to be the idol of the crowd, he was, nevertheless, loved and venerated as few leaders in history have ever been. . . .

"Standing on the fringe of the tribune, he cast his little winking eyes over the assembly, apparently deaf to the immense and prolonged ovation given him. When it was finished, he said simply:

" 'We will now turn to the construction of the Socialist order.'

"Once again a roar of frenzied cheering shook the assembly-hall.

" 'In the first place, practical measures must be adopted to secure peace. . . .'

"His broad mouth, which gave him the appearance of always smiling, opened wide when he spoke; his voice was harsh but not displeasing; it sounded as if it had been hardened by long years of public speaking; it flowed on, level and monotonous, and gave the impression of being never able to stop. . . . When he wanted to emphasise a point, he bent slightly forward. He did not gesticulate. At his feet a thousand simple faces looked up at him with a kind of intense adoration."

THE GREAT DECREES

The "theses" which Lenin had made public in April had now to be carried into practice; peace was to be proclaimed, the land handed over to the peasants and the dictatorship established.

The Congress of Soviets first passed the decree concerning peace: "The Workers' and Peasants' Government, sprung from the Revolution of 24–25 October and supported by the Soviets . . . invites all belligerent nations and their Governments to open without delay negotiations for the establishment of a just democratic peace."

The decree defined a just democratic peace as "an immediate peace without indemnities and without annexations" (which meant without territorial gains and without the union, under compulsion, of one nation with another). The decree announced the abolition of secret diplomacy and the publication of secret treaties.

Lenin next read the famous decree which gave the land to the peasants. This measure was to bring the Soviet Government immense popularity. "If we succeed in promulgating this decree," Lenin had said, "I defy anyone to repeal it." The measure of which the Soviet revolutionaries had always been talking was carried into practice by the Bolsheviks, thus robbing the party recently in power of the programme which had given them a hold over the country districts.

In drawing up this decisive pronouncement, Lenin had been prompted by 242 reports on claims forwarded by rural Soviets.

"Private property," read the decree, "is straightway abolished without the payment of indemnities." The property of landowners, monastic domains, churches, etc., with all their stock, whether alive or dead, passed into the peasants' hands. While dispossessing the landowners of their estates, the decree did not abolish private ownership of land, but brought the solid block of peasants, whether poor or of moderate means, rallying to the support of the Soviet councils.

Once in power, the proletariat carried through the middle-class revolution in the country districts. The Soviets did for the Russian peasantry what the Tiers-État had done in 1789–1793 for the French peasant by allowing him to acquire property and by liberating him from feudal service.

What advantages could this decree confer on the peasants? As a result of the October Revolution, up to 18 million dessiatins were allotted and distributed. Peasant holdings increased from 16 millions on the eve of the Revolution to 24–25 millions. Further, the peasants who had hitherto been crushed with taxes, debts and feudal obligations were now to find their burdens considerably lightened.

Finally Kamenev read the decree dealing with the formation of the "Council of People's Commissars." (The phrase had been proposed by Trotsky to obviate the further use of the word "minister.")

The first Council of People's Commissars was composed of Lenin as President, Rykov as Minister for the Interior, Milutin as Minister for Agriculture, Trotsky as Minister for Foreign Affairs, Lunacharsky as Minister for Education, Stalin as Minister for the Nationalities. A committee of three—Antonov-Ovseenko,[1] Krylenko and Dybenko,[2] —were in charge of affairs at the Ministry for War and Marine.

The Social-Revolutionaries had refused to accept the

1 Antonov-Ovseenko was an outcast intellectual.

2 Dybenko, a sailor from the Baltic, belonged to this triumvirate. He married Madame Kollontai, an ambassadress of the U.S.S.R., and, intoxicated by his good fortune, allowed a life of disastrous folly to lead him to his death.

Bolshevist proposal that they should have a share in the government.

The Second Pan-Russian Soviet Congress dispersed on the morning of 27 October.

KERENSKY'S DEPARTURE

Kerensky had taken refuge with General Krasnov's Cossacks. The latter's troops were in occupation of Gatchina and Tsarskoie Selo, less than twenty kilometres from Petrograd, when the students of military schools (Junkers) in the capital suddenly rose in rebellion. The Red Guards and sailors from the Fleet held up the Cossack advance on the Pulkovo heights (30 October). Surprised by this unexpected resistance and demoralised by propaganda, the Cossacks showed themselves willing to surrender Kerensky and did in fact give up Krasnov. Donning a disguise, Kerensky managed to escape by motor-car. He was to experience the greatest difficulty in getting out of Russia. Later, commenting on this event in the course of a controversy with the Whites, whom he accused of having followed a most unwise policy, Kerensky made this extraordinary statement:

"The Provisional Government was overthrown. . . . It only remained to carry out the second, and most important, part of the programme, which was to finish off the Bolsheviks in three weeks and re-establish a national (and above all strong) government in Russia" (Kerensky). These three weeks certainly seem to have been very long ones!

EVENTS IN MOSCOW

While the Petrograd insurrection was organised, the movement in Moscow was spontaneous. There was a scarcity of bread in the city and the situation was grave.

The workers vainly attempted to obtain the acknowledgment of their claims by the factory committees. Strikes occurred in many establishments. Led by Bukharin and Smirnov, the Bolshevist Party, which had a majority in the Moscow Soviet, passed a series of insurrectionary measures. At one conference of the party the question of the insurrection was put to the vote. "Figures and statistics in hand," wrote an eyewitness, "the speakers pointed out that if the proletariat, which alone could end the War, did not seize the supreme power, Russia would be ruined, there would be a total lack of bread and fuel and the railways and factories would be unable to carry on. . . ." Their speeches were scientific, even academic in character. This was not, so it seemed to him, an assembly of revolutionaries planning a social upheaval, but a meeting of some learned society. The spectators, of whom half were representatives of military organisations, seemed indifferent to what was going on. No one seemed anxious to contradict. When the motion was put to the vote, every hand was raised; the conference voted unanimously for the insurrection.

On 24 October the Soviet voted for the organisation of the Red Guards, and on 25 October for the establishment of a revolutionary Military Committee.

The municipal Duma, on its part, set up a Committee of Public Safety which ordered the dissolution of the revolutionary Military Committee. Street-fighting ensued; it lasted six days and was particularly bloody.

During the night of the 28–29 October the Junkers surrounded the Kremlin, which was in the hands of the Reds. The latter surrendered, and in the morning were massacred. Fighting redoubled in violence. The Whites surrounded the Moscow Soviet, but were themselves hemmed in by mutinous regiments and Red Guards. The Red artillery fired upon them from the Sparrow

Hills. On 2 November the Whites capitulated. The victors spared their lives and gave them their liberty.

The guns were still thundering out in Moscow and the Junkers' rising had been barely suppressed when the Soviet Government promulgated on 2 November the Declaration of Rights of the Russian Peoples, of which the main points can be summed up under three headings:

1. The equality and sovereignty of the peoples.
2. The right of the peoples to settle their own affairs even to the extent of separating in order to form independent states.
3. The abolition of all national and religious privileges and the free development of all national and ethnographic minorities.

THE RESISTANCE OFFERED BY GENERAL HEADQUARTERS

The General Headquarters Staff at Mohilev, where Dukhonin, who had been promoted Commander-in-Chief following Kornilov's dismissal, was senior officer, refused to recognise the Council of People's Commissaries. On 9 November, Lenin, Stalin and Krylenko communicated by telephone with General Dukhonin and enjoined him to open negotiations with the Austrians and Germans. Having given an evasive reply, Dukhonin was dismissed and Krylenko, formerly a second-lieutenant, was appointed Commander-in-Chief. The same day Lenin despatched a message to the soldiers calling on them to take a hand in the cause of peace. The Headquarters Staff prepared to flee into the Ukraine, but the troops prevented their escape and imprisoned the Commander-in-Chief in a railway carriage. On 20 November the soldiers went to meet Krylenko, and, despite all appeals to calm themselves, assassinated Dukhonin.

FRANCE'S AMAZEMENT

In France, public opinion had been very ill-informed as to what was going on in Russia. M. Noulens, a former Minister for Finance and War, the deputy for Le Gers, an honourable man with no experience of revolutions, was called to fill the post of French Ambassador to Russia on M. Paléologue's departure. He had come expecting to hold converse with a parliamentary republic and instead stumbled up against a social revolution: he was much too dumbfounded to be able to give his country any information of much value.

". . . While the military representatives kept Chantilly informed of the sudden changes in the Russian higher command, the diplomats were noting the declarations made by Kerensky, Nekrassov, Vinnitchenko and others. But we still remained ignorant of the people's inner life; we were blind to the rising tide of anarchy, or certainly of Bolshevism, which was now revealed by Russia's refusal to continue the War and by the desire on the part of a destitute majority to divide up among themselves the wealth belonging to an oppressive minority" (Raoul Labry).

The letters written to Albert Thomas by Sadoul, who as an eyewitness showed great perspicacity in his comments, were totally ignored or misunderstood. France continued to base her knowledge of Russia on a collection of out-of-date formulae.

"Are we going to lose Russia?" Marcel Sembat asked in amazement. "Have all Russian leaders sold themselves to the Germans? Is civil war in progress or will they make separate peace with the enemy? After all, what do the revolutionaries of Moscow and Petrograd really want? From a distance, we have heard nothing about them but their risings, their sudden attacks, their dealings with the Germans. How events have jostled each other! We saw the revolutionaries defeated in July, victorious in November; we saw Lenin seize the supreme power after escaping from cells and cellars; and we saw Kerensky, the dictator of the day before, fleeing, hidden under straw in a motor-ambulance!"

THE HIGHER COMMAND OF THE VICTORIOUS BOLSHEVIST PARTY

The two great leaders of the Revolution were Lenin and Trotsky. But they had the assistance of a staff of professional revolutionaries:

Sverdlov (1885–1919), five times imprisoned under the Tsarist rule and exiled to the extreme north of Siberia; returned in 1912, handed over to the police by an *agent provocateur* and deported once more to Siberia. Later he was one of the most able assistants of the new Government until he died prematurely in 1919;

Stalin (born 1879, his real name being Djugachvili) was a Georgian peasant, a bootmaker's son. Socialist at seventeen, deported at twenty, an escaped prisoner at twenty-five, he was continually being arrested and escaping. After the Revolution, he was Commissar for the Nationalities, then a little later Secretary-General of the Central Committee of the Communist Party;

Dzerjinsky (1877–1926), of Polish origin, became a Marxist in his youth. He was five times imprisoned, thrice deported and often made good his escape. He was condemned in 1912 to five years' hard labour. Liberated from the Moscow prison in February, 1917, he took part in the October Revolution as member of the revolutionary Military Committee. Soon—in December, 1917—he was appointed president of "*the Extraordinary Pan-Russian Commission for the struggle against the counter-revolution*," better known by its other awe-inspiring name of *Cheka*. Commissar for the Interior in 1919 and for Highways and Communications in 1921, he was elected president of the Supreme Economic Council when the State industries were in danger. It appears that, although sending many to their deaths, he had a tender heart, and that a "bloody mysticism" was the cause of his extreme harshness. This kindly-looking man was to die of rage in the tribune during a congress meeting;

Zinoviev, a Jew, who in 1917 was forty years old, was by profession a journalist and orator. He acted in a very ostentatious manner as Lenin's second-in-command. Even on the eve of its outbreak, he refused to believe that the October Revolution was threatening, just as Kerensky failed to foresee, up to the very last moment, the coming of the February Revolution. He was entrusted with the administration of the Petrograd commune, an office which he diligently performed. He became president of the Executive in the Communist Internationale from 1919–1926. In 1928 he was banished from the party for having co-operated with Trotsky. Since then he has been re-admitted;

Christian Rakovsky, Bulgarian by birth, became Roumanian after the Treaty of San Stefano, since his parents eventually chose to live in the Roumanian half of the Dobrudja. He was the most intellectual, the most encyclopaedic and gallicised of all the revolutionaries sent from the Balkan countries to Paris to study historical precedents. He was expelled a record number of times from various countries, and had ample opportunity of comparing prison conditions in several towns in more than one State before entering upon a new way of life which was full of unexpected activities. He negotiated the agreement between Soviet Russia and the Ukraine, became leader of the Soviet Government in that country, received appointment as Ambassador to London and later to Paris. In 1927 he was recalled to Moscow and dismissed from the party as being an obstinate supporter of Trotsky's policy. Then he was more or less banished to Astrakhan and, later, to Siberia, where French friends, anxious for his safety, could find no trace of him;

Arrested as early as 1902 for taking part in the 1st of May demonstration, and involved in the Revolution of 1905, Rykov was again arrested and deported. He showed great administrative ability during the Revolution. He organised the food-supply in the Moscow district, and in 1918 became president of the Supreme Economic Council; in 1921 vice-president of the People's Commissariat; and, on Lenin's death, president. He was a realist, and was for that reason deemed to be a Conservative revolutionary;

Kamenev, a Jew, having joined the Social-Democrats in 1901 at the age of nineteen, eventually became a follower of Lenin. He left the country in 1908, returning in 1914. He led the Bolshevist party in the Fourth Duma and supervised its labours. Arrested in February, 1917, together with his colleagues, deported and then liberated in February, 1917, he became co-editor of *Pravda* with Trotsky, who was his brother-in-law. Like Zinoviev, he placed no trust in the insurrection of October. Plenipotentiary at the Conference of Brest-Litovsk and afterwards president of the Moscow Soviet, he showed himself specially gifted as a municipal councillor and possessed of an easy-going temperament. An opponent of Trotskyism from 1923 to 1924, he later compromised himself in its support (1926–1927); but everything turned out well for him and suited his plans;

Bukharin, the Benjamin of "the Bolshevist Old Guard," a strike-agitator, was deported to Siberia, whence he escaped and fled abroad, not returning to Russia until 1917. Pamphleteer, doctrinaire, scholar, lecturer, professor, disputant, he was a kind of interpreter *ex cathedra* of Marxism, and for twelve years a "Doctor of the Science of World Revolution." In 1929 he was removed from responsible posts, having shown "Conservative tendencies";

Kalinin, the child of moderately well-to-do peasants, was a manual worker—a turner in the Putilov factory. He joined the Social-Democratic Party, which became anti-militarist in 1916, and, like many of his colleagues, he came straight from prison to shoulder the responsibilities immediately thrust upon him by the triumphant progress of the Revolution. He was to become president of the Central Executive Committee of the U.S.S.R. in 1923, that is to say, *mutatis mutandis*, President of the Republic.

There are other burgraves of Communism who are better known outside Russia, but despite their striking personalities they were less important in the initial stages of the Revolution than those discussed here: Chicherin the diplomat, the aristocrat from the Extreme Left, who remained Minister for Foreign Affairs from 1917 to 1930; the learned engineer, Krassin (1870–1927), Ambassador in Paris in 1925 and Commissar for Foreign Trade in London in 1926, who was "very enthusiastic over the plan (for which he was practically speaking responsible) of obtaining a monopoly of foreign trade: he was the most 'Western' of all the Kremlin chiefs" (Count Sforza); Karl Radek, who was the foremost journalist of the new regime; Maxim Litvinov, Deputy-Commissar for Foreign Affairs, who came to the front after Chicherin's withdrawal; Lunacharsky, Commissar for Education—the Alcibiades or Barras of modern times. These were the men who served as lieutenants under that unique leader Lenin, in the period immediately following the Revolution. He himself, hidden behind the Provisional Government of workers and peasants, was to be the soul, the brain, the will of the New Russia.

CHAPTER III

THE CIVIL WAR

Counter-revolutionary skirmishes — The Constituent Assembly—The decree cancelling the debts (28 January, 1918)—The Soviets faced with the "infamous peace" —Consequences in Europe of the Brest-Litovsk Treaty —The Czechoslovak insurrection (the modern anabasis) —Red Terror—The dreadful death of the Romanovs— —The situation at its worst: War Communism— Social-Revolutionary outbreaks and Boris Savinkov's rising: the Red army—Effects of the Allied victory— Prinkipo and a curious opportunity missed—The Koltchak affair—Yudenitch in sight of Petrograd— Honest Denikin's attempts to play a hero's rôle—The war with Poland—Wrangel's departure—Economic results in 1921—The Cronstadt rising and its lessons.

THE COUNTER-REVOLUTIONARY SKIRMISHES

So great was the general stupefaction at the outbreak of the Revolution of October that no one had time to offer any resistance. Dukhonin, the Commander-in-Chief and Kornilov's successor, did not carry out the order, which reached him by telephone, to open negotiations with the enemy. Of this, instant dismissal was the result. Second-lieutenant Krylenko was made Commander-in-Chief. It seemed as if someone had laid a wager—and had won.

The Stavka (General Headquarters) showed signs of resistance. Dukhonin was assassinated in the Mohilev Station, just as Krylenko arrived to complete the necessary formalities before taking up his new post. Other members of the Staff fled or had already escaped towards the South, to the Don and Kuban countries, which were in the hands of the generals.

Kornilov, who had been insecurely imprisoned by

Kerensky in a girls' school after his attempted *coup d'état*, escaped with his gaolers, who proceeded to act as escort, and reached the Don country, where the aged Alekseev, another former Commander-in-Chief, was trying to build up an army of volunteers. Officers, Junkers, students, even soldiers were there, anxious to defend their country against the Bolshevist invasion, but they did not constitute anything approaching a real army. The ataman Kaledin, a Cossack and the chief of the Cossacks, the same who had taken part in the Moscow Conference, soon realised that this attempt to stem the tide of Bolshevism was doomed to failure; he committed suicide on 29 January, 1918. The Cossacks' hour was passed: it was not long before his successor was shot; the Reds occupied the Kuban country and established themselves in Ekaterinodar, being equally victorious in the Urals against General Dutov.

But the Ukraine was a more difficult proposition. The country had been expecting a grant of autonomy since the February Revolution. The promises of Prince Lvov and Kerensky, which were continually being amended, had in no way appeased it. The Rada, a national assembly which had been established immediately after the downfall of Tsarism, was composed of a Social-Revolutionary majority which desired to see the establishment of Socialism and democratic rule, but which was even more anxious to obtain independence for the Ukraine. Its leaders were the novelist Vinnitchenko, and Petlura, formerly a minor Government official, who had been promoted to high office after becoming suddenly a popular idol. The Rada's sole objective was to secure the autonomy of the Ukraine; it was prepared to welcome the support of the Entente and the Central Empires, whether acting in concert or independently of each other. It desired peace, but an independent peace, and the Bolsheviks, having defeated Kerensky, attempted to destroy the Ukraine. Therefore the Red Guard marched for the first time on Kiev, which they seized on 26 January, 1918. But this was only one phase of the battle which had begun at Brest-Litovsk and in the surrounding district.

THE CONSTITUENT ASSEMBLY

The Bolsheviks, who had been impatient for the elections to be held while they were opposing Kerensky, had lost all interest in the Constituent Assembly when, after being so often and so long deferred, the day at last came for the nation to go to the polls. Lenin had explained that the Constituent Assembly represented democratic power at its greatest in a bourgeois republic, but that the Soviet was a superior type of administrative body. This theory was used in support of a clever stratagem, for the Social-Revolutionaries, who expected to return to power under the aegis of accepted principles, were sure of a majority in advance.

The Social-Revolutionaries obtained 267 seats, the Bolshevist die-hards 161, the Ukrainian Social-Revolutionaries and Mensheviks 41, National Minorities 33, Cadets 15 and Mensheviks 3. In an electorate of 36,262,560, the Social-Revolutionaries and Mensheviks obtained 22,600,000 votes, or 60 per cent. of the total. Only in the two capitals and in the army had the Reds secured a majority at the polls.

Then, on 8 January, 1918, the Constituent Assembly met at the Taurida Palace, "*making ready to legislate and to govern, and taking care to omit nothing of the beautiful parliamentary ceremonial of the Western type*" (Victor Serge). Attempts had been made to excite the interest of the masses in the men they had chosen to represent them. But those who had organised this entertainment, and were at the same time to benefit from it, employed discretion, and the people remained indifferent.

The session was opened by Sverdlov, a Bolshevist organiser, aged thirty-two. Chernov, the leader of the Social-Revolutionaries, who had been elected president by 244 votes, gave an interminable harangue, to which Bukharin made a churlish reply. After Tseretelli had intervened, the withdrawal of the Bolshevist Party was announced. It was four o'clock in the morning: the plans for agrarian reforms were being outlined.

The chief of the guard of sailors, Anatole Yalezniakov, who was semi-officially described as an anarchist, but who was certainly a humorist, advanced towards the President's tribune and bending over Chernov, who was no hand at *repartie*, said simply:

"The guard is tired. I beg you to leave the assembly-hall."

All the majesty of the Assembly collapsed at this injunction. The Constituent Assembly broke up. On the morrow it was dissolved. But its hasty dispersal and dissolution was of little importance. The Russian people had not learnt to love parliamentary government.

THE DECREE CANCELLING THE DEBTS

The Provisional Government had recognised the debts of the former regime in a declaration dated 8 (21) March, 1917, less for reasons of principle than in consideration of the special circumstances in which Russia was situated at that time: "Inspired solely by its conception of the modern State in which individual rights are rigorously safeguarded and each citizen scrupulously carries out his obligations, and bearing in mind that, if the basis of the financial administration were shaken during the War, the country would be threatened by irremediable misfortunes, the Provisional Government declares that it assumes without fail the financial obligations imposed on the Treasury under the last Government, as under: contract-payments, wages of employees and all other payments to be made by the Treasury, as laid down by law, contract, or agreed upon any other legal basis . . ." (Professor A. N. Slack).

The leaders of the October Revolution did not at first decide either for or against the recognition of debts. Lenin's first decree dealt with the suppression of war and of private property. In January, 1918, the deposits (security and specie) in all private banks were confiscated and handed over to the State Bank. Only on 28 January, 1918, was the decree promulgated cancelling, among others, State loans contracted abroad.

In the interval, the Allied Governments had been prevailed upon to change their attitude of expectancy into one of hostility: M. Pichon's speech in the French Chamber on 27 December, 1917, explained this hostile attitude which, in practice, took the form of sending aid to those who had already declared themselves adversaries of the revolutionary regime in the Ukraine and in Bessarabia.

It was in these circumstances that the following ordinance was drawn up and published:

DECREE CANCELLING STATE LOANS

(Code of Laws, No. 27, Art. 353)

I.—All State loans contracted by Governments for which Russian landowners and Russian bourgeois were responsible (they are enumerated on a separate list), are cancelled as from December, 1917. Dividend-payments due in December from the above loans will not be paid.

II.—Loans guaranteed to various institutions and industries by the above Governments are likewise cancelled.

III.—*With no exception, all foreign loans are cancelled.*

IV.—Short-dated bills and Treasury bonds remain valid. Interest on these vouchers will not be paid out, but the bonds themselves are legal tender equally with bank-notes.

V.—Citizens not in affluent circumstances, who hold State-vouchers for a sum not exceeding 10,000 roubles (nominal value) in the cancelled loans, will receive in exchange nominal certificates for the new loan contracted by the Russian Socialist Federal Soviet Republic, for a sum not exceeding 10,000 roubles. The conditions of the loan will be drawn up later.

VI.—Deposits made in the State Savings-Banks, together with the interest on them, are inviolable. All bonds held by the Savings-Bank in cancelled loans will be entered in the register of National Debt of the Russian Socialist Federal Soviet Republic.

VII.—The Co-operatives, local autonomous administrations and other democratic institutions or institutions of public utility, which hold bonds in cancelled loans, will receive compensation as provided for by the regulations to be drawn up by the Supreme Economic Council, working in agreement with the representatives of these institutions, if it is proved that these bonds were acquired before the publication of the present decree.

NOTE.—The local organs of the Supreme Economic Council will settle which local institutions are of a democratic character or of public utility.

VIII.—The general control of the liquidation of State loans is entrusted to the Supreme Economic Council.

IX.—The liquidation of loans is entrusted to the State Bank, which must proceed immediately to register all bonds held by the various holders as well as all others which are, or are not to be, cancelled.

X.—The Councils of workers' and soldiers' and peasants' representatives, in agreement with the local councils of the Supreme Economic Council, will set up Commissions to settle what citizens shall be considered as being in poor circumstances.

These Commissions have the right to confiscate wholly savings that have not been gained through work, even if these savings do not exceed the sum of 5,000 roubles.

Signed: The president of the Central Executive
Pan-Russian Soviet Committee: J. SVERDLOV
Secretary: J. SVERDLOV

The *corps diplomatique* protested in a note which declared

that it considered "all the decrees of the workers' and peasants' Government dealing with the cancellation of State loans, the confiscation of property, etc., to have no force where foreign interests were concerned."

By a significant coincidence, Roumanian troops launched an offensive this same day, 31 January, 1918, against Odessa. Thus a duel was beginning between Eastern Russia and Russia's creditor-Allies. There was every reason for agitation.

THE FIRST NEGOTIATIONS AT BREST-LITOVSK

But people's attention was elsewhere. The vision of peace alone kept alive the hopes of an exasperated, harassed people who had applauded the downfall of Tsarism and Kerensky's discomfiture, so that they might be freed from war; but they had not yet undergone the humiliation of defeat in peace-time.

When they came into power, the Soviets had announced that peace was declared: their first decree (26 October) implied an immediate request for an armistice. This armistice was signed on 2 December, 1917, at Brest-Litovsk, a little frontier town in the Grodno province, situated at the confluence of the Mukhavee and the Chlerka. The Germans had been informed of the Russian request by General Hoffmann, Chief of the Staff of the Eastern army, who telegraphed at once to Ludendorff: "Your Excellency needs troops, here is the first contingent." Actually, the signing of the armistice on the Eastern Front left the Germans free to send reinforcements to the Western Front. It was understood that peace negotiations would be opened during the following weeks between the Central Empires and the Soviets: the Allies were invited but by their silence intimated their refusal to attend.

Thus the Allied representatives had already refused to enter into official relations with the Soviet Government, in spite of that most unexpected telegram which President Wilson had sent the victors of the 25 October. Only M. Noulens was in communication with Trotsky, and even then unofficially, whilst General Pellé, on the other hand, had notified the unfortunate General Dukhonin of this rupture and had, at the same time, informed him that he hoped to see the Russian command "able to keep the Russian army facing the common enemy." Mr. Balfour announced in the House of Commons that he was awaiting a direct communication from Germany in order to be able to confer upon the question with the Allies. This obviously banished all hopes of an Allied delegation being despatched to Brest-Litovsk. M. Pichon, Minister for Foreign Affairs in the Clemenceau Cabinet which was formed on 16 November, 1917, was more explicit and more pessimistic. "Will the Russian delegation," he said, "be able to brave the dangers of this meeting? Is it not fated, I fear, to be misled, surrounded as it will be by enemy delegations?" (Chamber of Deputies, 27 December, 1917).

Events took a different course to what had been prophesied, and unexpected influences came into play. Negotiations were reopened on 27 December, 1917, not at Stockholm, where the Soviets had once hoped they would, but at Brest-Litovsk. The representatives of the Central Empires were the aged General Hoffmann, a giant with a bushy face and a peremptory manner, von Kuhlmann, an astute diplomat educated in London before the War; and to represent Austria-Hungary came Count Czernin, a poor imitation of Metternich, a Thugut who had missed his mark. On the Soviet side there were Trotsky, the imperturbable Kamenev and Ioffe—three persons but only one personality. Besides these, there was a party of Ukrainian delegates who took advantage of a recent proclamation by the Rada to intervene in the discussions on an equal footing with the Bolsheviks. These Ukrainians had received encouragement from both sides, from the Allies and from Austria. Soon it was to be known that the "people from Kiev had opted for a treasonable peace" (*Temps*, 30 January, 1918).

But, yielding to Bolshevist pressure, the Rada had lost the Ukraine while engaged in negotiating on its behalf. There was fighting at Kiev between Ukrainians and Bolsheviks, but there was also strife at Brest-Litovsk between delegates of the Rada and representatives of the Ukrainian workers' and peasants' Government which had been hastily set up at Kiev as a direct result of the Bolshevist invasion. Count Czernin declared on 17 January, 1918, that only the Rada delegates represented independent Ukraine, and on 25 January a treaty was signed with that country by Germany, Austria, Bulgaria and Turkey. On 26 January, Kiev was taken by the Reds and the Rada dispersed. But its delegates returned to their country by way of Volhynia in railway wagons supplied by the foreigners. On 16 February Kiev, which was in immediate danger of being bombarded, was delivered from its precarious situation by Saxon troops. The Rada, once more set up, was again dissolved, just as simply as the Constituent Assembly had been. A little Prussian lieutenant made ready the way for the hetman Skoropadsky, who was installed by Field-Marshal von Eichorn (29 April, 1918) as a step towards the formation of the "Mittel Europa."

THE SOVIETS CONFRONTED WITH THE "INFAMOUS PEACE"

Trotsky's thesis can be summed up in four words: *neither peace nor war*. But by the end of December an important section of the Bolshevik Party from the Extreme Left called for negotiations to be broken off. Lenin, who believed in the urgency for an immediate peace, was continually out-voted up to 18 January, 1918. That day the German offensive was renewed; a series of *communiqués* was issued announcing the capture of Dvinsk and the occupation of the Ukraine. At last, by seven votes to six (Trotsky having taken his side), Lenin carried the day. The supporters of revolutionary war resigned: Piatakov, who later held high appointments, was among them.

Four days later an offer of assistance from the French and English reached Trotsky. It came too late. The Germans brought fresh pressure to bear on the Bolsheviks. Lenin threatened to resign if some kind of a treaty was not immediately signed. Sokolnikov affixed his signature, "his teeth clenched," to quote his own phrase, supported by Chicherin (returned from exile), Karakhan, the future Ambassador, and Ioffe. He did, in fact, sign the most disadvantageous treaty ever drawn up in thirteen clauses, for by its terms the Russian army was to be demobilised and Russia was to renounce all rights to the Baltic States, to Lithuania and Poland, and was also to evacuate Asia Minor. The Ukrainian people's Republic was to be recognised and a treaty signed by that country with the Central Empires. Russia was required to promise the evacuation of Finland and the Aaland Islands and the payment of three milliards of gold-roubles in reparations.

"General Hoffmann's artfulness was the only real driving-force in all these negotiations," wrote Trotsky. As far as Lenin was concerned, he was willing to lose ground in order to gain time.

But Russia had, indeed, lost a great deal of ground that day, 3 March, 1918, when the Treaty of Brest-Litovsk was signed! She had lost 90 per cent. of her coal output, 70 and 55 per cent. of her metallurgical and cereal productions respectively. Red Finland was left to her fate, which meant that she was to suffer under a vigorous system of repression introduced by Svinhufvud, the head of the Government, acting in concert with the German general, von der Goltz. The Transcaucasian Republic was destroyed by the Turk general, Vekhir Bey, in accordance with the terms of one of the clauses in the treaty; a similar fate overtook the Georgian, Armenian and Azerbaidjan Republics, built up on the debris of a Bolshevism which had gone before: disasters followed one upon another, to engender ever-increasing despair. The victors of October could console themselves with the thought that their regime had already lasted longer than the Paris Commune itself.

CONSEQUENCES IN EUROPE OF THE BREST-LITOVSK TREATY

The Brest-Litovsk Treaty caused immense, but short-lived, jubilation in the Pan-German camp. Fifty-three infantry and thirteen artillery divisions, or more than one million German soldiers, exclusive of Austrians, had been kept inactive, standing to arms, facing the Bolshevist sphinx. Forty divisions were now, therefore, withdrawn and despatched to the Western Front.

But the Ukraine, which was to revictual the armies, furnished but a meagre supply of cereals under the never relaxed menace of German bayonets. This system could only be carried out by the employment of a great number of troops; material results were poor and moral consequences odious, for the Ukraine found unity in her suffering and in her resistance to oppression. The Social-Revolutionaries of the Left assassinated Count Mirbach, the German Ambassador to Moscow, and the Field-Marshal von Eichorn at Kiev (July, 1918).

The Entente, however, looked upon the separate peace signed at Brest-Litovsk as a treasonable peace and a veritable catastrophe. France calculated what immediate damage had been done by Russia's defection; England calculated what would eventually be the effect of Russian propaganda. M. Clemenceau feared that Alsace and Lorraine might be freed; Mr. Bonar Law feared the loss of India, for the route to that Empire would be certainly cut if Russo-German Imperialism were to make Persia its vassal. Every country reacted according to its national temperament, but they were all agreed henceforth to exclude Bolshevist Russia, who had deserted the common cause, from the comity of nations.

One of the consequences, which it was impossible to foresee, of the Russo-German agreement was the annexation of Bessarabia by Roumania, who, on 3 January, 1918, had with the greatest difficulty seized Kishinev. All possibility of friendly negotiations being opened between Roumania and Russia was, in fact, removed as soon as the German occupation of the Ukraine was officially recognised and had become a serious menace to Roumanian territory. It was in these circumstances that, in March, 1918, the decree proclaiming the annexation of Bessarabia was issued, and ever since the Soviets have never ceased to raise active and vehement protests against Roumania's action.

The peace of 3 March, 1918, had not caused the Allies the inconvenience they had feared or had given their enemies all the advantages they had anticipated to reap from it. "Neither in a military nor in an economic sense was the Peace of 3 March advantageous to the Central Empires. It was a Pyrrhic victory. It brought them every kind of trouble in the East and plunged them into a sea of contradictions. It led them to reveal their aims as regards annexation and, in spite of themselves, to ensure the maintenance of the Bolshevist regime in Moscow . . ." (André Pierre). General Hoffmann, who drafted the treaty, later perceived his error, and from his death-bed urged the countries of Western Europe to launch a crusade against Russia (*vide* his book published in 1925: *An allen Enden Moskau*). The Kaiser's last Government, led by Max von Baden, broke off relations with the Soviet State as soon as 5 November, 1918, the same day as the United States agreed to open negotiations with Berlin: the result of the Brest-Litovsk Treaty had been fatal, not only to Count Mirbach, but also to the Reich itself, for its whole framework came near to collapsing when it had to face a revolution of the Moscow pattern. By 9 November, 1918, the Hohenzollerns were no more; on 11 November the armistice of Rethondes was signed. On 13 November the Treaty of Brest-Litovsk was but a scrap of paper torn in half by the Central Committee of Moscow.

THE RISING OF THE CZECHOSLOVAK TROOPS (THE NEW ANABASIS)

Despite the fact that he had issued drastic decrees ordaining the confiscation of land and capital, Lenin would have liked, in the early months of 1918, to have had a breathing-space—to have let the country pass through a stage of State Capitalism—in order to have had an opportunity of examining the Russian economic system which was so lacking in uniformity and in which the patriarchal, and particularly small bourgeois, type was found, or ought to be found, in coexistence with operative Socialism. But succeeding events did not allow him the respite which he had deemed necessary.

By May, 1918, the rising of the Czechoslovaks was to put the strength of the revolutionary movement to the test. But who were these Czechoslovaks?

In order to understand the part they played, it is necessary to go back a stage, to the beginning of the War. Milan Stefanik, the son of a Slovak pastor, an astronomer of distinction and a naturalised French subject, joined the French Flying Corps on 4 August, 1914. He was invalided during the retreat from Serbia, being then a second-lieutenant, and was taken to a hospital in Rome. As soon as he was convalescent, he embarked on a recruiting campaign among his compatriots scattered about the world, with the idea of forming Czechoslovak contingents which would fight shoulder to shoulder with the soldiers of the Entente and set an example which would cause Czech subjects serving under the Austrian flag to desert *en masse* and join the Russian army.

In fact, during General Brussilov's offensive in Galicia (1916), the Russians captured in the neighbourhood of 400,000 prisoners, the majority of whom were Czech or Slovak by birth. The *Ceska Druzina*—the Czechoslovak battalion of volunteers formed at Kiev on 20 August, 1914—had grown to a brigade by May, 1916. But the Russian Government (of which Sturmer was at that time head) disliked admitting among regular troops a corps composed of rebels and deserters from the enemy and would have preferred to employ these alien troops in the munition factories. Therefore, Stefanik came to Russia in July, 1916, to arrange for the transfer of the Czech contingents to the French Front. Objections were raised, and the matter was still under discussion when the Provisional Government came to be established.

In April, 1917, Prince Lvov authorised the formation of the Czech brigade as an independent and autonomous force, with the result that numbers of enthusiastic Czech and Slovak workmen hastened to swell its ranks. A national Czech Council was set up at Paris with Masaryk, the famous historian, as president. Masaryk, who arrived in Petrograd on 15 May, 1917, solemnly blessed the re-birth of this Czechslovak army of which history had nothing to record since the Battle of the White Mountain in 1620. The Czech troops showed conspicuous bravery on 3 July at Sborov during General Brussilov's ill-fated offensive.

Following the disaster, the brigade, having received reinforcements, was attached to an army corps of which the Russian general Chokorov had been given the command. Masaryk would have liked to transfer this army corps to France, where a Czechoslovak army was in process of formation: only two contingents embarked at Archangel in July and November, 1917.

The remainder, who were posted to the Ukraine, found themselves faced with an unprecedented situation after the October Revolution and even more so following the armistice which effected a reconciliation between Soviets and Germans. It was now impossible to maintain that attitude of neutrality which President Masaryk had ordained that his army commanders were invariably to adopt—a rule never to be broken. The order was given for the Czechoslovak army corps to proceed towards their port of embarkation at Vladivostok, 9,000 kilometres distant from Moscow.

"From Kiev to France by way of Siberia! It's a fantastic plan, I sometimes said to myself; but having thoroughly weighed the matter, it appeared the most practical, despite the length of the journey" (T. G. Masaryk, *The Resurrection of a State*).

The Germans advanced into the Ukraine and, on the other hand, the local Soviets showed opposition to the movement of the Czechoslovak troops. "In April, 1918, Maxa and Cermak, delegates to the National Czech Council who had been sent to Moscow to arrange for the repatriation of the army were held by the Bolsheviks as hostages. They were forced to sign first an agreement which directed the Czechoslovak troops to proceed in the direction of Murmansk and Archangel, and later (27 May) were obliged to agree to the disarmament and internment of the whole army. Faced by this ultimatum, the volunteers decided to fight their way through. On 14 May a clash occurred between Czech troops stationed at Cheliabinsk and the local Soviet, which arrested several volunteers. The Czechs then seized the station and the town.

"On 25 May, 1918, the Czechoslovak contingents were attacked at Marianovka and, on the following days, there was fighting at Irkutsk and Zlatoust with local Communists. On the other hand, a military Directorate of eleven members was elected" (Charles Henry and de Méans). Then the volunteers manœuvred along the Trans-Siberian railway to found an anti-Bolshevist Government at Samara (8 June, 1918), to seize Ufa (4 July, 1918), and Irkutsk, at the other end, on 11 July; and to set up a Directorate at Omsk in August. These events were taking place while the Japanese were disembarking five divisions at Vladivostok and the English were landing war material at Murmansk.

Between the Volga and the Pacific Ocean a vast territory was slipping out of the hands of the Soviets. And the march of the Czechoslovak army to the sea was the beginning—that odyssey which Marshal Foch ventured to describe as "a modern anabasis."

THE DREADFUL END OF THE ROMANOVS. THE RED TERROR

On 7 December, 1917, an Extraordinary Commission had been created. It bore the name of Vecheka, but was popularly called the Cheka and has since been known as the O.G.P.U. This was the "iron fist of the revolution," "the proletariat's granite citadel," "the sword of the Red Terror."

The Cheka had not been responsible for the early political assassinations; it simply set its seal on any spontaneous acts of violence. Moreover, it was the Ochrana's natural successor and claimed to be the Bolshevist answer to this detested machine of Tsarism. The existence of the White Terror, and still more of the Terrorist methods employed by the enemy, justified or excused the doctrine of the Red Terror. It is right to remember, also, that Russian revolutionaries were cognisant of all the precedents of the English and French revolutions; that they willingly invoked Cromwell, and that Robespierre was held in highest honour by these extremists as a proud forerunner of their type.

At the outset of the Bolshevist rule, only robbers and *agents provocateurs* could be sentenced to death. But soon the death-penalty was applied more generally. In September, 1918, the Sovnarkom (the People's Commissariat) decided to sentence to death "all persons belonging to White Guard organisations who were guilty of having laid plots or planned revolts." This decree was a direct result of the fury aroused by the attempted assassination of Lenin. From this moment onwards the grants of money made to the Cheka by the State—almost negligible in 1917—and the, originally, very limited powers conferred upon it, were to increase to such an extent that this revolutionary police system was finally entrusted—to quote the historian Pokrovsky's phrase—"with the essential work of the Revolution."

But the Cheka's reign opened in a sinister manner with the murder of the Imperial family.

* * * * *

On 26 April, 1918, the Tsar had been moved from Tobolsk to Ekaterinburg, the chief industrial city of the Urals, where he arrived ahead of the Tsarina and Tsarevitch, who came on 10 May with another convoy. All the prisoners were confined in the Ipatiev mansion, named "the house with the special purpose." The life of the Imperial family at Ekaterinburg was the same as it had been at Tobolsk, until the day came when the guard of workers, recruited from among the local population, was replaced by a Lettish Guard.

"A curious incident occurred the day before the Lettish Guard took up its duties, on the last occasion Mass was celebrated for the Tsar and his family in the Ipatiev mansion. According to the rites of the Greek Orthodox Church, a certain prayer is said in an undertone at ordinary Mass and is sung at funeral services. The congregation kneels at this point in the service. But on this occasion—the last on which Mass was celebrated—the priest made an error and loudly intoned the prayer; according to practice, the Imperial family fell to their knees. . . . The incident created a profound impression . . ." (Nicholas de Berg Poggenpohl).

On 16 July, 1918, at midnight, Nicholas II, the ex-Empress Alexandra, the Tsarevitch Alexis, the Tsar's four daughters, Doctor Botkin, the cook, his assistant and a female servant were all killed by revolver-shots. Their bodies, piled into a lorry, were taken to a disused quarry, soaked in petrol and burnt. Only buttons, medals, and fragments of crucifixes remained as means of identification.

On 18 July, 1918, the Grand Duke Serge Mikhaïlovitch, the Grand Duchess Elisabeth Feodorovna, sister to the Empress, Prince Constantinovitch and his wife Helen Petrovna, the Serbian Princess, Prince Igor Constantinovitch and Prince Vladimir Pavlovitch Paley were assassinated at Alapaievsk, where they were leading a tolerably comfortable life in exile, though closely guarded. Their bodies were thrown down a mine-shaft in the neighbourhood.

On 25 July, 1918, Ekaterinburg and on 28 September Alapaievsk were wrested from the Bolshevist grasp by troops belonging to the Siberian army and by the Czechoslovaks. A judicial enquiry was opened, or rather, enquiries were ordered to be made; but owing to the rabid formalism which existed even at this time in these troubled areas, the judicial enquiry was not opened before March, 1919.

If the advance of the Whites and the Czechoslovaks explains in some measure the reason for taking the murderous precautions which spelt death for the Tsar and Tsarina, the princes of the Imperial family and their faithful servants, that in no way lessens the horror of these massacres, which will for ever stain the records of the Soviet Revolution with their dreadful memory.

The Pan-Russian Executive Committee was in session at this time: a measure relating to public hygiene was being debated. Sverdlov entered and requested permission to speak: "I have learnt," he said, "that Nicholas has been shot at Ekaterinburg by the orders of the local Soviet: Nicholas wanted to escape. The Czechoslovaks were approaching. The Vtsik Committee approved the action taken."

Nothing more; the Committee returned to the business of the day. Nevertheless, the future had further difficulties in store.

THE SITUATION AT ITS WORST. WAR COMMUNISM

The territory of the Soviet Republic continued to diminish in extent and its boundaries were barely wider than those of the old Muscovite principality of the sixteenth century. On all sides stretched the enemy's battle-lines: in Finland, a German-Finnish force, in the south and west, the Germans; on the Volga, the Czechoslovaks;

in the north, the English. The peasants were rising in rebellion. No corn supplies were forthcoming from the Ukraine or coal from the Donetz. Famine was threatening. "Here we are brought back to the primordial task of all human societies: to fight famine." So remarked Lenin. An exceptional situation was to be met with exceptional measures.

A strict rationing system, the nationalisation of all industrial undertakings, the pooling and requisitioning of economic resources which were to be distributed on the card-system as wages in kind—this was War Communism, a safety measure and an imitation of the system employed by the belligerent nations.

Since the workers' control of production had been revealed as inadequate and uncertain, the Soviet State nationalised all industries, not so much as part of a definite economic policy, but rather as a reprisal for sabotage and for bad workmanship and failure in production. In view of the ever-increasing confusion in industry, a decree, issued on 28 June, 1918, arranged for the immediate nationalisation of all mining, metallurgical and transport concerns operating with a capital exceeding 500,000 roubles.

The well-to-do peasants (*kulaks*) rose in rebellion against the corn monopoly. The dispossession of the landowners had brought Lenin the gratitude of all country workers and he still retained it. But when the currency depreciated in value, the kulaks refused to give up their corn for distribution. Moderately well-to-do peasants were torn between their fear of the counter-revolution and their horror of the requisition agents: attempts to restore confidence were far from being successful.

But the committees composed of poor peasants were ranged against the rich peasants, while the inhabitants of the principal urban centres rid themselves of the hordes of revictualling agents who were authorised to confiscate any grain found in the people's barns.

SOCIAL-REVOLUTIONARY RISINGS: BORIS SAVINKOV AT YAROSLAVL. THE RED ARMY

July, 1918: a recrudescence of Terrorism. The extremist Social-Revolutionaries repudiated the Treaty of Brest-Litovsk. "The uncertain attitude adopted by the Bolsheviks in the struggle against the Germans, the Government's appeals to them to offer a stout resistance to the enemy and to carry on the struggle, contrasting strangely with its own terror and inertia, placed the workers in a most awkward predicament," wrote Irene Kashovskaya in her *Memories of a Woman Revolutionary*. No one knew what course to take. Count Mirbach's assassination was simply an isolated act of murder—nothing more. The Social-Revolutionaries attempted an attack on Moscow, gained possession of the post-office and fired on the Kremlin. The street was promptly swept with rifle-fire. This was only an alarm, but it revealed the rift between the Social-Revolutionaries and the Soviets in power. Dora Laplan's attempt on Lenin's life (end of August, 1918), which inspired the vehement protests of Karl Radek (who had himself on a previous occasion endangered the life of the great leader), must be considered as a Terrorist action and the responsibility for it assigned to the Social-Revolutionaries with whom this Jewish Charlotte Corday was connected.

Boris Savinkov (1879–1925) was also a former Terrorist and a Social-Revolutionary of the period preceding the Revolution of 1905. He was a novelist, poet and man of action, all at one and the same time; he was Azev's dupe as well as the dupe of his own courageous nature; converted to patriotism by the War, he served in an unfortunate capacity as intermediary between

Kerensky and Kornilov; he was suspected by everyone but universally admired for his chivalrous bravery. He had founded the *League for the Defence of the Fatherland and of Liberty*, which, in a few months, had a membership of several thousands. Relying—one cannot imagine why—on the landing of Allied troops at Archangel, Savinkov induced his friends to choose Yaroslavl, which is situated on the line between Vologda and Moscow, for a model counter-revolutionary experiment. When their activities began the conspirators had only a dozen revolvers between them, but they plundered the artillery depot and the Bolsheviks were obliged to bombard Yaroslavl for twelve whole days before being able to drive out the victorious rebels who, led on by Boris Savinkov's daring, had stumbled on success. The punishments inflicted were terrible: the Cheka inaugurated its system of mass-execution.

But these outbreaks, coupled with the victories obtained by the Czechoslovaks, brought with them the widespread conviction that the formation of an army was necessary: in this, Kerensky had not succeeded.

The soldiers of the Red army had spirit but no cohesion; their officers no technical ability. Trotsky was invited by Lenin to reorganise the army. "They resolved with one accord to have recourse to professional soldiers. Up to that time officers were always liable to assassination." The dictators declared that the Revolution needed live, energetic generals. A ukase declared: "The Soviet Government is not responsible for the attitude of hostility adopted towards the officers as a body." An ordinance was issued pointing out that officers deserting to the enemy ran the gravest possible risks. . . . "These turncoats betray Russian workers and peasants into the hands of those robbers, those English, French, Japanese and American tyrants. Deserters should realise that the consequences of their guilt will fall upon their own families, wives and children. I give the order . . . for the families of deserters and traitors to be seized" (Valerio Marku). This was something after the style of Saint-Just. Trotsky, in common with the revolutionary *élite*, knew—almost as well as our great historian, Mathiez himself—all the most important principles which had governed the revolutionary struggle in France. But in adapting these principles to Russian conditions, he infused into them something of his own force, his "red" genius, that gloomy eagerness which he inherited from the prophets of his Jewish race.

The real miracle of the Red army was the manner in which the Staff was improvised. "Kamenev, Lebedev, were appointed to the General Staff; there was also Yegorov, Brussilov, Vatsetis, Nicolaïev, Stankievitch, who had been general officers or held important appointments in the Tsarist army; but the most striking figures of all were Azim, who was twenty, Budienny, formerly a non-commissioned officer of cavalry—a kind of red-capped Murat—and Frunzy, who was thirty. . . ." (Pierre Fervacque). And lastly there was Mikhaïl Tukhatchevsky, a young aristocrat, barely eight months previously a prisoner in the fort at Ingoldstadt, appointed a colonel almost by guess-work. In appearance he recalled the shadowy figure of Napoleon at Brienne, and, before preaching, like Trotsky, the doctrine of the Revolution, had, like Sorel, preached the doctrine of his own ambitions. Profiting from the lessons of 1793, Trotsky succeeded without much experimenting in amalgamating these two categories of leaders—the one drawn from the *tchin*, the other from the professional military class. In this way the Red army was made to appear the work of the Red Revolution.

FIRST SUCCESSES OF THE RED ARMY

Trotsky was People's Commissar for War and president of the Soviet, responsible for the conduct of the revolutionary war. But the Soviet's deliberations caused him very little embarrassment, as this council met in a troop-train which was hastily got together between 7 and 8 August, 1918, in order to proceed in the direction of Kazan.

Sviajsk, a little township on the banks of the Volga, seventy kilometres from Moscow, had become at that date Central Russia's last bastion of defence against the attacks of the Czechoslovaks who were in victorious vein. The Reds broke and fled under machine-gun fire. Trotsky rallied them and drove back the enemy; the next day, embarking on a torpedo-boat and followed by four other similar vessels, so old as to be almost unnavigable, he burnt the White ships anchored at Kazan. On 10 September the capture of Kazan was the first of a series of victories. On 12 September Simbirsk was in the hands of the Reds and the Volga was freed.

Here and there the exploits of other Red supporters met with success: the metal-worker Blucher, leading a small army of workers, crossed the Urals and joined the main Red force. In the north of the Caucasus, 16,000 men who had been cut off following the defeat of the Kuban army forced their way into the impregnable fortress of Tuapsy which was held by a Georgian garrison. By the autumn of 1918 the fact was established that "on the warm cinders of the Great War, the Bolsheviks had built up a new army" (Trotsky).

Of this, however, the nations of the Entente, their thoughts occupied with their own victory, were ignorant: they had been duped by this ignorance and gulled into the bargain by a policy of metaphor.

CONSEQUENCES OF THE ALLIED VICTORY

Soviet Russia paid no regard to the Allied victory except in so far as its consequences might influence world revolution. At the news of the overthrow of the German Empire, Lenin was filled with great hopes. The opposition of the Spartakusbund, of Rosa Luxemburg and Karl Liebnecht to the Social-Democrat Government, which succeeded the Imperial rule, appeared in his eyes the German counterpart of the Russian Revolution of October, 1917. His elation led him to conceive the fantastic notion of an army of two million men carrying with them to Berlin the might of Bolshevism and the ideas of Moscow.

In the meanwhile, the German troops, hitherto in occupation of the Ukraine, fell back in disorder upon the Reich, having become infected with the Bolshevistic influences with which they had come in contact when weighed down by despair, while the Red armies were received with open arms by the peoples of the Ukraine, White Russia and Lithuania. Skoporadsky, liegeman of the Germans in the Ukraine, was outlawed by Petlura, who established a National Government, later to be confronted with a branch of the Soviet Government under the presidency of Christian Rakovsky. The strict, methodical and severe rule of the Germans when in occupation was followed by a period of civil war with guerilla fighting: brigandage and pogroms became widespread. Then Makhno appeared, the anarchist nobleman who "abolished the infantry, artillery and even the cavalry as being bodies not easily handled, and substituted for them an army of *britchkas* (light tanks) which bristled with machine-guns (approximately 300 machine-guns being employed in all)" (Isaac Babel, *Red Cavalry*). The Ukraine was destined to be a theatre of incessant warfare.

In 1918[1] the French fleet dropped anchor off Odessa.

[1] December.

The troops, under the command of General d'Espérey, since created a Marshal of France, were intended for action in Southern Russia, for once the Ukraine was in their hands, Central Europe would automatically fall under their control. The Inter-Allied forces, numbering 45,000 to 50,000 men, were divided up and sent both to the Odessa region and to the Crimea, where the French held Sebastopol and Simferopol. To the north of Odessa the zone of occupation stretched from Tiraspol to Nicolaev and Kherson. The Allied intervention in Russian affairs had been planned previous to 11 November, 1918, for military and strategic reasons, and it was to assume the character of a hostile intervention in Soviet affairs from the very fact of the existence in Southern Russia of a White army and of counter-revolutionary agitation.

But those whom M. Clemenceau was anxious to assist received no definite advantages from this intervention: the French troops would not fight beside the Whites. On the other hand, the mutiny in the Black Sea fleet, imprudently stirred up and sternly suppressed, gave French Communists a powerful, sentimental theme with which to arouse post-war republican opinion in favour of an unobtrusive reconciliation with the Soviet Republic. These painful incidents caused the Governments of the Entente to let "the Russian experiment" henceforth develop on its own lines without pledging their soldiers' lives in the struggle between the old and the new Russias.

PRINKIPO, OR A CURIOUS OPPORTUNITY MISSED

A definite stir, if not amazement, was created among the victorious Allies when it became known that the Peace Conference, of which the first meeting had been held in Paris, had decided—at the suggestion of the British delegates—to arrange a discussion-meeting with the Russians, despite the fact that the Soviet Republic was still suffering an economic and diplomatic blockade. But the invitation which was passed on 23 January, 1919, was addressed to all *de facto* Governments existing on the territory of the former Russian Empire, whose representatives were to meet, together with the plenipotentiaries of the Entente, at Prinkipo, an almost unknown island situated not far from Constantinople. There the new Eastern Question was to be discussed "*without ceremony*."

Chicherin accepted this invitation in the name of the Soviets, without being in the least concerned about the risk of seeing the *status quo* sanctioned. His note in reply, in addition to other matters, stated:

> "The Soviet Government declares itself ready to yield to the demands made by the Powers of the Entente with regard to the question of loans. It does not refuse to recognise the obligations towards its creditors, subjects of the Entente Powers. . . . It proposes to guarantee the payment of interest on its loans in raw material, the quantity to be agreed upon. It is disposed to grant nationals of the creditor Entente Powers mining, lumber and other concessions on definitely established conditions, the internal management of the aforesaid concessions being in no way permitted to injure the economic and social order of Soviet Russia. . . . The fourth point, to which, in the opinion of the Soviet Government, the proposed negotiations might turn, concerns territorial concessions, the Soviet Government having no intention of excluding at all costs from the negotiations the question of the annexation by the Entente of certain Russian territories. . . ."

An irreconcilable attitude was adopted to these proposals by those from whom it was least expected—the counter-revolutionary leaders, Koltchak in Siberia and Denikin on the Don. They had given support to the Powers responsible for the invitation and yet were prompted to take up an uncompromising attitude by the defeat of the proletarian revolution in Berlin.

As a result of this obstinacy, the curious opportunity of a conference at Prinkipo was missed, thus enabling the Soviets, even while civil war was raging on every hand, to reconstruct their Republic so that finally its territory embraced one-sixth of the earth's surface.

THE KOLTCHAK AFFAIR
(18 NOVEMBER, 1918–6 FEBRUARY, 1920)

The Government of the Soviets had been unable to make any real progress in Siberia during the first few months of its advent to power. A Duma met and broke up in February, 1918. Transbaikalia was dominated rather than ruled by the ataman Semenov. Four different groups contended for power in Vladivostok. A so-called ministerial decree announced to the Siberian peoples that a Government had been formed which would summon a regional Duma in the place of the one to which the members of the autogenous ministry had belonged. In actual fact, between the Urals and Vladivostok there were more than twenty pseudo-Governments of different types and with different tendencies, from the Constituents' Committee which sat at Samara down to the *Regional and Directoral Government* of Siberia which was established at Omsk. The country was an immense caravansary of petty, ever-changing powers, a lumber-room of contradictory whims and fancies. The conference at Ufa (8–25 September, 1918) decided in principle on the co-ordination of efforts in the campaign to be launched against Bolshevism, and nominated a Directorate of five members, in which the Demosthenes of the Social-Revolutionaries, Avksentiev, consented to work with General Alekseev, a deputy-director and an ex-commander-in-chief, who was bowed down with age and tortured by monarchic nostalgia.

This Directorate, which was recognised by the Omsk Government and by General Horvat, solicited the approbation of foreign Powers who were duly notified of its creation. It next appointed Admiral Koltchak as Minister for War. The chiefs of the Allied Missions which had already been given authority to thwart, if possible, the aggressive action of the Bolsheviks—presumed to be tools of the Germans—were to make all arrangements with this Directorate. The plan was to effect a junction of the Czech and Siberian contingents with the Allied forces at Archangel: America and Japan were acting in co-operation, but not wholeheartedly.

When General Janin arrived in Siberia, bearing detailed instructions, the situation had undergone a curious change. The great victory of 11 November increased the Allies' prestige but did not make up for the insufficient strength of the armies of which the Allies now assumed control.

The Czechoslovaks, having taken and then lost Samara (October, 1918), were very elated at having captured the town of Perm with the aid of one of their compatriots who had become commander of a White army. But the troops were tired and, moreover, upset by the rival commands: the ataman Semenov, who enjoyed the confidence of the Japanese, ruled as a tyrant in Irkutsk and refused obedience to the Government at Omsk.

During the night of 18–19 November, 1918, Koltchak had proclaimed himself to be the *Supreme Government*: the members of the Directorate having been previously arrested and all the resistance on the part of the Social-Revolutionaries broken down by a few rounds of machine-gun fire, the Siberian Government changed from a verbose democracy into a military autocracy. For this former officer of the Imperial fleet was impatient to gain sole control of the situation. "I need nothing," he said, "but material aid—boots, for instance—and I'll go to the enemy for them if necessary."

"He suffered too much from nerves to be a statesman" (Philippe Berthelot), and as seen by his entourage, he was "a saucepan always on the boil, but in which the stew was never cooked." He was jealous of the foreigners who assisted him.

But amongst the foreigners themselves jealousy was none the less rife. There was no common object, no unity of command. Obstacles were placed in the way of President Wilson's secretly laid plans for the formation of a new Directorate. President Masaryk looked upon the leader under whom, willing or unwilling, the soldiers of his country were to serve, as an adventurer. England and France alone made no secret of their support. A telegram from M. Clemenceau (21 December, 1918), which was published later, defined the nature and scope of this policy of succour: "The Allied plan is to effect the encompassment, in an economic sense, of Bolshevism simultaneously with the establishment of ordered conditions in Russia through the efforts of certain elements among her people." England had invented Koltchak, France adopted him on her Ally's recommendation; Japan was to furnish the necessary war material. Thus, with the forces at his disposal, Admiral Koltchak met with considerable success in his operations and was able to approach close up to the Volga. But Bolshevist propaganda agents profited by the enforced suspension of the advance owing to the thawing-out of the river and by the admiral's increasing unpopularity. "By reason of its monarchist plots, the Government has aroused, both among the people and in the army, a feeling of distrust and hostility which is so marked that internal order and the morale of the troops are in great danger. The army lacks supplies and is unwilling to fight" (Report of Commandant Lasies, a former Bonapartist deputy). Some companies went over to the enemy, wearing brand-new English uniforms.

As regards the Czechoslovaks who were guarding the Trans-Siberian railway, it was impossible to prevail upon them to take part in the operations owing to their having been enjoined to maintain a neutral attitude. Two generals of distinction, the Czech Garda and Pepelaiev, the brother of one of Koltchak's Socialist ministers, had left the dictator, being driven away by the intrigues of suspicious coteries.

Safety was now only to be found in retreat. That retreat was carried out in July and August. Fortune once again smiled upon them: Tobolsk, recently seized by the Reds, was torn from their grasp. But the White army, now nearly exhausted, could no longer stand the pace.

Between 5 and 10 November, Omsk was evacuated, and by 15 November was invested by the Bolsheviks. Worn out by this seemingly endless, and now entirely aimless, struggle, the Czechoslovaks demanded their repatriation with greater insistence than ever before. From one end of the railway to the other there was a series of insurrections. On 17 November the Social-Revolutionaries seized the supreme power and offered it at once to General Gayda, whose followers had been rounded up and shot by Koltchak's last remaining supporters. "Admiral Koltchak's adventure ended in a Siberian tragedy."

On 25 December, 1919, a Social-Revolutionary outbreak occurred which was witnessed by the Allied Missions from their train which was drawn up outside the station, preparatory to their evacuation. The troops of the ataman Semenov, which had been despatched to bring aid, were commanded by Skipetrov, a kind of bandit chief: they retired after carrying off and massacring thirty-one hostages. When Admiral Koltchak reappeared at Irkutsk in January, 1920, he was arrested, imprisoned and shot (6 February, 1920), without it being possible to assign the responsibility for his murder either to the Czechoslovak General Staff or to General Janin, the head of the French Military Mission. "The unrest created by the massacre of the hostages was so intense that the rescue of Admiral Koltchak *manu militari* would have required the employment of considerable armed forces which were non-existent, since the only troops at the disposal of the Military Mission were the Czechoslovaks, who were obliged to remain neutral" (General Rouquerol).

After the evacuation of the Czechoslovak troops in March, 1920, the whole of Siberia, freed from foreign intervention, was restored to Soviet rule.

The resistance offered by the ataman Semenov continued for a short time in the form of a swashbuckler's romance. Its hero, the Baltic baron von Ungern Sternberg, the grandson of an alchemist, awoke, in twentieth-century Mongolia, memories of the great *reiters* (German horse-soldiers) of the sixteenth. Made a prisoner by the Reds, von Ungern died bravely in September, 1921, shot by his captors. "I've lost the game," he said. But no, it was the Allies who had been worsted in the Ukraine.

YUDENITCH IN SIGHT OF PETROGRAD

In July, 1919, General Yudenitch was appointed Commander-in-Chief of the White army in the north-west: he was acting in conjunction with Koltchak, whose subordinate he was—at any rate, in theory. Yudenitch, whose attack was very well timed, received assistance from the British fleet lying in the Gulf of Finland. The seventh Red army (there were sixteen Red armies) was driven back, either as a result of treachery or of inefficient leadership, and sustained serious losses. Following this disaster, Petrograd was in danger, and in so great danger that Lenin thought seriously of giving it up. Trotsky violently opposed the idea of surrendering the capital. "Well, let us try," Lenin concluded. They were, indeed, destined to be sorely tried. Yudenitch took Luga on 13 October, Krasnoie Selo and Gatchina on 16 October; in another ten days the White army had taken Tsarskoie Selo (the Tsar's town) where formerly the Imperial family resided—the Russian Versailles—only thirty kilometres from Petrograd. The Soviet Government was thrown into confusion, and confusion was to reign supreme until 21 October. On that day the Red army, entrenched at Pulkovo, repulsed the White attack, and so completely was the situation changed that in a fortnight Yudenitch's troops were obliged to take refuge in Esthonia, where they were disarmed. On the testimony of his adversaries, the honour of having brought about this change of fortune was due to Trotsky alone. The Carnot of the Revolution, he has been called, and on this occasion in particular he showed himself to be no mean strategist.

HONEST DENIKIN ATTEMPTS A HERO'S RÔLE

All that remained of the Russian Imperial army had been mustered in the south by the time the French carried out their intervention in Southern Russia. The officers, who were naturally alienated from the Soviet regime by the murder of the Tsar, after surmounting the greatest difficulties, had fled into the Ukraine and to the territory of the Don, where the Cossacks, now cured of their infatuation for Bolshevism, had elected General Krasnov as their ataman. They also escaped to Rostov, the provincial capital of the colony of White exiles, which had been planned under the aegis of Generals Alekseev, Kornilov and Denikin, two Commanders-in-Chief and a Chief of the General Staff, all unemployed as a result of the Revolution.

Faced with the possibility of a German invasion, an army, 35,000 to 45,000 strong, was successfully got together. The civil population was made responsible for the supplies of food, and munitions were forthcoming from the Entente. Except in the cavalry, which was recruited from amongst the Cossacks of the Kuban and the Circassians, there were not enough soldiers. There was no lack of officers, but men capable of leadership were not forthcoming.

Honest subordinates like Alekseev and Denikin, who were born always to be nothing more than seconds-in-command, became standard-bearers. Denikin was still young enough to fill this heroic rôle; he was brave, honest and scholarly: he had a reputation for openness and as an upholder of common honour. People remembered that he had been a prisoner at Bykov and Kornilov's Chief of Staff. The story of his famous deeds was handed down from officers to men, crowning his loyal head with glory. In the war with the Germans his was called "the iron division." That was sufficient reason to make him the central figure of this concourse of volunteers, all yearning for an incentive to common effort. Denikin's collaborators, however, who agreed to work under his magic spell, would not obey each other. "Not one among them," said Denikin of his general officers, "will carry out the orders given him by one of his own rank." He had authority, but did not confer it on others.

Nevertheless, the beginnings were magnificent. The whole of the Ukraine, Central Russia and Kursk were conquered. Denikin was approaching Tula. Beyond was Moscow, his mystical objective.

Denikin's army advanced northwards to the cry of "Moscow, Moscow." But those in close touch with the Commander-in-Chief had the gravest doubts concerning the eventual success of this overwhelming advance. The local assemblies were restless, General Sidorin, commanding the Don army, pessimistic, likewise General Wrangel, Denikin's deputy. . . . Why? Because of the incessant disputes which rent the anti-Bolshevist parties, influenced, as they were, by conflicting Cossack opinions; because the Entente hesitated between Denikin, the man who stood for Russia as one and indivisible, and the separatist policy which the diplomats were still in favour of applying to the Caucasus, the north-west and even the Ukraine.

Denikin had no idea of the ever-mounting difficulties until the Council of War met at Kharkov on 2 November, 1919, when the hopeless inefficiency of the army staffs was revealed.

There was still one minor success to come—the taking of the Tsaritsin by Wrangel. And then, helped by discord in the White ranks, the Bolsheviks gained the ascendancy, thanks to the cavalry led by Budienny, a sergeant-major promoted to leadership. They took possession of Novo Cherkask and soon afterwards Rostov. Suspicion crept into the ranks: the troops from the Kuban were accused of being traitors. The Whites spent their time quarrelling and babbling. Local Soviets were set up: profiting by the confusion in the enemy's ranks, the Reds threw back the Cossacks from the Urals and drove the volunteers out of Odessa. A general collapse was threatening; above all, the alliances with England, France and Petlura were breaking down. Denikin, who understood nothing of politics, was much taken with the idea of drawing up a political programme—a form of madness that often attacks generals. On 15 December he published this programme, and on 17 December formed a Cabinet: though his ministers styled themselves "directors," they were in reality merely puppets. But all around him generals were quarrelling. As a means of getting rid of him, Wrangel was shipped aboard a torpedo-boat. The troops and their leaders lacked a common aim and object, and this had crushed the spirit which would otherwise have crowned their efforts with success.

On 20 March, 1920, Denikin had become discouraged, and having arranged the appointment of his successor, General Wrangel, the most able man of the counter-revolution left Theodosia *en route* for London. There his time was spent in meditation and in writing his memoirs.

THE WAR WITH POLAND

The Soviets had hardly finished with Koltchak and Denikin when they turned to making preparations for war against Poland. At any rate, Pilsudsky firmly believed in their hostile intent. He was the saviour of Poland, her national hero, and in 1920 her undisputed master. A Socialist and patriot, he loathed the Russian Bolsheviks with religious fervour, with the fierce hatred which, as a young conspirator, he had nursed against his Tsarist oppressors. He was awaiting the attack—at any minute now it might be delivered—of which he had been forewarned by Trotsky's fiery utterances. He preferred to attack rather than be attacked, and on that account, following the signing of an agreement on 21 April, 1920, between Poland and Simon Petlura's Government in the Ukraine, the Polish troops marched into that country. Kiev surrendered without fighting.

But almost at once, on 4 May, 1920, the Russian forces suddenly took the offensive and threw back the Polish troops for 100 kilometres: Tukhatchevsky, the Polish commander, formerly a second-lieutenant in the Imperial Guard, was twenty-eight years old, and an exceptionally capable leader. At the end of June, 1920, the situation was entirely reversed and found the Poles once again victorious. Then a second Soviet offensive forced the

Poles, outflanked on their left, to retreat on a front of 600 kilometres. "Who could give Warsaw a guarantee of the fidelity or even the neutrality of the Ukraine population?" (Maurice Pernot).

In Warsaw and the capitals of Europe the panic hourly grew more intense. Mr. Lloyd George advocated the opening of peace negotiations and offered to mediate. A Polish coalition Cabinet, led by the peasant deputy Witos, addressed a direct request to the Soviets for an armistice. Chicherin declined Lloyd George's proposals and cunningly exploited the Polish predicament in order to give the Red troops time to reach their goal. And their goal was Warsaw. "Lenin had drawn up a very definite plan of action: to carry the affair through to the end, or, in other words, to march to Warsaw and assist the Polish working masses to overthrow Pilsudsky's Government and to seize the supreme power" (Trotsky). "Lenin was incapable of understanding that the situation could present a factor so foreign to Marxist principles and so human as nationalism; he was incapable of foreseeing the inevitable reaction by which the Polish people would be roused to combat the invaders of their native land" (Isaac don Levin). France despatched to Warsaw, on 25 June, 1920, her greatest military expert, General Weygand, formerly Foch's Chief oi Staff and now Commander-in-Chief of the French army. M. Millerand, who succeeded M. Clemenceau (January to October, 1920) as President of the Council, announced that his country, deeply anxious for Poland's safety, sympathised with her in her understandable distress.

It was then that Pilsudsky struck northwards with his Polish divisions which had been mustered and equipped in haste. In six days he had covered close upon 200 kilometres, and by a miracle righted the strategical situation. This success of Polish arms robbed Tukhatchevsky's praise, "the experiment of exported revolution," of all its meaning. "The pressure exerted by General Wrangel's forces had contributed to save Warsaw" (M. Millerand's declaration to *Le Temps*).

The victory at Warsaw (15 August, 1920) was, it seems, Pilsudsky's personal achievement—a feat which had far-reaching results, since 250,000 Reds had either been taken prisoner or driven back into Germany. The Bolshevist disaster was aggravated by the attacks of Ukrainian *francs-tireurs*. In the south, the White army held its ground and gained fresh victories. Once again the Soviet regime was threatened by danger—this time in a different, but very definite, form. It was necessary to negotiate and quickly. Poland expressly declared that she "sincerely desired peace." Negotiations were opened on 18 September, 1920, and on 12 October peace preliminaries were signed between Poland and the Soviet Union. In the meanwhile, the Bolsheviks, having occupied Vilna, were forced to evacuate it on 25 August. Then General Zeligovsky seized the town during a raid which was undoubtedly planned beforehand, proclaimed the existence of a central Lithuanian State and prepared to annex the territory. His action, though sanctioned on 15 March, 1923, by the Ambassadors' Conference, continued to be deemed irregular by Lithuania and the Soviet Union. A final treaty was concluded on 18 March, 1921, at Riga, of which the following were the main clauses:

Article II.—The two contracting parties, in conformity with the principle of self-determination, recognise the independence of the Ukraine and of White Ruthenia and decide that the eastern frontier of Poland, that is to say the frontier between Poland on the one hand and Russia, White Ruthenia and the Ukraine on the other, shall be fixed as follows: [Here the frontier is traced.]

Article III.—Russia and the Ukraine renounce all rights

and claims to the territories situated to the west of the frontier as fixed in Art. II of the present treaty. On its part, Poland renounces in favour of the Ukraine and White Ruthenia all rights and claims to the territories situated to the east of this frontier. The two contracting parties agree that, in so far as the territories situated to the west of the frontier fixed in Art. II of the present treaty include territories subject to dispute between Poland and Lithuania, the question of the grant of these territories to one or other of these two States exclusively concerns Poland and Lithuania.

Article V.—The two contracting parties give a mutual undertaking fully to respect the political sovereignty of the other party and not to interfere in its internal affairs and, particularly, to abstain from all agitation, propaganda and intervention whatever, and not to facilitate such movements.

The two contracting parties undertake not to create nor to protect organisations which aim at armed attacks on the other contracting party, nor to seek to strike at its territorial integrity, nor to abolish by force its social or political systems; nor to create and protect organisations which seek to rule a part or parts of the territories belonging to the other contracting party. In consequence, the parties undertake to prohibit the existence on their territory of such organisations, their official representatives and other organs, to prohibit military recruitment, as well as the importation into this territory and the transport across it of armed forces, of arms, of munitions and war materials of every kind, destined for these organisations.

Article VII.—Russia and the Ukraine confer on persons of Polish nationality dwelling in the territory of Russia, of the Ukraine and of White Ruthenia, according to the principles of equality among the peoples, all rights guaranteeing their free intellectual development, the use of their mother-tongue and the exercise of their religion.

Reciprocally, Poland undertakes to grant these same rights to all persons of Russian, Ukrainian and White Ruthenian nationality dwelling in Poland.

Persons of Polish nationality living in Russia, in the Ukraine and in White Ruthenia, have the right, in so far as permitted by the internal legislation of these countries, to cultivate their mother-tongue, to organise and protect their own educational systems, to develop their intellectual movement and, to that purpose, to create associations and societies: persons of Russian, Ukrainian and White Ruthenian nationality dwelling in Poland shall enjoy the same rights, in so far as permitted by Polish legislation.

The two contracting parties mutually agree not to interfere directly or indirectly in questions pertaining to the organisation or life of the Church, as well as with religious societies existing on the territory of the other party.

The Churches and religious associations to which persons of Polish nationality in Russia, in the Ukraine and White Ruthenia belong, will be entitled, in so far as permitted by the internal legislation of these countries, to organise their own internal life in an independent manner.

The aforementioned Churches and religious associations shall enjoy, in so far as is permitted by internal legislation, the right of acquiring and utilising real or personal property, necessary to the exercise of their religion and the maintenance of their clergy and ecclesiastical institutions.

In conformity with the same principle they shall have the right to attend the churches and institutions necessary for the practice of their religion. Persons of Ukrainian and White Ruthenian nationality will enjoy identical rights in Poland.

ARTICLE VIII.—The two contracting parties reciprocally renounce the repayment of war expenses, that is to say, State funds applied to the war, as well as indemnities for damage caused by the war, that is to say, damage caused by the war to them or their nationals in the field of operations or by military measures taken during the Polono-Russo-Ukrainian War.

ARTICLE XV.—Russia and the Ukraine undertake to pay Poland 30 million gold-roubles in specie or in bars, in virtue of the active participation of the Polish Republic in the economic life of the former Russian Empire, a participation recognised by the peace preliminaries of 12 October, 1920; the sum to be paid within a year at the latest after the ratification of the present treaty.

ARTICLE XIX.—Russia and the Ukraine release Poland from all responsibility for debts and liabilities incurred by the former Russian Empire, among others, for liabilities contracted as a result of the issue of paper-money, treasury bonds, vouchers and certificates; for internal and external loans contracted by the former Russian Empire, for the guarantees given to all institutions and enterprises whatever, as well as for the debts guaranteed to the above institutions.

WRANGEL'S FINALE

On 20 March, 1920, overpowered, disheartened and beaten, General Denikin resigned in favour of General Wrangel, whom he had previously removed from his Staff and whose appointment was made by the almost unanimous wish of the volunteers. Wrangel had looks, courage and a stainless past. But that he belonged to the old regime there was no question; he found it quite impossible to acknowledge the new order, and it would be easy to represent him as an impenitent and uncompromising monarchist.

General Baron Peter Wrangel was not blind to the realities of the situation when he succeeded Denikin, for his first care, before reorganising the army, was to prepare a plan for the evacuation of his troops by way of the sea, should this course be rendered necessary by a catastrophe. Civil administration was non-existent; in one country—the Crimea—all food-supplies were exhausted owing to the enormous forces of troops and refugees which it had been called upon to feed; whole regiments were broken up, decimated, demoralised and lacked war material. England had notified that her support was to be withdrawn and advised the signing of an armistice with the Bolsheviks.

Wrangel sent for M. Krivochein, who had formerly collaborated with Stolypin, and chose Struve, a disillusioned Socialist who had made a reputation in Paris, to carry out negotiations abroad.

On 18 April, Maklakov, the Russian Ambassador in Paris, who had been appointed by the Provisional Government, and who remained at his post waiting to be relieved, telegraphed as follows: "French Government hostile to an agreement with Bolsheviks. Will exert no pressure to secure capitulation of the Crimea. Will take no part in similar mediatory proceedings if undertaken by other Powers. Favours the idea of defending the Crimea and Tauric province. Regarding Bolshevism as Russia's principal enemy, French Government favours Polish offensive. Unwilling to accept idea of camouflaged annexation of the Dnieper region. If an Ukrainian Government is established it will only be recognised *de facto.*"

Thus the sympathy which the French Government showed towards Wrangel's efforts was actuated by the deep sympathy which France felt for Poland. This declaration was given special significance by the fact that at this moment the Polish troops had been thrown back by the Reds. But England persisted in her plan of breaking off hostilities in South Russia. Wrangel was not justified in thinking that any change of British policy would result from the Polish offensive. Viscount Curzon in his note to Wrangel warning him of the British intentions was as harsh as M. Millerand in his note of encouragement was prudent: "I am pleased to assure you," wrote M. Paléologue, Secretary-General for Foreign Affairs, to M. Krivochein, "that the French Government recognises the importance of a territory which is the last refuge of Russian patriots, the last sanctuary of Right and of the Russian conscience." To match this kindly note from La Châtre, assistance in the shape of food-supplies and war material was immediately forthcoming.

Between 25 and 30 May, Wrangel attacked and repulsed the thirteenth Soviet army: this victory was only made possible by the fact that the Soviets were making a definite effort on the Polish front, where they had gained a great victory. But the effect which it produced in Paris was such that M. Millerand did not hesitate to recognise General Wrangel's Government *de facto*—an act of recognition which has often been questioned and which M. Raymond Poincaré refused to approve. As a result of this fictitious legal measure, the volunteers' army, which was now called the Russian army, received a part of the Russian stocks held in bond in several countries since the Great War.

And the fighting continued. First, fortune favoured the Whites, who, between 15 and 28 June, took 11,000 prisoners, 60 guns and 300 machine-guns. An expedition to the Kuban, after a successful beginning, had, by 20 August, become a complete failure. But the French Government, carrying out M. Millerand's declaration to the Chamber (20 July, 1920), decided to publish its official recognition of the Wrangel Government and to accredit it with a diplomatic representative, Comte Martel, who arrived at Sebastopol on 6 October, 1920.

General Wrangel begged the Poles not to cease hostilities on their front, nor to yield to Lloyd George's suggestions. "It was clear that after the Armistice and the conclusion of peace with the Poles, the Bolsheviks would turn their forces against the Crimea and that the White army would be worsted in the one-sided struggle."

These apprehensions were fully realised. After the Peace of Riga was signed (18 September, 1920), the Soviet Government concentrated on the front held by General Wrangel's troops some 500,000 men and the whole force of Red cavalry, which Budienny, a substitute general, had brought to the highest pitch of efficiency. As the sea had receded, the Reds were able to make their way round the famous positions at Perekop, reputed to be impregnable. The isthmus which protected the Crimea on its north side was forced. General Wrangel's army was crushed.

The Whites fell back by forced marches on the seaports; 126 ships took on board 145,000 people in one day (31 October, 1920). General Koutepov, who later disappeared in a mysterious manner (January, 1930), made the arrangements for this departure *en masse* of the last remaining soldiers of the civil war.

The same day, following an exchange of notes between General Wrangel, Comte Martel and Admiral Dumesnil, all the available Russian ships were handed over to France as a security for the expenses incurred by her in the evacuation. This agreement was to arouse the protests of the Soviet Government, and in the course of time they have not become less vehement.

The Russian refugees were distributed among military camps on the island of Lemnos, or sent on to Serbia, Roumania, Bulgaria and Greece, and have gradually scattered all over the world. Some have gathered together in the West to form a Union of Russian Combatants, others have joined the Balkan armies; there are others still who are fighting side by side with the Chinese.

Peter Wrangel—he whom the Bolsheviks nicknamed the Baron of the Crimea—died in 1928 at Brussels, an embittered, forgotten man.

ECONOMIC RESULTS IN 1921

The tragic year of 1919 terminated victoriously for the Soviets. In the course of that year, delegates from the Communist parties in several countries had met at Moscow and founded the Third Internationale.

The civil war seemed at an end, and the problem arose of how the demobilisation of 5½ million Red soldiers was to be carried out. In view of the complete breakdown of all transport arrangements, this demobilisation seemed fraught with danger, for, in the event of fresh trouble arising, it would have taken several weeks to mobilise them again. It was therefore resolved, acting on Trotsky's proposal, to transform the armies of fighting men into armies of workers. These armies were to be employed on tasks of economic importance, being at the same time subjected to strict military discipline and coercive methods.

The militarisation of the economic services and transport systems produced but the poorest results.

Attempts to revive activity in certain branches of industry were hardly more successful. In giving one pound of bread a day to workmen employed in industries which it was desired to resuscitate, it was necessary to deprive workmen in other industries of their bread.

The organisation of industry in the years 1919–1920 constituted a rigid and highly centralised system. All the great factories were divided up according to the branch of industry in which they were engaged. At the head of each branch there was a central office (*glavok* or "centre"). The *glavki* were under the control of the Supreme Economic Council, which allowed neither the *glavki* nor the "basic" factories any independence whatsoever. All industrial products were at the disposal of the Supreme Economic Council, which drew up the plans for production and distributed the products according to the needs of the moment. In 1920 there were fifty-six *glavki:* a *Glavtextil* (textile), *Glavugol* (coal) and a *Glavbum* (paper), etc.

Industry did not, therefore, produce for the market. It was controlled by the State service. The economic system of the Soviet Republic represented an organisation, which was centrally controlled, like a factory.

The main characteristic of the industrial system was the "militarisation of labour." Work was declared obligatory for everyone. Special bodies were entrusted with the mobilisation and distribution of the working forces. The worker was not entitled to leave the factory where he was employed. His "working power" was at the service of the central bodies, which disposed of it just as they did raw material.

Under these conditions, money became valueless. The peasant was forbidden to trade and the country districts had returned to the stage of natural economy. In the towns also, what the economist Kritzmann called "the natural proletarian economic organisation" had been reached. Bread was supplied, not through ordinary trade channels, but on requisition. The Soviet Government's object was the abolition of the monetary system, and the unrestrained inflation of prices, which was followed by a rapid depreciation in money-values, attained this end.

The Soviet economic system of the period was an all-embracing one, in which production was regulated according to specially drawn-up plans and distribution effected through the intermediary organisations of the State; in which there was an exchange of products between town and country, the town providing the country districts with manufactured goods and the country districts providing the towns with agricultural products.

Such a system resembles the Socialist order. But in the conditions of that period it only faintly resembled it. It was the prefiguration of Socialist economy in its true form. Actually, it was a "Communism of supply" whose only effect was to socialise poverty; it was a form of Communism imposed by ruin, famine and the war. The military organisation of the Soviet economic system in the years 1918–1920 was not Socialism, neither could it serve to build up Socialism. But it enabled the Soviet Government to hold its enemies at bay and to defeat them, to establish in an economic sense the military alliance of workers and peasants.

Due to the effects of the War, its devastation, the

blockade and to epidemics, the level of production continued to fall. In 1921 it reached its lowest ebb. In the various branches of industry the output was only 10 and 15 per cent. of what it had been before the War. The consumption of bread, which had been 14 pouds per head in the towns, fell to 8 pouds. In 1920 5½ million people contracted typhus. The railways carried only 12 per cent. of their pre-war traffic. On the other hand, the system of forced requisitions became increasingly less profitable. Between 1918 and 1919, of the 260 million pouds of wheat anticipated, only 107 million were forthcoming. There was a falling-off of acreage under crops. There was a decrease of 40 per cent. in industrial plants, since they had ceased to be remunerative. On large-scale collective farms there was a shortage of horses and implements. Peasants came out on strike at sowing-time. There was a decrease in the area under crops of all kinds—a fall in flax of 19 and in sugar of 71 per cent.—in comparison with pre-war levels. The decrease in the number of live-stock was equally marked. For Russia without the Ukraine and Turkestan, the figures for 1921 compared with those for 1916 show that the decrease in the number of cattle, sheep and pigs was 20·5, 41·5 and 50 per cent. respectively. During the three years of civil war the rural population received 292,000 ploughs, whereas in pre-war years the normal demand was in the neighbourhood of 1½ million ploughs per annum.

In the opening months of 1921 the situation became particularly acute. Food and fuel were unobtainable; there was a scarcity of everything. Industry, which in 1920 provided work for 43 per cent. of the number of workmen employed before the War and whose output was only 18 per cent. of the pre-war figure, was paralysed. Nearly all the factories ceased work, the railways came to almost a complete standstill and the peasants responded to the forced requisitions by increasingly frequent armed insurrections and acts of robbery. The whole of the moderately well-to-do peasantry threatened to rise against the Soviets.

The working classes became more and more discontented. During the "non-party" conferences at Moscow, Communists were prevented by the workers from speaking. The Red army, which was composed of peasants, could no longer be relied upon to support the Soviet regime; certain detachments sent to put down country risings refused to fire on the mobs.

THE CRONSTADT RISING (MARCH, 1921)

On the 1st of March, 1921, at the news of the scarcity of bread in Petrograd, there was unrest among the naval ratings at Cronstadt, and at a meeting of the first and second brigades from the vessels of the Fleet, a resolution was passed demanding the suppression of requisitions and, in particular, the re-establishment of private trading and of liberty in industry. This was also the peasants' programme, and was summed up in this somewhat paradoxical phrase: "Long live the Soviets!" "Down with the Communists!" On 3 March the mutineers appointed a revolutionary committee. On 5, they presented their ultimatum. On 7, there was an exchange of salvos from heavy guns. On 20, the Red army attacked but did not succeed in suppressing the mutiny.

On 13, at the opening of the Tenth Congress of the Communist Party, Lenin announced the abolition of requisitions; Trotsky came to Petrograd, put himself at the head of the detachment charged with suppressing the insurrection and crossed the ice at the mouth of the Neva to attack Cronstadt. The survivors of the rebel force, who had taken refuge in a battleship, surrendered. On 18 March, 1921, the Communist rule was completely re-established, while the Soviet Press commented on the signing of the Peace of Riga and the fiftieth anniversary of the Paris Commune.

On this occasion the movement had been spontaneous; it showed the temper of the peasants whose adherence to the Bolshevist cause was the deciding factor in its triumph. Lenin understood the lesson of the Cronstadt rising; on 19 March he proclaimed the withdrawal of all restrictions hitherto imposed upon internal trade and the immediate application of a tax in kind to take the place of the requisitions; on 24, a decree was issued guaranteeing the peasants' right to the possession of their property; and on 29, other decrees re-established unrestricted trade in wheat, oats and potatoes.

The markets reopened on the 1st of April, 1921. Here was the new economic policy which was to become famous as the NEP.

CHAPTER IV

THE DRAMA OF THE ANNEXATIONS

The shrinkage of Soviet territory—The annexation of Bessarabia—Roumania and the U.S.S.R.—Georgia loses her independence—The Russian exodus.

THE SHRINKAGE OF SOVIET TERRITORY

The advent of the Leninist NEP system marked a definite stage in the formation of the U.S.S.R. The people were enabled to relax after the dreadfully tense period of pitiless war and breadless Communism. Certain regions (3·8 per cent. of the territory belonging to the former Empire of the Tsars) were separated from the Federation of Soviet Republics:

I.—Finland, formerly an autonomous Grand Duchy.

II.—Esthonia, composed of the former province of Estland and a part of Livonia.

III.—Latvia, composed of parts of the provinces of Livonia and Courland, as well as a portion of the Vitebsk region.

IV.—Lithuania, which represents the former province of Kovno.

V.—Russian Poland (that is to say Plock, Lomza, Warsaw, Kalisz, Siedlce, Piotrkov, Kielce, Radom, Lublin and Vilna —formerly provinces under Empire rule).

VI.—The Pashalik of Kars, ceded to Turkey by the treaty of 16 March, 1921.

VII.—Bessarabia, whose history deserves to be related side by side with the history of revolutions.

Regardless of her wishes, Georgia has recently been brought back to the Russian fold. The sudden turns of fortune which brought her emancipation, independence and then forced her once again under Soviet control makes the history of her annexation one of the most painful of all: and there is a general feeling in France and elsewhere that the epilogue to this tragedy is yet to come.

In 1921 the figures for the shrinkage of territory and the loss of population were as follows:

		Square Kilometres	Population
1. Finland	..	286,500	3,348,000
2. Esthonia	..	36,000	1,750,000
3. Latvia	..	61,000	2,500,000
4. Lithuania	..	51,500	2,246,000
5. R. Poland	..	218,500	16,022,000
6. Bessarabia	..	39,000	2,213,000
7. Kars ..	..	17,500	492,000

But how much more serious was the loss of wealth and brains resulting from the wholesale emigration of Russian people which reached its height towards the end of 1921!

The drama of the annexations! There are many reasons why the union of Bessarabia with Roumania, the seizure of enfeebled Georgia by Muscovite Russia, the wholesale emigration of the Russian people, seem to fall logically under this mournful heading.

BESSARABIA. STAGES IN ITS ANNEXATION TO ROUMANIA

Immediately following the Russian Revolution of 1917, a movement started in Bessarabia in favour of local autonomy. In October a Moldavian military congress decided to establish a local council, the Sfatul Tseri, which was to govern the province until the opening of a Bessarabian Constituent Assembly.

On 21 November, 1917, the Sfatul Tseri began its labours. On 2 December it passed a resolution declaring that "Bessarabia, ever mindful of her past, proclaims herself to be the 'Moldavian Democratic Republic,' forming part of the Federated Democratic Russian Republic." It then proceeded to appoint its first Government, the "Council of Directors-General."

At that moment the Bolshevist disorders assumed

such alarming proportions that the Sfatul Tseri appealed to Roumania. The "Council of Directors-General" gave its assurance that the entry of Roumanian troops into Bessarabia would be a purely military measure which "could have no possible influence either on the present political situation or on the future of the country" (January, 1918). As soon as order had been restored the Roumanian forces were to return to their own country (General Prezanu's declaration to the Bessarabian people, 27 January, 1918).

Despite every assurance to the contrary, the presence of the Roumanian troops exercised an inevitable influence on the conduct of the Sfatul Tseri. On 24 January, 1918, this assembly broke off all relations with Russia. Annulling its decree of 2 December, 1917, it proclaimed the country to be the "Free and independent Republic of the Moldavian People."

The Sfatul Tseri justified its action in proclaiming Bessarabian independence by pointing to the "insurmountable obstacles" standing in the way of reunion with the Federated Russian Republic and, above all, to the declaration of independence issued by the Ukraine, which separated Bessarabia from Russia.

Bessarabia's independence lasted sixty-one days.

On 27 March the Sfatul Tseri, led by Inkuletz, voted for the reunion of Bessarabia with Roumania on the basis of provincial autonomy. Finally, by 28 November, 1918, there was no further mention of autonomy: Bessarabia was purely and simply reunited to Roumania.

Thus, in less than a year, four successive, contradictory measures had been voted:

1. 2 December, 1917: Union with a Russian federation.
2. 24 January, 1918: Rupture with Russia.
3. 27 March, 1918: Autonomy under Roumania's aegis.
4. 28 November, 1918: Unconditional reunion with Roumania.

Was it possible that, while its troops were still in occupation of the country, Roumania had influenced the voting in the Sfatul Tseri? Grave accusations were made at this time and brought before the Peace Conference by the Russian Political Conference in Paris and by a Bessarabian delegation. The Peace Conference held no enquiry to establish the truth of these accusations.

Acting upon the final resolution of the Sfatul Tseri, the Roumanian Government decreed all Russians domiciled in Bessarabia before 1914 to be Roumanian subjects, introduced conscription into the province and made it obligatory for all Bessarabians to take part in the elections.

The Bessarabian elections took place in November, 1919, the province being still occupied by Roumanian troops. The 120 Bessarabian delegates to the Roumanian Constituent Assembly, who were, however, suspected of not representing the free, unfettered will of the people, voted for definite union with Roumania.

The protests of the Russians—Whites and Reds—became more and more vehement. On 22 March, 1920, the Russian Political Conference in Paris demanded a plebiscite "hedged round with the most definite international guarantees" and the establishment of a provisional regime while awaiting the reconstitution of Russia as a nation. In other words, it proposed to entrust the government of Bessarabia to the League of Nations, which was to be looked upon as watching over the interests of Russia in her absence: as to the plebiscite, it would be taken after Russia was rid of the Soviet regime.

The Western Powers did not keep these suggestions in mind. Leaving the United States as the sole champion of Russian integrity (Cilby's note of 10 August, 1920—*vide* the *Temps* of 13 August), they considered that they would be able to settle the Bessarabian problem internationally.

THE TREATY OF 28 OCTOBER, 1920

Adopting the Roumanian point of view, the British Empire, France, Italy and Japan concluded a treaty with Roumania which was signed in Paris. It recognised Roumanian sovereignty over Bessarabia. In the preamble it was declared that the immediate recognition of Roumanian sovereignty over Bessarabia had become necessary "in the interests of general peace in Europe."

This treaty was inspired by a spirit entirely new to international relationships, for, contrary to Russia's express wishes, it disposed of a portion of Russian territory and gave a foreign Power sovereignty over it. It entrusted the Council of the League of Nations "with appointing a Russian representative to the Commission which was to fix the new frontier between Bessarabia and Russia." Finally, "while Article 9 provided for the admission of Russia to the League as soon as she had formed a Government which was recognised by the Powers, and while it provided for the right of the contracting parties to submit questions which might be raised by the Russian Government for arbitration by the League of Nations Council, it nevertheless stipulated that the frontiers, as fixed by the treaty, as well as Roumanian sovereignty over territories bounded by these frontiers, were not to be called in question" (Ernest Lagarde). A well-known jurist, M. André Dandelstam, wrote that the immediate cession of Bessarabia to Roumania was contrary to International Law for the following reasons:

1. The Russian State having been the ally of the principal Powers and of Roumania in the War, no right of conquest can be legitimately invoked against her in order to justify the action of 28 October, 1920.

2. The character of the general political relationships between the principal Powers and Roumania cannot, in virtue of compensation for concessions on other territories, justify the immediate cession of Bessarabia to Roumania.

3. Neither does the absence of responsible government in Russia create a political situation necessitating the recognition by the Powers of Roumanian sovereignty over Bessarabia. This absence of responsible government merely authorises them to set up a provisional regime under the auspices of the League of Nations. In consequence, the treaty of 28 October, in its present form, appears an unjustifiable attack on the rights and dignity of the absent Russian State (*The Slav World*, August, 1925).

Naturally, Chicherin also protested against this treaty and posed as the champion of Russian integrity. It is certain that Roumania's policy and that of the Allies with regard to this question has brought about a kind of sacred union of all classes and shades of opinion. Chicherin has made repeated requests for a plebiscite to be taken in Bessarabia, as MM. Maklakov and Milukov had done before him. (In this connection, it is illuminating to compare his attitude towards Bessarabia with that of the Soviet Government towards Georgia. In the case of Georgia, it was the Government of Moscow which refused a plebiscite which had been demanded since 1921. . . .)

Article 9 had, in any case, never been carried out. The U.S.S.R. was recognised *de jure* by the Powers, but she was never invited to adhere to the treaty of 28 October, 1920. It was well known in Paris and London that she would definitely refuse.

THE RATIFICATION OF THE TREATY

The ratification of this treaty was not accomplished without some difficulty. Great Britain and France were the first to sign. Only on 16 March, 1924, did the French Chamber pass the resolution in favour of ratification.

When the Franco-Roumanian Treaty was signed—a treaty which guaranteed the territorial *status quo* in Roumania—the Government of Moscow made vehement protests against it in a note which M. Rakovsky despatched to M. Poincaré. The following passage is of particular interest:

"By promising Roumania France's aid in the eventuality of war and by proclaiming the identity of French and Roumanian interests, the French Government encourages the aggressive tendencies of the Roumanian leaders. By so doing it lessens the chances of a peaceful settlement of the Bessarabian question on the basis of the people's right of self-determination and increases the dangers which threaten peace in the east of Europe.

"I declare that my Government is reluctantly obliged to consider the conclusion by France of the treaty with Roumania as an unfriendly act directed equally against the interests of the U.S.S.R. as against the interests of the Bessarabian people."

A similar incident occurred a few months later when the Italo-Roumanian Treaty was signed (16 September, 1926). A note of protest was delivered to Signor Mussolini on 6 October, 1926, by M. Kerjentsev. One passage read as follows:

"The friendly relations between the U.S.S.R. and Italy had developed so smoothly up to this moment that my Government was led to hope that the Italian Government would not take up, as regards the political status of Bessarabia, a hostile point of view and one contrary to Bessarabian interests."

The only difference between the French and Italian attitudes was that in October, 1926, Italy had not yet ratified the Treaty of Paris concluded on 28 October, 1920, whereas France had a few months previously recognised *de jure* the U.S.S.R.

However, the ratification by Italy of the treaty followed soon after in March, 1927. Signor Mussolini in his note of 7 March announced that if he had postponed the ratification of the treaty until that moment, it was only in the hope that the Bessarabian question would be amicably settled between the U.S.S.R. and Roumania.

No hope of such a settlement remained in June, 1927. Fresh protests were raised by the U.S.S.R. (17 March). The last paragraph of the Soviet note read as follows:

"I feel that it is indispensable to point out that the Government of the U.S.S.R. has in no way altered its views and considers, as it did in the past, that the annexation of Bessarabia by Roumania constitutes an act of pure violence, and that the protocol of 28 October, 1920, which has now been ratified and concluded by Italy without the U.S.S.R. having had any part in the proceedings and without the consent of Bessarabia, is, in its eyes, an action which is robbed of all legal force; and is not only powerless, contrary to the Italian Government's opinion, to ensure peaceful conditions in Eastern Europe, but is also violently opposed to the principles of a peaceful policy.

ROUMANIA AND THE U.S.S.R.

From 1918 onwards the U.S.S.R. continually denounced Roumania's annexationist policy. Attempts were made to settle the matters in dispute between the two countries (besides the Bessarabian question there was the seizure by the Bolsheviks of the Roumanian Treasury): but the efforts made in Warsaw in 1921 and at Vienna in 1924 to obtain a settlement were doomed to failure. The Soviet Government demanded a plebiscite in Bessarabia, and on every occasion Roumania rejected the proposal. An outburst of anti-Roumanian feeling and protest marked the tenth anniversary of the annexation of Bessarabia by Roumania (26 January, 1928).

As an off-set to Roumania's action, the U.S.S.R. created a Soviet "Moldavian Republic" towards the end of 1924. This republic played the same rôle as had the White Russian Republic in the struggle with Poland. On 27 January the president of the Central Executive Committee of the Moldavian Republic declared, at the opening of the session:

"The opening of our session coincides with the tenth anniversary of the occupation of Bessarabia. Ten years ago the Roumanian boyars, employing force, became masters of the greater portion of our Moldavian Republic—Bessarabia."

And the president of the Council of People's Commissars, on his part, exclaimed: "We persist in regarding the Pruth as our frontier. We demand the union of the two parts of the autonomous Soviet Socialist Moldavian Republic."

Thus the U.S.S.R. (as did all anti-Bolshevist Russians) had reason to look upon Bessarabia as an "irredentist" country.

GEORGIA FROM MARCH, 1917, TO THE DISSOLUTION OF THE RUSSIAN CONSTITUENT ASSEMBLY

During the first stage of the Russian Revolution the Georgian people threw in their lot with the other Russian peoples. Georgia, which was joined, for purposes of administration, to Transcaucasia, Armenia and Azerbaidjan, considered herself an integral part of liberated Russia. The Soviet of Tiflis was in the hands of the Georgian Social-Democrats, who for thirty years had obtained the support of the workers and peasants of the country. The leader and president of the central Committee of the party was Noah Jordania. He became automatically president of the Tiflis Soviet.

Throughout 1917 Georgia remained faithful to Social-Democracy. While the masses in Russia were deserting in ever-increasing numbers the Democrat and Socialist parties (Social-Democrats and Social-Revolutionaries) and had allowed themselves to be led away by the Bolshevist slogans: "The land for the peasants!" "Immediate peace!" the Georgian people continued to place its trust in the Social-Democrat leaders. There was definite evidence of divergence of opinion at the time of the elections for the Russian Constituent Assembly. Whereas in Russia the Mensheviks suffered an overwhelming defeat at the polls, in Georgia they obtained 640,230 votes out of a total of 892,304. Therefore, Georgia sent to Petrograd the same delegates as had always represented her in the various Dumas under Tsarist rule. The Bolsheviks obtained but little support, only polling 24,513 votes.

FROM JANUARY TO MAY, 1918

What took place in Georgia after the dissolution of the Russian Constituent Assembly by the Bolsheviks who then controlled Petrograd? The regional centre of the Transcaucasian Soviets (to which Georgia belonged) voted the following resolution:

"The dissolution of the Russian Constituent Assembly has snapped the last bond which guaranteed the unity of Russia and of the entire revolutionary, democratic movement."

In actual fact, unity in Russia was non-existent at this time. Independent States had been constituted in the Ukraine, the Kuban and on the Don, etc. Transcaucasia alone remained to face the Turkish invasion. The Turkish army, commanded by Pasha Vekhir Bey, advanced, meeting with no opposition. Despite this fact, Transcaucasia sent no delegates to Brest-Litovsk.

On 3 March, 1918, the Bolshevist Government signed a peace with the Central Powers, Bulgaria and Turkey. Transcaucasia naturally refused to cede her territories. She reopened hostilities against Turkey (April, 1918). It was a very one-sided struggle and she was defeated. On 22 April, 1918, the Transcaucasian Seju made two important decisions:

1. To negotiate peace with Turkey.
2. To separate finally from Bolshevist Russia.

In the second resolution it was stated that the Transcaucasian Diet had decided to proclaim Transcaucasia as an independent, democratic, federal republic.

This republic, which was a makeshift union of dissimilar elements, was not likely to endure. It lasted five weeks (22 April–26 May, 1918). It broke up under the Turkish attacks.

From its ashes three separate republics arose—Georgia, Armenia and Azerbaidjan. Baku, the capital of Azerbaidjan, was the centre of the most intense race-conflicts, party-struggles, and was never free from foreign intervention. The Baku Soviet, led by Chaumyan, made itself supreme in the country in the spring of 1918; but under the continuous attacks of the Turks, Whites, Georgians and of English troops from Persia, Bolshevism was swept away for the first time on 14 August, 1918. Twenty-six commissars were captured on their arrival from across the Caspian Sea and executed on a railway line (20 September, 1918). This massacre is often quoted by Bolshevist and anti-Bolshevist martyrologists and has been a cause of much controversy.

The Georgian people then devoted every effort to the creation of their own State.

Summoned by Noah Jordania, the Georgian National Council (elected on 5 December, 1917, by the Georgian National Assembly) proclaimed the independence of Georgia on 26 May, 1918. Georgia became a democratic Republic (*vide* the Treaty of Independence in Voytinsky's *Georgian Democracy*, pp. 159–160. Alcan, 1921).

INDEPENDENT GEORGIA (1918–1921)

The young Republic encountered great difficulties; its very existence was continually threatened. It was forced to defend its liberty on every front against the Turks, Germans and Russians—both Whites and Reds. In

Bolshevist eyes Tiflis was the stronghold of the Mensheviks and therefore of "traitor-Socialists." In the opinion of the White generals, Georgia had committed a crime in that she was ruled by Socialists who wanted to carry into practice the programme of the 1917 Revolution and would not join in the movement to restore the old regime.

Profiting by the lack of agreement existing between the Turks and Germans, Georgia took refuge from the Turkish invasion behind the might of Germany. She offered this Power certain economic advantages but refused her alliance. Her foreign policy consisted, on the one hand, of combating the attempts of the Turks to secure a monopoly in her country and, on the other hand, of resisting Germany's endeavours to make her abandon her neutral state.

After the Allied victory Georgia had but one desire—to obtain recognition of her independence at the Peace Conference. The Georgian delegation (led by Sheidzy and Tseretelli) arrived in Paris at the end of 1918.

A campaign against the recognition of Georgian independence was conducted by Russian refugees who were champions of the integrity of the former Russian Empire. They continually reproached Georgia for not facilitating the policy of intervention. Though the diplomats of Western Europe saw in this policy of intervention a means to solve the problem of Bolshevism, Georgia's attitude only provoked distrust. This attitude was only understood and appreciated in English and French official circles when all hope of the White generals' success had been removed.

On 10 January, 1920, the Supreme Council recognised *de facto* the independence of Georgia.

If the Russian counter-revolutionaries hated Georgia —too democratic to their liking—the Bolsheviks did not loathe her less. They still looked upon her as a nest of "traitor-Socialists" and of opponents of their ideas. She had committed a crime by not allying herself with them against Denikin.

After trying in vain to crush Georgian resistance and foment rebellion in that country, the Government in Moscow came to the conclusion that the Georgian people would defend their liberty to the death. It decided to recognise the independence of the little rebel republic.

THE TREATY BETWEEN TIFLIS AND MOSCOW (7 MAY, 1920)

Soviet Russia, recognising unreservedly the independence of the Georgian State (Art. 1), renounced all claims to intervention in its internal affairs, and recognised as belonging to Georgia the Batoum region, the cantons of Zakataly and Sukhum and a part of the Black Sea province (Art. 4). Georgia undertook not to permit the assembly or sojourn on its soil of armed forces operating against the Moscow Government, and in the same way Russia undertook not to allow on its territory preparations to be made for hostile acts against Georgia and her Government. Economic relations were resumed on the basis of a "most favoured nation" clause.

On the eve of the conclusion of this treaty, the Allied Supreme Council had decided to restore to Georgia the Batoum district which was occupied by British troops. It was, however, two months before this decision was carried out. Only on 7 July, 1920, was Batoum restored to Georgia. Throughout 1920 the attention of Europe was attracted to this little Socialist republic which had been able to resist the Russian counter-revolution, the Bolshevist attacks and the designs of the Allies—England in particular. In the autumn of 1920 a European Socialist delegation, composed of Mr. MacDonald, Mrs. (now

Viscountess) Snowden, MM. Vandervelde, De Brouckère, Renaudel, Kautsky, etc., was solemnly received at Tiflis.

In order to secure her legal position, it remained for Georgia to obtain her recognition *de jure* by the Supreme Council and her admission to the League of Nations.

With this end in view, a Georgian delegation went to Geneva at the end of 1920. On 15 November, at the first meeting of the League, it presented a memorandum requesting Georgia's admission. The question was the subject of grave debate in committee. The president of the Assembly, Dr. Nansen, declared himself in favour of her admission and Lord Robert Cecil was of the same opinion. The representatives of England and France, however, opposed Georgia's request, declaring that the League of Nations could not assume the responsibility of aiding Georgia in the event of her being attacked. When the resolution was put to the vote, ten States were found in favour of her admission, fourteen were opposed to it (England and France being among them) and fifteen abstained. Thus Georgia's request was refused by the League of Nations, and she was only given authority to join certain technical organisations and the International Labour Office.

On the other hand, on 27 January, 1921, Georgia's international status was fixed by the Powers. The Supreme Council recognised the independence *de jure* of the Republic. (It had, shortly before, recognised in the same way the independence of Latvia and Esthonia. For further information see Lagarde's book, *The Recognition of the Soviet Government*, pp. 95–96, and Paul Gentizon's excellent work, *The Georgian Resurrection*.)

SOVIET GEORGIA

The Bolshevist Government in Moscow had signed a treaty with the Menshevist Government at Tiflis on

7 May, 1920. But this was only a temporary agreement. There was every sign that the Bolsheviks would not long tolerate the existence of a hostile Socialist republic at the very doors of Soviet Russia.

Nine months after the treaty had been signed, in February, 1921, the Red army opened hostilities against Georgia. This military offensive was but the continuation of a political offensive which had been systematically conducted for a long time. The Moscow Government had succeeded in exploiting all the defects in a State which had but newly sprung into existence and had been reduced to a pitiful plight by foreign and civil wars: it had established on Georgian soil secret commercial organisations, which were responsible for an intense campaign of propaganda among workers and peasants. In fact, the old duel between Bolshevism and Menshevism was being fought out once again on foreign territory. Moreover, Russia was lured by Georgia's immense natural wealth. She produced no naphtha, since the borings were at Baku, but supplies were transferred across the Caucasus through Georgian territory in order to reach Batoum, whence they were exported. Russia needed this naphtha for her reviving industries and was unwilling that it should fall into the hands of the English. This was, therefore, a new episode of the ancient Anglo-Russian rivalry.

The Red army penetrated into Georgia both in the north and south. The Republic made a valiant defence of its territory, but its troops were beaten after a few days' fighting and the Government of Tiflis forced to take refuge abroad (21 February, 1921).

Less than a month after her recognition *de jure* by the Entente, Georgia, as an independent State, had disappeared. When M. Chenkely, Georgian Minister in Paris, handed his letters of credit to the President of the French

Republic, Tiflis had already been four days in Bolshevist hands.

In place of the National Government, a Council of People's Commissars was set up. The National Assembly was dissolved. An administration of the Soviet pattern was created. Terror reigned. All Mensheviks who refused to recognise the new regime were either imprisoned or shot.

Thus forcibly united to the U.S.S.R., Georgia has become one of the three autonomous republics of the Transcaucasian Federation. (The two others are Armenia and Azerbaidjan.) There, as elsewhere, the general administration is controlled by the Russian Communist Party. But the Government is in the hands of Georgian Communists. In the Government services, schools and universities, etc., Georgian is the official language and its use compulsory. (Relevant information can be found in *Alone in Russia*, pp. 297–298, by Andreé Viollis, who visited Georgia in 1926–1927. She considers that the movement to "Georgianise" wherever possible is carried to absurd extremes. She had an interview with the president of the People's Commissariat, Eliarva, and discussed with him, among other matters, the question of the industrialisation of Georgia, hydro-electric stations, and the manganese mines which have been conceded to the American firm of Harriman and Co.)

The attitude of the Moscow Government towards little Georgia has often been compared to that of the German Imperial Government towards Belgium. The invasion and annexation of Georgia aroused strong protests in Europe, particularly in Socialist circles at the Second Internationale. Even at the present time protests are still being raised. In November, 1930, the International Peace Bureau addressed a note to M. Litvinov, asking him whether he intended to withdraw the Red army from Georgia and to institute a plebiscite which would permit the Georgian nation to make a free declaration as to what form of government it preferred.

THE RUSSIAN EXODUS

The Russian Revolution altered the very standards of human suffering. Before its advent there were, here and there, mass migrations—after the revocation of the Edict of Nantes, after the first acts of brutality in the French Revolution, after the Tsarist repression in Poland in 1831: but then a few thousand only fled their countries. In Russia, since October, 1917, the exodus has numbered millions—in the neighbourhood of two millions. High officials of the Imperial Court, bureaucrats, governors, generals of the old regime, manufacturers, shopkeepers, landowners—ruined and driven out by the fear of what might befall them—officers and men of the White armies, condemned by defeat to suffer the horrors of exile; Cossacks and atamans, likewise forced to flee on the morrow of disasters in the field, republicans and Russian Socialists, whom Kerensky's defeat had banished from their land; workless aristocrats, intellectuals, writers,[1] barristers, who were once the hope of Russian democracy; Jews who were driven by fear of the Whites, Greens and Reds to flee from the Ukraine and had finally broken away from the ghettoes of the East; disillusioned Bolsheviks, Georgians, irreconcilable Ukrainians, who even in lands far distant from Russia held themselves aloof from Russians—such were the infinitely varied, ever-changing elements that went to make up the great Russian exodus.

The flight of the Russian exiles began immediately after the Bolshevist *coup d'état*. After Denikin's downfall

[1] Among the writers were Aldonov, the poet Balmont, Bunin, Kuprin, Merejkovsky and Remizov.

and the departure of Wrangel in 1920, whole armies of people left Russian soil. It seemed almost as if they wished to take their country with them. Wrangel and Koutepov managed to keep their troops—still strictly disciplined—in the Gallipoli peninsula for twelve consecutive months. Finally, Jugoslavia and Bulgaria opened their doors to these hordes of unfortunate creatures who were endeavouring to keep the General Russian Military Union something approaching a united body.

Moreover, the defeats of Koltchak in Siberia, General Miller at Archangel, Yudenitch on the Baltic frontiers, Savinkov and Balakhovitch on the Polish and Soviet borders, scattered far and wide a host of weaponless soldiers and shiftless civilian supporters. In the wake of each body of troops, engineers and barristers—almost all the members of the old Bar in Petrograd and Moscow—moved along these paths of misery, seeking refuge; some destined later to find themselves stranded on the quays in Galata or herded together in Polish concentration camps; others to wander starving and shelterless in German ports or lost amidst the confusion of Kharbin (cf. Pierre Benoit's *Soleil de Minuit*).

In 1921 Europe was faced with the problem of how to provide collective assistance: a High Commission was set up to manage the refugees' affairs. But it was seven years before a scheme was drawn up (30 June, 1928); it was sanctioned in France by the decree of 11 January, 1930. According to the arrangements made, the High Commission of the League of Nations was to carry out the duties of registration, etc., ordinarily devolving upon national consular officials. In virtue of this arrangement, Russian and Armenian exiles retain the privileges existing under the personal statutes, or at least a recommendation in this sense was addressed to all countries which were members of the League.

But in the interval, exiled Russians have adapted themselves with wonderful intelligence and resignation to their seemingly hopeless situation. An immense effort has been made to provide educational facilities, and the most generous support has been forthcoming from the Czechoslovak and Jugoslav Governments, as well as from a committee in Boston. In the neighbourhood of 170 million francs have been spent in assisting young Russian students to carry on their studies: the income of the Union of Russian Wounded amounted in 1928 to five million francs.

But the great majority of Russian refugees have been absorbed into French industry, mines and the electro-chemical trade; colonels have become taxi-drivers and officers of less exalted rank restaurant waiters in French Riviera towns. Doctors sometimes practice among Russian communities in virtue of special permission accorded them.

Russian men of letters first improvised a university at Prague, then, when this was closed, opened a Franco-Russian Institute in Paris, a scientific Institute in Jugoslavia and another in Berlin.

There naturally exist as many factions among the *émigrés* as there were parties before the flight from Russia—perhaps more. The Union of Zemtsvos has been split up and divided into two. The Extreme Right and the Nationalists, who joined the counter-revolutionary movements, became disunited after the revival of Russian freemasonry (the Lodge founded by Alexander I has, in fact, been reconstituted). General Romanovsky, formerly Denikin's Chief of Staff, was assassinated, probably because he became a member of this Lodge. Wrangel was accused of extravagance by the Democrats and Milukov of treachery by the Military Union. A split has occurred among the charitable societies, and, following the example of the Press, they are divided up between the Right and the Left. In the exiled Russian Church there are similar antagonisms—if possible more violent than ever before: the Metropolitan Antony, after the election of the Patriarch, proclaimed himself chief of an independent Church and engaged in Tsarist propaganda. The Metropolitan Eulogios, on the contrary, is understood to look to Moscow for his authority, although in exile he has been obliged to cut himself off from the clergy in Soviet Russia, who have been driven in no uncertain fashion to accept the Bolshevist regime! The charges brought against each other by the various parties in the Church are quite incomprehensible to French people: Antony's spirit has been broken by the accusation made against him of monophysite heresy.

But nothing has been able to prevent the spread of a religious mysticism among the Russian exiles, and this has not only affected idealist philosophers like Berdiaev and Bulgakov, but even those who were formerly atheists —the Jewish writer Chestov, for example.

Under the aegis of the refugees' official Committee, over which M. Malklakov, the ambassador appointed by Kerensky but never accredited—at least officially—presides in Paris with calm dignity, not altogether successful attempts have been made to bring about a reconciliation between the various factions existing among the refugees, whose longing for their home-country has accentuated the varying shades of opinions in their worn-out disputes. "The *émigrés* fight against adversity, work and recover their self-confidence; they struggle against sickness and poverty—always honestly. Here is a proof: if you ask at the head police-office which community has the smallest proportion of evil-doers, you will be told that it is to be found among the Russian refugees" (Jean Delage, *La Russie en exil*). But these Russians do not go without tea, music or razgovor (endless discussions).

It would be impossible to enumerate the subjects discussed at these razgovor, or where they are held. It is easier simply to describe the principal political groups into which Russian exiles are divided.

On the Extreme Right there is the Union of Legitimists, which was formed at Karlovitz: it supports the Grand Duke Kyril and his son, the Grand Duke Vladimir.

The Higher Monarchist Council, founded at the Congress of Reichenhall (1921), has recognised the Grand Duke Kyril as Emperor.

The Young Russians recognise equally the authority of the Tsar, but they represent both a Fascist and Trades Union tendency and claim to be governed by a peasant and Christian autocracy.

The Brotherhood of Russian Truth comprises Monarchist Terrorists and orthodox fanatics who resort to secret activities and attempt to organise peasant insurrections in Soviet Russia.

Equally Monarchist are the following: the General Military Russian Union, founded by Wrangel after the dispersal of the White army interned in Gallipoli, and which has had, in succession, as presidents (following Wrangel), the Grand Duke Nicholas, General Koutepov and, after his disappearance, General Miller; the Union of Nationalist Youth; the Patriotic Union; the People's Monarchist Union; the Cossacks' Union, which has branches in all countries of the world; the Gallipoli Veterans; the Struggle for Russia; and the National Russian Committee, a group which includes those remaining faithful to the White army.

Supporting the political activities of the Right, the Committee of Trade and Industry (Tsugprom), which was concerned in the proceedings against Krylenko when the counter-revolutionary *saboteurs* were brought to trial in November–December, 1930, at Moscow, includes the most influential members of the upper bourgeoisie who were robbed of all their possessions by the Revolution. Among its members were men who were formerly big manufacturers and financiers: Denissov, Tretiakov, Nobel, Gukassov, etc. This is the Union of Russian Economic Interests.

Opposed to the numerous organisations of the Right and Extreme Right, the political groups of the Left are divided into three parts.

The Republican Cadets and Democrats are led by Milukov. Their influence is preponderant in refugee circles thanks largely to their newspaper, *Les Dernières Nouvelles,* which is published in Paris and has a large circulation.

The Social-Revolutionaries of the Right, under the leadership of Kerensky, have their head-office in Paris, and those from the Left, with Chernov and Sukhomlin as leaders, at Prague.

The Social-Democrats, led by Dan and Abramovitch, continue to uphold Menshevist principles.

Mention should be made of the Social-Populists and the Russian peasants' group, an anti-Bolshevist peasant party which is in favour of Terrorist methods.

Besides these purely political parties, two unions of Zemstvos, which have been formed, one on the Right, the other on the Left, display considerable activity. Finally, scholars and barristers of the Right and Left have formed professional associations, some definitely monarchist in character, others influenced by the political theories of the Cadets.

CHAPTER V

THE STABILISATION OF THE REGIME

The NEP and its immediate consequences—The "scissors" crisis and its results—Lenin's death—His political last will and testament—Struggle between Stalin and Trotsky—Reinstatement of the U.S.S.R. in international relationships—Improved internal conditions: settlement of the Ukrainian question—Stalin encounters opposition from the Right—The "liquidation" of the kulak—Military operations in Eastern China.

THE NEP AND ITS IMMEDIATE CONSEQUENCES

"The weak point in the Socialist economic system was the impossibility of wresting from the peasants enough wheat to feed the army and the officials, and of forcing them to increase the acreage under crops. It was, therefore, on these grounds that the retreat was begun towards the 'new' system. The NEP (new political economy) took the place of the SEP (Socialist political economy). . . ."

Lenin hoped that the peasant would sell his wheat in exchange for manufactured goods with which the State-controlled industries would supply him as required: thus the Socialist ideal of the "exchange of commodities" would be preserved. But Lenin was equally aware that the Socialised industries would not in any case be able to furnish the peasants with "all products." It was therefore necessary to permit "an exchange which was private and not State-controlled"—that is to say, trade, or in other words Capitalism; but this Capitalism was to be guided "towards the channels of State Capitalism" (Milukov). The immediate consequences of introduction of the NEP was the re-establishment of the money-system and of a currency which, if it was to serve its purpose, had to be, or had to become, stable. If the monetary system was introduced the State industries would be forced to obey the fundamental rule governing cost-prices and to pay the workers wages which corresponded to the value of their work; and the State would be obliged to abolish or, at any rate, reduce in number its *rationeers* —those whose needs it satisfied without taking into account the productivity of their work. Lenin had foreseen all these possibilities, but he was prepared to prevent at all costs the rupture between peasantry and proletariat.

Now, as formerly, the population of Russia numbers a vast majority of peasants—more than 100 millions—who were neither swept away nor deprived of their property by the Revolution. Lenin was anxious to carry on the military alliance of workers and peasants as an economic alliance, in order to weld the Socialist economic system, which was in the process of elaboration, to the backward economy of the peasants. Part of the lands taken from the peasant would be restored to capital; it would be necessary to retreat to the positions of 1917–1918, and replace the system of rations and requisitions by an agricultural tax in kind. The peasant would be recognised as owning commodities produced by him and would be entitled to place these on the market.

"Private property" was, in fact, to be restored.

"Dating from the decree of 8 August, 1921, Soviet law recognises the establishment of 'denationalisation,' that is to say, the restoration of nationalised articles, etc., to their original owners. . . . The system of wholesale confiscations is abolished by the decree of 17 April, 1921 . . ." (Timatche).

The re-establishment of internal trade involved other consequences and, first and foremost, necessitated the use of money and, as a result, the stabilisation of the currency; it required the suppression of inflation and a balanced budget. The deficit could only be made up if the notion of making a profit in commerce and of keeping down cost-prices was substituted for the principle of State-controlled industries.

In the autumn of 1921 Lenin issued his slogan: "Learn to trade!" Bukharin went as far as translating into Bolshevist terms Guizot's famous words of advice: "Get rich!"

But the Soviet economic system did not abandon its doctrinal ambitions: a system of nationalised industry and the twenty-five million private enterprises, which had been legalised by the NEP in view of the peasants' attitude, existed side by side. There was a socialised sector and a private one. A kind of rivalry arose between these two systems of production.

But the future was to decide the question. The NEP at once proved very beneficial to the peasants, who found themselves in a position to dispose of the surplus of their crops, having first paid the tax in kind. This tax was proportionate, and, by the application of basic reductions, the poorest class of peasants was exempt from paying imposts which would have ruined them. The peasantry paid off their taxes in rye or in corn after the in-gathering of the cereal crops. Finally, the State levy, which under the system of forced requisitions had risen to some 6,768,000 tons of wheat, had been reduced to 3,840,000 tons, and the balance, which was required for food-supplies, was made up by purchases through the channels of free trade.

Even in industry the situation was not untroubled. In 1921 the drought and the lack of food reserves caused an unprecedented famine, which was so severe that hundreds of thousands died of hunger: the plight of Soviet Russia became so distressing that America was roused to take action. An American committee, with Mr. Hoover as chairman and a number of committees under the direction of the celebrated Norwegian explorer, Dr.

Nansen, set about collecting supplies in an endeavour to assist the famine-stricken people. The Pope organised a service of succour, *The Pontifical Aid*, which had the same charitable object. All nations took part more or less effectively in this dash to aid starving Russia.

Despite the horrors of this crisis and the popularity of the NEP amongst the agricultural populations, there were signs of opposition to this new policy in the Communist Party, which took as its theme and as a pretext for its protest the economic concessions, which were looked upon by some as being the prelude to political concessions. Kamenev tried to reassure the Communists by arguing that "Soviet power still held the five dominating positions [this expression was often subsequently employed] which were as follows: nationalisation of industry and transport, nationalisation of the land, nationalisation of banks, nationalisation of foreign trade." "Not omitting the Cheka," added Lenin, who did not mean to be ironical.

Already a workers' opposition party had been formed under the leadership of Shlyapnikov, later attached to the Paris Embassy as councillor, and Alexandra Kollontay, the Amazon ambassadress who represented the Soviets in Sweden. These leaders complained of the interference of Communist Party busy-bodies in the administration of the Trades Unions: the object of their reaction was to obtain increased power for the bureaucratic machine. But an increase in the authority of the Trades Unions would have been advantageous to the Mensheviks and Social-Revolutionaries, whose prestige among the workers seemed to have been strengthened by the crisis, the famine and the long-drawn-out period of sacrifices. That is the reason why Lenin remained adamant.

He was just as stubbornly opposed to Trotsky, who, moving in the opposite direction to Shlyapnikov and Madame Kollontay, aimed at making the Trades Union movement a bureaucratic and State-controlled machine —an action which could not have failed to aggravate the disaffection of the masses. As usual, Lenin's opinion prevailed, and the Trades Unions were relieved of all administrative functions, being at the same time authorised to recruit without restriction. On the whole, apart from certain criticisms revealed in August, 1922, by Zinoviev and in April, 1923, by Trotsky, the application of the NEP stirred up no controversy either dangerous or even embarrassing to the Government, which, moreover, gained in prestige in the eyes of the world what it lost in revolutionary fire.

THE "SCISSORS" CRISIS AND ITS CONSEQUENCES

It was the condition of Soviet industry—stricken, it seemed, with a kind of creeping paralysis—which caused the first serious disagreements after the NEP had been in force for some eighteen months. Cost-prices had not fallen, individual output showed no increase, the costly bureaucratic system had lost none of its power. In the spring of 1923, as a result of a plentiful harvest, agricultural products fell 40 per cent. in value by the simple process of demand and supply. The peasants hastened to the shops to set themselves up with tools, cloth and manufactured goods; they had money and definite needs —needs which were all the more pressing since for six years they had been left unsupplied. Retail merchants raised the prices of all commodities, which had been already brought to a high figure by the State Trusts. In less than a week prices rose by 60 per cent. If the curves showing the prices of agricultural produce and of manufactured goods between September, 1922, and September, 1923, are traced on the same graph, it will be seen that the two lines run wide apart from each other and that the graph resembles a pair of scissors left open. In October, 1923, a farmer who wanted to buy a reaping-hook had to sell three times more corn than he would have had to do in 1913 to procure the money sufficient to make this purchase. Having made a figurative analysis of this economic anomaly, Trotsky declared brutally: "*The scissors must be closed.*"

But how was this to be done? Dictatorship methods had gone out of fashion. A few NEPmen—people who had become enriched through the excessive rise in prices—were denounced; this was the age-old method of satisfying, under similar circumstances, outraged consumers in Paris. But the main effort to root out this economic anomaly was made by resorting to ordinary methods of commerce: the purchase by the Commissariat for Foreign Trade of corn, which it resold in Europe to former customers of Russia who were amazed at such unexpected good fortune: the careful revision of expenditure in State industries which, sure of disposing of all their stocks, had increased their general running expenses by 40 and sometimes 100 per cent., unconsciously imitating the privately owned industries of former times; the closing of all factories which were found too costly to run; the dismissal of managers who were extravagant; economies, reductions and reorganisation—of which nothing was allowed to temper the severity. The desired result was quickly obtained. In February, 1924, a fall was announced in the State industries; the curves showing the rise and fall in price of manufactured articles and agricultural produce drew nearer each other: the scissors closed.

But the struggle opened. Trotsky, who was supported by forty-six Communists, accused the Central Committee of leading the party astray and the country into an abyss of torment. Basing their protests on the erratic course taken by the NEP, Trotsky and his followers relied upon the support of discontented workers, who were not at all disposed to suffer further hardships in order that the peasants' portion might be increased in consequence. Trotsky claimed that these workers should be given a hearing, that the party should be democratised and young blood be introduced into the party staffs, which he declared to be degenerate: but Lenin was still alive. The fear of causing disunity in the party dominated all these dialectical attempts at reform. Trotsky gave in and even agreed to resign from his post as People's Commissar for War—an appointment in which the force of his "Bonapartist" temperament was liable to alarm "established authority"; finally, he joined in the long-drawn-out, universal, almost religious mourning into which Lenin's death plunged all the Russian republics, bringing together workers, peasants, Communists and non-party people, as if in death the great leader had finally torn himself from the grasp of dogma to become simply a great man.

LENIN'S DEATH

For many months Lenin had been ill. Superhuman labours, sleepless nights and perpetual nerve-strain had undermined his robust constitution and brought on an attack of cerebral sclerosis. In May, 1922, following a stroke, his right side became paralysed, but with marvellous strength of will he gradually overcame his affliction, and in 1923 wrote a treatise on co-operation which was to be his last written work. He lived with his wife in a little country-house at Gorky. On 21 January, 1924, a terrible attack struck him down. He was fifty-four years old.

The entire Central Committee of the Soviets came to Gorky.

On the morrow of his death, the Communist Party issued a proclamation:

"Lenin is dead, but he lives on in the soul of each member of the party. Each member of the party is a particle of Lenin. Our entire Communist family is the collective incarnation of him."

All the way to Moscow, massed close up to the railway line a dense throng of human beings.

The coffin, borne by members of the Central Committee of the party, was laid in the great assembly-hall of the Trades Union House. For three days hundreds of thousands of men, women and children passed before his coffin. The queue of devoted followers stretched day and night over several kilometres, with the temperature at thirty degrees below zero.

On 27 January the coffin was borne to the Red Square and placed in front of the Kremlin wall in a vault surmounted by a mausoleum with the single word "Lenin" on the pediment.

The body, embalmed according to the most recent scientific methods, rested under the crystal dome-shaped covering, with the flag of the Paris Commune lying close at hand: and still the crowds filed past his mortal remains.

"His private life," wrote Gorky, "was such that in a religious age he would have been held a saint." "*Der Paulus des Sozialismus*"—The St. Paul of Socialism, Maximilien Harden described him.

Never had there been a more exaggerated form of religion than this adoration of Lenin, or one that brought so vast a number of human beings together for so long a period to mourn for a reformer. "The enigma of this poor, honest man, who from exile to Kremlin remained the harsh disciple of a single idea, must be explained—as Ludovic Naudeau has already done—by looking upon him as a counterfeit Messiah. Listen to this phrase which is most certainly borrowed from Messianic writings: 'We do not fear our faults! Men have not become saints because the Revolution has been set in motion' " (Lenin, *Letters to American Workers*). "He knew Marx and was worthy of Nietzsche" (de Monzie, *Du Kremlin au Luxembourg*, 1924).

Pierre Daye, the Belgian writer who was present at Lenin's obsequies, gave his impressions as follows: "We are in the hall where Lenin's body is exposed to view. Wooden barriers intersect the approaching crowds and keep them two or three yards from the funeral couch. The room is small and low, with scarlet silk hangings on every wall, and it is brilliantly lighted. Under-foot, red carpets. At the head of the couch, his head resting on a scarlet silk cushion, Lenin seems to be musing ironically. He has almost the appearance of a waxen statue in an anatomical museum. . . . The extraordinary impression created by this vision is augmented by the way in which the body is illuminated, lying as it is, in the full light of invisible electric globes hidden all round the couch after the manner of stage footlights. A sort of dome-shaped glass cover is over the whole. . . . I have never experienced such a feeling of horror and dread before the tomb of any other famous man. I have been able to contemplate the monuments where a St. Paul, a Napoleon or a Charles V sleeps peacefully beneath his marble tombstone. . . . But here, in the midst of this strange hypogeum . . ." (*Moscou dans le souffle d'Asie*).

LENIN'S POLITICAL LAST WILL AND TESTAMENT

Among Lenin's papers found after his death were some notes on certain Communist Party leaders who had been his closest collaborators. It is these notes which were later called his political will.

Lenin wrote that at any cost unity within the party must be preserved and divisions avoided. He saw that the danger of a split lay in the growing antagonism of the two most striking figures in Communism—the two who were eventually to succeed him.

"In the relations between Stalin and Trotsky lies, in my opinion, the greatest danger of this division, and it could be avoided. In order to prevent it, the first step should be to increase the membership of the Central Committee to one hundred and fifty.

"Comrade Stalin, on becoming Secretary-General, has gathered into his hand an immense power, and I am not certain that he will always employ sufficient prudence in the exercise of it. On the other hand, Comrade Trotsky is not remarkable for very great ability, as he has already shown in his struggle against the Central Committee over the question of the People's Commissariat for Highways and Communications. Personally, he is the most capable man of the present Central Committee, but he is much too inclined to over-assurance and is, besides, attracted to the purely administrative side of affairs. . . .

"These outstanding characteristics of the two leading men in the Central Committee may involuntarily bring about a division: if our party does not take measures to prevent it, this scission may occur with unexpected suddenness.

"I am not going to describe the characteristics of the other members of the Central Committee as regards their personal qualities. I will only point out that the incident, which occurred in October and in which Zinoviev and Kamenev were concerned, was not evidently an isolated occurrence, but that now they can no more be reproached for it than Comrade Trotsky could be reproached for 'non-Bolshevism.'"

THE STRUGGLE BETWEEN STALIN AND TROTSKY

As soon as he knew the contents of Lenin's will, Stalin tendered his resignation from the post of Secretary-General of the party, but was kept in office by the Central Committee.

As Lenin had foreseen, the struggle between Stalin

and Trotsky was to begin immediately. But it did not cause a division, because Stalin had almost the entire party behind him.

In the autumn of 1924 Trotsky published a book entitled *The Lessons of October*, in which, taking up once more his theory of revolution as a permanent state, he pointed out that he had not entered the Communist Party in 1917 but that he and Lenin had met at that time. Trotsky showed in this book his contempt for the present leaders of Bolshevism, notably Zinoviev and Kamenev, who had withdrawn at the decisive moment of the October Revolution.

The Central Committee vigorously denied the truth of Trotsky's charges and accused him of under-estimating the part played by the peasantry, and therefore of endangering the alliance between peasants and workers. Zinoviev and Kamenev requested the Bureau to remove Trotsky, but their demand was refused.

Soon an even more bitter altercation arose between Trotsky and Stalin. Trotsky did not think that Russia could by herself build up Socialism. According to his view, the most advanced proletarians of Western European countries must seize the supreme power if Socialism was to triumph. Soviet Russia should sacrifice everything to set a world revolution in motion, for, owing to the backward condition of her technical industries and of the greater part of the peasant masses, her strength alone was insufficient to create Socialism. To persist in holding on to the supreme power while Socialism in Europe made no progress was to run the risk of bureaucratic or Thermidorian degeneracy.

Zinoviev and Kamenev, who had recently been opposed to Trotsky, now rallied to him, and in 1925–1926 formed an opposition rather different to its predecessors—the "Troïka," the Bolsheviks called it, seeing that there were three in the team. This opposition "party" was called the NOP (new opposition party).

In answer to the theory formulated by Trotsky and Zinoviev of the impossibility of Socialism triumphing in one country at a time, Stalin replied:

"We can establish Socialism and we shall establish it, with the peasants' aid, under the leadership of the working class, for, under the rule of the dictatorship of the proletariat, we are in possession of all the necessary data to make Socialism a reality by surmounting all internal difficulties, and we must and we can surmount them through our own resolution."

The opposition raised by Zinoviev was serious; he held appointments both as president of the Third Internationale and of the Leningrad Soviet. But Stalin did not hesitate to dismiss his opponent and even drove him out of the Politbureau.

In 1927 opposition was suddenly raised for the third time, following the failure of the revolution in China. Trotsky accused the leaders of the party of having supported Chang-Kai-Chek when the working masses should have been stirred up against the Kuomingtang and the slogan taken: "Supreme power for the Soviets!"

On this occasion there was serious discord within the Communist Party. Secret meetings were held and methods of conspiracy so much in vogue under Tsarist rule were again employed.

On 7 November, 1927, the tenth anniversary of the October Revolution, the opposition showed their dissatisfaction with the party leadership by street demonstrations.

Following these manifestations of disapproval, Trotsky was excluded from the party, as well as several leading members of the opposition. Zinoviev and Kamenev were obliged to make amends and submit to temporary exclusion. Still irreconcilable, stiff with the arrogance of a Red Titan, Trotsky, who had already been exiled to the snow-clad slopes of the Alma-Alta (January, 1927), was banished to Constantinople (January, 1929).

Even in his banishment he continued, with wonderful spirit and force, to attack the administration of the Communist Party and of the Third Internationale. He had previously obtained the support of Communists in various countries, Germany in particular, with the result that "Communist parties of the Left" had been formed outside the official Communist parties and in opposition to them.

REINSTATEMENT OF THE U.S.S.R. IN INTERNATIONAL RELATIONSHIPS

The isolation of the Republic of the Soviets from European affairs had been complete since the October Revolution, though diplomatic relations had been established with Germany by the Treaty of Brest-Litovsk: but the ties which united them were so precarious, so uncertain, that neither Russia nor Germany reaped any advantages from this relationship. Only from the Near East, from a country which was likewise anxious to break with the past, was Russia to receive sympathetic understanding.

It was with Nationalist Turkey, which had been shaped by the National Pact and by the efforts of Mustapha Kemal Pasha, that the Soviet Republic established its first diplomatic relations. On 16 March, 1921, the new Turkey, cut off from the whole of the Western world and on the eve of great struggles which were to decide her future, signed at Moscow a treaty of friendship with Soviet Russia.

"The Government of the Great National Assembly of Turkey and the Government of the Russian Socialist

Federal Republic," it was stated in the preamble, "being in mutual agreement concerning the principles of the fraternity of nations and of the people's right to self-determination, also declaring their solidarity in the struggle against Imperialism and their recognition of the fact that any difficulties which came to trouble one people would aggravate the situation of the other, and being animated with the desire to see cordial relations and ties of sincere friendship based on *reciprocal* interests always existing between the two countries, they have decided to conclude a treaty of friendship and fraternity." Thus a secular rivalry came to an end: Russia received the province and the port of Batoum as her perquisites. The same kind of treaty was signed at Kars on 13 October, 1921, with the Soviet Republics of Armenia, Azerbaidjan, Georgia—and on 2 January, 1922, at Angora, with the Ukraine—while in the meantime Mustapha Kemal became Ghazi, and Turkey, having overcome Greece, became a nation of importance, with which Franklin-Bouillon, in the name of France, signed a belated agreement on 30 October, 1921.

Notwithstanding her hostile attitude to the Russo-Turkish dual alliance, and Messrs. Churchill and Lloyd George's anti-Soviet policy, revealed during the debates in the House on 16 April and 29 July, 1919; despite the supplies furnished to Poland for use in her war against Russia, England—following the San Remo Conference (April, 1920)—resolved to make use of the motto adopted by the City, "Peace and Trade," in a trade agreement with the Soviets. Moreover, England only opened these negotiations with Russia because she had failed to come to an agreement with the Allied delegates to the Supreme Economic Council. "You cannot afford to have prejudices if you are a trading community. Certainly not. You cannot always examine the records of your customers."

Mr. Lloyd George declared in the House of Commons (7 June, 1920). Krassin met Mr. Lloyd George in London on 30 June, 1920, when Poland and Russia were still at war. The negotiations, which were temporarily interrupted by the reopening of hostilities, ended in the signing of a trade agreement (16 March, 1921) which implied on the part of Great Britain the recognition *de facto* of the Soviet Government. Mr. Hodgson went as English agent to Moscow and Mr. Lloyd George attempted at the Cannes Conference to gain general support for his move. Since the Cannes Conference (January, 1922) had contemplated the establishment of a European plan of economic reconstruction, the Russian problem, for this reason alone, was brought up for discussion, as it was bound to be, by the very nations who had hitherto refused to recognise the Soviet regime. At Boulogne on 25 February, M. Poincaré, who had succeeded M. Briand in office, obtained support for his proposal that no agreement should be signed with the Soviet Government unless that Government recognised the debts contracted by previous Russian Governments. Nevertheless, at Mr. Lloyd George's express wish, a conference was held at Genoa, and thirty-four nations accepted Italy's invitation to attend. MM. Chicherin, Ioffe, Litvinov and Krassin were accommodated at Rapallo under the protection of the guns of an Italian guardship anchored in the roads. By 10 April it was obvious that the Soviet delegation had aroused, and would remain an object of, international curiosity throughout *"the momentous proceedings at Genoa."* At the Hotel Genoa, near the Royal Palace where the Conference assembled, Rakovsky received deputations of journalists and propounded the theories of Bolshevism. The proceedings opened pleasantly with lunches and congratulatory speeches. But intentions ran counter to each other. On 17 April, sensation: the scandalised Allies and neutrals learnt that on the day before, at Rapallo, the Russians had signed a treaty with the Germans in due and proper form (16 April, 1922). Notwithstanding the general disgust, the conversations were continued, and the King of Italy, who was on board the *Dante Alighieri*, showed M. Chicherin special favours. "The fact is," wrote M. Pinon, "that the Bolshevist delegates appear at Genoa as the ambassadors of King Petrol and the dispensers of his favours." It was of no great moment that through the irreconcilable attitude adopted by the Bolsheviks and the Belgian Prime Minister, M. Jaspar, the Conference ended without accomplishing anything. For the Soviets, the new members of this international Academy, Genoa was a definite step towards the re-entry of Soviet Russia into the comity of nations.

Because Chicherin possessed what Montaigne called "the science of tact," he was henceforth to be looked upon as an Asiatic Mazarin, while his long service as Minister for Foreign Affairs was to make him doyen of his European colleagues and an object of envious admiration.

After the fiasco at Genoa, the sham conference at The Hague (20 June–26 July, 1922). Here there were more retrospective debates and an exchange of figures and statistics. But these two meetings set a precedent for the invitations received by the Soviets on 26 October and 14 November, 1922, to attend the Lausanne Conference, which was to revise the Treaty of Sèvres with Turkey, and at which Russia was called upon to "take a part in the discussion concerning the question of the Straits." The assassination at Lausanne of the Soviet delegate Vorovsky only gave rise to complications of a temporary nature with Switzerland.

France, who was Russia's principal creditor on behalf of her bond-holders in Russian stocks, remained satisfied with the legal reservations formulated by M. Poincaré and with which she met every move on the part of M. Chicherin, particularly his claims in connection with the ships of the Russian fleet which had been interned at Bizerta since 1920. The visits to Russia of MM. Edouard Herriot (1922) and de Monzie (1923); the general desire for improved relations or of reconciliation which was, moreover, manifested during the general elections in 1924; more important still, the example given by Mr. MacDonald, the British Prime Minister, in recognising *de jure* the Soviet Government (January, 1924), had as a result—after conversations at Dover between Rakovsky, Soviet Ambassador in London, and de Monzie—the official recognition by M. Edouard Herriot, President of the French Council, of the Soviet Government. M. Herriot's Note was couched in the following terms:

PARIS, 28 *October*, 1924.

The President of the Council, Minister for Foreign Affairs,
To M. Rykov, President of the Council of People's Commissars, and M. Chicherin, People's Commissar for Foreign Affairs.

In pursuance of the ministerial decree of 17 June, 1924, and of your communication of 19 July last, the Government of the French Republic, true to the friendship which unites the French and Russian peoples, recognises *de jure* from to-day onwards the Government of the Union of the Socialist Soviet Republics as the Government ruling over the territories of the former Russian Empire in which its authority is accepted by the inhabitants, and in these territories recognises it as the successor of former Russian Governments. It is ready, in consequence, to enter forthwith into regular diplomatic relations with the Government of the Union through an exchange of ambassadors.

"In notifying you of this recognition, which cannot alter the engagements entered into under treaties signed by France, the Government of the Republic believes in the possibility of a general agreement being reached between our two countries to which the reopening of diplomatic relations is but an introduction. On that account, it intends to reserve expressly all rights held by French citizens in the obligations contracted by Russia or its subjects under former Governments, obligations of which respect is guaranteed by general principles of the law which remains for us the rule of international life. The same reservations are made with regard to the responsibilities assumed since 1914 by Russia towards the French State and its subjects.

"Acting in this spirit and in order to serve once more the interests of peace and of Europe's future, the Government of the Republic intends to seek an equitable and practical settlement which will permit the re-establishment between the two nations of advantageous relations and normal exchanges when the confidence of France has been strengthened by signs of good faith. As soon as you make known your assent to the opening of negotiations of a general or more particularly of an economic order, we will welcome your representatives to Paris. They will doubtless be furnished with full powers in order to be in a position to meet our negotiators.

"Until the favourable termination of these negotiations, the treaties, conventions and arrangements which already exist between France or the citizens of France and Russia shall have no effect; the relations under private law, those created before the establishment of Soviet power, between French and Russian citizens, shall be regulated as they have been in the past, and all measures taken or about to be taken in France to secure the *status quo* shall in every respect be suspended until the accounts between the two nations are audited.

"Finally, it must be understood that from now onwards non-intervention in internal affairs shall be the rule in the relations between our two countries.

"HERRIOT."

Owing to the special position of France, this note had a more definite significance than any act of recognition. Bitterly criticised by refugees and looked upon as a sop to Communist agitators, it has, however, never been repudiated, despite the incidents which brought about the replacement of M. Krassin, the Ambassador in Paris (1926), by M. Rakovsky and the latter's recall (1927) in circumstances in which the pressure exerted in Paris seemed to coincide with the internal policy in Moscow. M. Jean Herbette has been France's representative in Moscow since the end of 1924, and M. Dogvalevsky the Soviet representative since the end of 1927. It is proper to recall that between March, 1917, and November, 1924, a man of great capabilities, M. Malklakov, who was appointed ambassador by Kerensky on the eve of his fall, continued to hold the appointment provisionally, although he was disgraced by the Government of the country whose representative he was in the diplomatic corps. The disputes which were the outcome of that situation have been materially settled by the sequestration of property belonging to the former Russian Empire in France.

In England, the regular relations established in 1924 were broken off by Mr. Baldwin in January, 1928, and re-established by his successor, Mr. MacDonald, in 1930. In April of that year a temporary trade agreement negotiated by Messrs. Henderson and Sokolnikov made these relations all the more secure. Excluding America, who is still opposed to resuming diplomatic relations, Soviet Russia has established contact with all the great Powers, Italy in particular. Her leader, Signor Mussolini, has always been on excellent terms with Moscow, even when he was tracking down and treating Communists in the most brutal fashion: a trade and industrial agreement (2 August, 1930) has strengthened Italo-Soviet relations, which have developed smoothly since 1922 and are now invested with all the characteristics of a true economic alliance.

In reply to M. Briand's memorandum proposing the establishment of the United States of Europe, Italy and

Germany have both demanded that the U.S.S.R. and Turkey shall have a place in the eventual consortium of European peace.

EUROPEAN PEACE.
IMPROVED INTERNAL CONDITIONS.
SETTLEMENT OF THE UKRAINIAN QUESTION

In his own way, Lenin was the second statesman to bring Russian territories under the same rule. Racial antagonisms, which, together with others, had been let loose by the Revolution, had not been suppressed; but, little by little, the various peoples had returned to the federal fold, with the exception of the Baltic countries, which, by reason of their origin, could not be reconciled to Soviet rule and which the Great Powers had opportunely emancipated. Georgia, the rebel against Communist rule and against the Cheka, was brought to obedience by force. But in the Ukraine, force was but an accessory.

The settlement of the Ukrainian question coincided with the improved conditions in international affairs from which the U.S.S.R. benefited in 1923 onwards. No problem could have been more complex. Separated from Poland in 1654, the Ukraine had, under Empire rule, kept her language, her civilisation and her independent desires as a sovereign State. Recognised as independent by the October revolutionaries, she gave the Allies the impression of being willing to continue the War. General Tabouis was even sent to Kiev as High Commissioner. Then the Rada delegates hastened to Brest-Litovsk and the Rada itself called in the Germans (12 February, 1918). This was the time when the hetman Skoropadsky made his appearance, later to be overthrown by Vinnitchenko and Petlura. The Allies landed troops at Odessa and Petlura allied himself to them. The Ukrainian people did not accept the Allied intervention; they rebelled against Petlura and set up a workers' and peasants' Government at Kharkov (January, 1919). On the first day of February, 1919, Petlura was thrown back by the Reds into Podolia, where he proceeded to make war on the Soviets, finally suffering defeat. On 20 April, 1919, Petlura signed a treaty with Poland at Warsaw, but his ill-fortune continued to dog him, when the first Polish offensive was thrust back and the western frontiers of the Ukraine settled by the Treaty of Riga. For some time yet he struggled on and then became exiled in Paris, where he fell a victim to a Jewish vendetta (he was assassinated by Schwarzbard). The memory of the pogroms carried out by his bands, with or without his consent, had ruined his prestige as a Ukrainian patriot.

But Ukrainian patriotism still existed, and it was the supreme triumph of Soviet policy (of Stalin in particular, in his capacity of Commissar for the Nationalities) to have succeeded in satisfying the claims born of this strong patriotic sentiment. When Christian Rakovsky resigned in 1923 from office as president of the Soviet of Commissars of the Ukraine People, the task was accomplished, the situation consolidated and a sound agreement reached between the Ukraine and the Soviet Union:

"Russia has largely contributed in restoring prosperity to the Donetz basin; she is financing the development of the Dnieper and the construction of a central hydro-electric station at Kitchkas. In every sphere there is evidence of the brotherly assistance given by the associated republics. . . . The Government of the Ukraine will be compelled to use the Ukrainian tongue, and officials who are not conversant with it will be dismissed. Ukrainian will be the language used in Ukrainian universities and schools. Private notices as well as official information must be worded in Ukrainian. But a Russian translation must accompany the Ukrainian text. . . . These measures show a great breadth of view . . ." (René Martel, *Le Monde Slav*, 1927).

They also show the care with which the U.S.S.R. is endeavouring to win the sympathies of ten million Ukrainians living in Sub-Carpathian Russia, in Galicia, Bukovina and Bessarabia, and on whom the various treaties have conferred, *volentes nolentes*, Czechoslovak, Polish or Roumanian nationality. Be that as it may, Soviet Ukraine, whose present capital is Kharkov, is no longer looked upon by Europe as an open, gaping wound or by Moscow as a hot-bed of trouble and revolt.

Nevertheless, more may yet be heard of Ukrainian patriotism. It has survived the dispersal of Petlura's bands, the "Ukrainisation" of the Soviet governmental machine and the brutal, cunningly exerted pressure of those whom the Supreme Council of Ukrainian Refugees calls "the Red Occupants." The proceedings begun in April, 1930, against the academician Efremov and forty-five Ukrainian patriots, the sentences pronounced on 19 April, 1930, by the Supreme Tribunal of Kharkov, condemning them to prison, the grotesque attacks made upon Yakovsky, the famous Ukrainian historian, on the grounds that he was a scientific *saboteur*, are only a few episodes in the hidden struggle for Ukrainian autonomy.

Peace will be restored here as elsewhere by the substitution of judges for soldiers and the punishment of individuals for mass repressions. It is enough to touch upon this stage in Ukrainian history without expressing an opinion as to the probable permanency of the present regime.

STALIN ENCOUNTERS OPPOSITION FROM THE RIGHT

Whereas progress in Socialised industry was rapid, in agriculture it was very much the reverse. The Fifteenth Congress of the Communist Party, held in December, 1927, revealed that, though the restoration period for industry was closed (the pre-war production level having been exceeded since 1926), the development of agriculture had been delayed owing to the splitting up of peasant-holdings and the backward methods employed in small-scale farming. If rural economy was to be prosperous, large-scale farming would have to be introduced, the sovkhozy and kolkhozy multiplied and agriculture, generally, collectivised.

Alarmed by the difficulties encountered by Socialist reconstruction schemes in the country districts, an opposition party from the Right was formed. This opposition put the party on its guard against the dangers of "the degradation of the rural economy" as a result of untimely collectivisation.

In 1928 a Five-Year plan for the main industries, which was to hasten the establishment of Socialism, was adopted. The Right opposition party considered that the figures for estimated output given in the Plan were exaggerated, that the rhythm of industrialisation was too intensive and smacked of the fantastic. "*You cannot build with non-existent bricks,*" wrote Bukharin, the licensed idealist of Communism, who had become leader of the Right opposition.

The chiefs of the party accused Bukharin of objectively supporting the kulak in his resistance to Soviet policy and of under-estimating the possibilities of establishing Socialism in the U.S.S.R.

In the domain of world politics, Bukharin expounded a theory of "organised Capitalism," which forecast a long period of stabilisation instead of the wars and revolutions predicted by the theorists of the Third Internationale. The opposition from the Right was accused of wanting to favour Capitalist elements within the country and without.

"They [the Right] think," said Stalin in his report to

the Sixteenth Congress of the Communist Party, on 28 May, 1930,

"that the village can be Socialised almost secretly, without any class-war, simply by co-operative methods which will supply and dispose of goods; for they are convinced that the kulak will be absorbed in Socialism.

"They think that it is not necessary at the present moment to accelerate the rhythm of production in industry and on the sovkhozy and kolkhozy, but that it is necessary to organise and free the market, to allow individual (including Capitalist) rural organisations more initiative.

"But since the kulak cannot be absorbed in Socialism and since the 'liberation of the market' means the arming of the kulak and the disarming of the working class, it follows that the Right do, in fact, deny the possibility of leading on the peasant masses to play their part in the building-up of Socialism."

THE LIQUIDATION OF THE KULAK

During the year 1927 class-strife in rural districts became intensified. As a result of the Soviet Government's propaganda and policy, whole bodies of poor and "medium" peasants entered the kolkhozy, which offered economic advantages, and while remaining vast Co-operative enterprises, provided them with a certain number of private small-holdings. The kulaks were dispossessed; there were immense tracts of land, in North Caucasus, for example, which were entirely collectivised.

The success of the Soviet scheme, which exceeded all expectations, brought difficulties and dangers in its train.

The Five-Year plan forecast the collectivisation of 25 per cent. of peasant-holdings by the end of the five-year period, that is to say, by the end of 1933. But, at the beginning of 1930, 50 per cent. of these holdings had been collectivised. The State was unable to supply these countless kolkhozy with tractors and petrol, for it had not foreseen that they would exist at all. If disappointment follows excessive enthusiasm the resultant reaction may be very terrible. If the Soviet Government does not make the peasants who have established themselves on the kolkhozy contented with their lot, it runs the risk of rendering them adverse to collectivisation and agrarian Socialism—and for a long time, perhaps for a whole generation.

On the other hand, the Soviets have counted to a great extent on the private sector for its corn supplies. In consequence of the mad rush for admittance to the kolkhozy, the private sector has been very considerably weakened, and the kolkhozy themselves, badly equipped with poor tools or with no tools at all, are in danger of not being able to supply the needs of the market.

Faced with this situation, therefore, Stalin has taken measures to limit the extension of the kolkhozy. He has advocated the consolidation of the progress already made and the adoption of the *artel* as the form-type of agrarian collectivism, the *artel* being a community of production in which the resources of production are pooled but whose members keep as their own private property the less important livestock, the farmyards and vegetable gardens.

MILITARY OPERATIONS IN EASTERN CHINA

In virtue of an agreement (1924) the railways in Eastern China, including the lines running through Manchuria to Progranitchaya and from Chang-Chow to Kharbin, had been entrusted to joint Russo-Chinese management, with the understanding that the ownership of the railways would be restored sixty years after 1896 to China, who in the meantime reserved all rights to buy back her share. This Sino-Soviet agreement was the cause of endless disputes—disputes which were stirred up as a result of Communist propaganda for which the Russians denied all responsibility and which were provoked equally by the united desire of the Manchurian and Nankin Governments to nationalise Eastern China.

In 1929, without any diplomatic warning, the Chinese expelled the Russian manager and his technical assistants and seized, first, the telegraphic and telephonic apparatus and then the railway itself.

Moscow was first content to address a note of protest to Nankin, then appealed to the solidarity of Japan, who had every reason to fear a similar assault on the South Manchurian railway, and, finally, sought to rouse France to action, for the French had every reason to fear Chinese Nationalist action in Yunnan.

"The rupture of communications on the Chinese Eastern railway, on the western side of Manchuria and to the east of Progranitchaya, held up the Trans-Siberian traffic, and trains had to take the secondary line from Amur, thereby losing two days and preventing the flow of merchandise to Vladivostok, which suffered in consequence a reduction of two-thirds of its traffic. Finally, losing all patience, the Soviet Government determined to put an end to the presumptuous attitude of the Chinese and ordered its troops to advance fifty kilometres. The forces of the Mukden Government then broke and ran, devastating the districts through which they passed in their flight to safety. The Mukden Government surrendered all along the line and re-established the *status quo*. Moscow, though not with right entirely on its side in this affair, had given the Powers—quite inexpensively—a lesson in clear-sighted energy" (G. Angoulvant, *Étapes Asiatiques*.)

This military demonstration was carried out in August, 1929, under the orders of Blucher, a former metal-worker, and the return to the *status quo* was officially recognised in a convention signed at Kharbin.

But China still remains the field for the great manœuvres of Russian Bolshevism, the revolutionary horizon on which the greatest hopes of all are fixed.

PART II

CHAPTER VI

PHYSICAL FEATURES AND GOVERNMENT

Physical geography — Area — Climate — Population — Agriculture—Forests—Cattle-raising, etc.—Fisheries—Mineral wealth—Communications—Administrative geography—The Constitutions—Administrative structure—The electoral law—The Soviet hierarchy—Prerogatives of organs of power—Administrative reform—The Communist Party—The Third Internationale.

I. PHYSICAL GEOGRAPHY

AREA

The total area of the Union of Socialist Soviet Republics, within its present frontiers, is 18,968,300 square versts, or 21,342,872 square kilometres, which represents approximately one-sixth of the earth's surface. The Soviet Union is, after the British Empire, the largest State in the world as regards the extent of its territory. The total area is divided up as follows between the republics composing the Union:

	In Thousands of Square Versts	Percentage
R.S.F.S.R. (Russian Socialist Federal Republic)	17,747	96·7
Ukraine Socialist Soviet Republic ..	393	2·1
White Russian Socialist Soviet Republic	52	0·3
Transcaucasian Socialist Soviet Republic	169	0·9

The immensity of the U.S.S.R. and its situation between Eastern Europe and Western Asia have given it special characteristics which have left their mark on the history and civilisation of the Russian Empire. The geographical situation has given Russia a mixed civilisation; besides, the enormous distances have exercised a decisive influence on the history of the country.

No State in the world has a greater uninterrupted

stretch of territory than the U.S.S.R. The natural frontiers, which are clearly marked by the Arctic Ocean, the Pacific Ocean and the mountain ranges of upper Asia, protect this land-unit. The frontiers are not to any extent open, except on the west, where the great central plain of Eastern Europe stretches into Central Europe and where several provinces which withdrew from Russia between 1917 and 1920 and formed independent States are situated.

"The sun takes eight hours to rise over the whole of the Union of the Socialist Soviet Republics" (Pilniak).

CLIMATE

The continental character of the country is shown by its climate. The difference in the maxima and minima of annual temperatures is accentuated between north and south and east and west. The winter is particularly severe even in the south. On the other hand, the summer is very warm. There is a difference of 60°, even of 80° (Turkestan), between the extremes of winter-cold and summer-heat. Temperatures of − 30° Centigrade are common at Moscow in winter.

The distance from the sea has yet another consequence—the slight importance of annual atmospheric precipitations, a maximum of 60 cm. in the north and 30 cm. in the south. Their regular distribution in the north throughout the year must be attributed to the forest zone, which stretches from the Baltic countries to the Pacific Ocean and which constitutes, with its 600 million hectares of timber, one of the great riches of the U.S.S.R. On the other hand, the immense steppes of the Ukraine and of Western Siberia receive only a moderate rainfall, precipitation occurring generally in the spring and summer.

POPULATION

At the census of December, 1926, the total population of the U.S.S.R. numbered 145½ million people. This population increases at the annual rate of 3½ millions. At the end of 1930 it exceeded 160 millions.

In the European part of the Union the urban population represents 16 per cent. and the rural population 84 per cent. of the whole.

Moscow has nearly three million inhabitants and Leningrad two millions.

The national composition of the population is very varied: there are more than 200 different nationalities on the territory of the U.S.S.R.

Up to the Revolution the Russians (Great Russians), who came from the forest zone in Eastern Europe and in the course of centuries colonised the south-east and Siberia, played the principal rôle in national life. All other nationalities were oppressed, culturally and politically. To-day, the political aspect of the former Russian Empire corresponds almost exactly to the ethnographical divisions. When a nationality is concentrated in compact, homogeneous masses in one region where it forms the majority of the population, it enjoys autonomy in the form of a united or autonomous republic or as an autonomous territory, according to its historical development and cultural level.

The majority of the population, approximately two-thirds, is of Slav race, being Russian Ukrainians and White Russians, who are culturally predominant throughout the greater part of Soviet territory. The Russians or Great Russians (71·3 millions, according to the census of 1926) represent a majority in the R.S.F.S.R., and in the Ukraine a marked minority of 3½ millions. Of the 23·6 million Ukrainians, 2·3 millions are scattered about in the European provinces and 1·2 million inhabit Northern

Caucasus. The White Russians, to the number of 3·3 millions, are principally concentrated on the territory of the White Russian Republic.

Among the peoples of Turkish origin, the Tartars, numbering 5·1 millions, form perhaps the most active element in the Soviet Union after the Slavs. The Tartars of Kazan, grouped along the Volga and numbering 1·3 million, form the autonomous Soviet Tartar Republic. Another group of 1·2 million Turco-Tartars inhabit Azerbaidjan and the Republic of Nakhitchevan; there are 200,000 others in the Autonomous Crimean Republic. Others of the same nationality are scattered about in the European parts of the Union and of Siberia. There are approximately 1·8 million Bashkirs, who form an autonomous republic on the slopes of the Urals. The territory of the Kazaks (Kirghizians), who number 5·6 millions, is situated between the Volga and the Altai, and forms an autonomous republic. The 3,500,000 Uzbeks (Sarts) and 500,000 Turcomen who live in what was formerly Turkestan, in the Bukhara and Khiva regions, have enjoyed since 1924 the largest measure of autonomy and their republics have been united with the Soviet Union. Living on the slopes of the Tien-Shan there are 800,000 Kirghizians who form an autonomous republic. In northern Asia 300,000 Yakuts of Turkish origin and 200,000 Buriats of Mongolian origin have set up autonomous republics.

The average density of population in European Russia is 25 per sq. km., 2 in Asiatic Russia, and 7 for the whole country. It must be remembered, however, that the density of population per sq. km. is 73 in France, 91 in Switzerland, and 257 in Belgium.

AGRICULTURE

Agriculture is Russia's principal source of wealth.

In the north the forest region almost coincides with

the zone which is continually receiving rainfall, but which is characterised by a light, mellow soil, poor in humus and not very fertile; this obliges the inhabitants to carry on various trades in their homes (the *kustari* or artisan communities) and to cultivate industrial plants (before the War Russia produced 80 per cent. of the world's supply of hemp). In the south the black soil lands (*chernozium*), rich in humus together with a climate favourable to the cultivation of cereal crops, make these regions one vast, overflowing granary. The average area under cereal crops in the U.S.S.R. (108 million hectares) represents one-third of the total area sown in the world. The sub-tropical regions such as the Crimea, the Caucasus and Turkestan, which are famous for their vineyards and tobacco-plantations, are also favourable to cotton-growing (Azerbaidjan and Ferghana), and tea-growing in the districts around Batoum.

FORESTS

As regards its extent, the area covered by forests in the U.S.S.R. is greater than that in any other country.

Before the War the administration of the forests was deplorable; only 18 per cent. of lumber available in European Russia and 1 per cent. in Siberia was regularly worked. Afforestation was likewise very limited. The efforts made by the new Government have resulted in a very increased growth. The Siberian forests, which cover an area of 370 million dessiatins, have an annual increase of 6 milliard cubic feet of wood (principally valuable woods, such as cedars, white firs, etc.), as compared with only 20 million cubic feet in 1913, that is to say, one-thirtieth of the present increase.

According to the statistics of the Central Administration of Forests, the afforested area in the European part of the U.S.S.R. (excluding autonomous republics) is 147·4 million dessiatins, and the exploitable area 117·9 millions.

The exploitable forest area is divided up between the three principal forest regions as follows:

	Millions of Dessiatins
North region	93·3
Central region	19·6
Southern region	5·0

This area, without exhausting the reserves, furnishes annually 21 million cubic feet of wood, of which 12·7 millions can be furnished by the northern region, 6·7 millions by the central and 1·7 millions by the southern region.

CATTLE-RAISING, ETC., AND FISHERIES

One of the causes of agricultural inferiority in Russia is, together with the almost complete lack of machinery, the insufficiency of national live-stock. Therefore, the lack of artificial manures is hardly compensated for by the use of the natural variety.

According to Professor Goldstein's estimate, the number of head of cattle (eight sheep or three pigs being taken as equivalent to one beast) per 1,000 inhabitants was: 390 in Russia, 860 in the United States, and 5,320 in the Argentine.

Russia is the classic country of the horse; if the statistics drawn up before the War are reliable, the horse population in the world numbered 60 million head, of which Russia possessed 33 millions, or more than half. In 1914 she had close upon 35 millions (24 millions being draught-horses) or about 20 horses to every 100 inhabitants. In France the proportion was only 8 (1913). In 1922 there were no more than 16 million draught-horses in Russia. To-day, the number of horses has reached the pre-war figure.

Sheep are very numerous on the grassy slopes in the

south and east. Certain breeds are worth noting individually: the Romanskovaya breed, which comes originally from Yaroslavl and which yields a warm, thick wool; the Karakul breed, which is confined to Turkestan and Central Asia and whose newly born lambs yield that black fur universally known as astrakhan; the Valak breed, which grows long white wool, is found principally in the south-west.

The breeding of pigs might be much more common in Russia than it is, for grain is cheap and there is an abundance of potato and beetroot parings to feed them on. But the pig is a much less important item in the food-supply in Russia than in Germany, for example. If pigs are bred it is for their bristles—a speciality of Russia and China—which are exported.

Russian live-stock—oxen, sheep and pigs—suffered a serious decrease as a result ot the Revolution. Since the inauguration of the NEP, however, there has been a marked improvement in the number of animals bred, although the pre-war figure has not yet been reached.

In all ages Russia has been a hunter's country. The great climatic variety prevailing in the country makes it the home of many different species of fauna; Russian hunters can shoot white bears in the Arctic seas as well as tigers in Turkestan. Game has been much reduced as the result of being over-hunted, but Russia will remain for a long time yet, with Canada, the chief fur-exporting country. The furs most sought after are the blue fox, ermine, sable, beaver, otter, skunk and the white fox. The export of furs, which previous to the War was valued at 16·6 million roubles per annum, was carried on chiefly with London and Leipsig. It remains to-day one of the chief resources of foreign trade.

Russia could easily be, but is not, a great fish-market. An infinite variety of species live in the seas which wash its shores and in the rivers which run through it. The Volga abounds with salmon and in sturgeon—from which comes caviare—carp, bream and lampreys. Sterlets are found in the Don. The Caspian Sea, which is swarming with fish, is the home of both freshwater and sea-water species. According to pre-war statistics, the total annual catch of fish in Russia put this country almost on an equal footing with the United States. It is quite probable that Russia would be by far the greatest fish-producing country in the world if the fishing were better regulated and the fishermen better equipped.

MINERAL WEALTH

Russian mineral resources are even more varied than her surface resources. Almost every metal and rock and most precious stones are found there, together with coal, petroleum, salt, mineral-springs—even ivory, in the shape of mammoth's tusks.

The majority of these resources is hardly exploited as yet: the metallurgical industry, apart from iron-founding, is of recent date. Moreover, the lack of roads and communications holds up the exploitation, even the exploration, of numerous bearings. In 1911, however, Russia ranked first amongst the countries of the world in the production of platinum; second in the production of petroleum, asbestos and manganese; fourth in the world's gold-yield; fifth in cast-iron production, and seventh in copper and asphalt output.

The reserves of iron and chromium ore in the deposits in the Urals, at Krivoi Rog in the Ukraine, at Kertch in the Crimea, in Central Russia, Siberia and Turkestan are estimated to be of more than two milliard tons; and to that must be added the deposits recently discovered in the Kursk region, of which the extent is not yet known.

The reserves of coal in the Donetz basin, in the Urals

and Siberia are estimated at 700–800 milliard tons, three times more than in Germany; the Kuznetsk basin in Western Siberia contains alone more than half Germany's reserves.

The manganese deposits in the Caucasus are the richest in the world and their reserves amount to 65 million tons. But the recent discoveries in French Morocco have somewhat taken away from their value.

Copper is found in the Urals, the Caucasus and in Siberia; gold in the Urals and Siberia; platinum, above all others a Russian metal, in the Urals (95 per cent. of the world's production).

Precious stones, silver, lead, zinc, nickel, asbestos, chromium, magnesium and gold still lie hidden in the sub-strata of the Soviet Union.

But more than hydraulic power and its reserve, which is estimated to be 30 million horse power, it is petroleum which constitutes the most important source of mineral wealth in Russia and which is at this time the principal cause of the disputes occasioned by attempts at reconciliation with the Soviets.

MEANS OF COMMUNICATION

The exploitation of all these riches has not yet emerged from its preparatory stage owing to the lack of means of communication.

For the railways, the statistics for 1913 gave the length of lines in operation as 57,906 km. in European Russia and 17,036 km. in Asiatic Russia, or a total of 74,942 km. Of this total, 16,000 km. have been ceded with the territories which have been separated from the former Russian Empire.

Russian railways have gradually developed in the form of lines radiating from Moscow, the natural centre of the country, according to a methodical plan, which is all the more easy to carry out, since on the Russian plain obstacles to its construction are few and far between. The Centre and the mining basin of the Donetz are the regions best served by railways.

During the War and the Revolution great damage was done to rolling stock, which was not repaired nor to any real extent replaced. As the civil war was fought to a great extent up and down the railway systems, the result was that a great number of trucks and locomotives were destroyed. Even more than that, the track itself was also destroyed: the rails were torn up over long distances and in the Ukraine peasants were seen sowing wheat on what had formerly been the railway line.

The Soviet Government has applied itself to restoring the railway system. Plans have been drawn up for the construction of lines. The important system, called the Turksib, 1,800 km. in length, which links Turkestan and Western Siberia, was completed in 1930.

With vast rivers flowing through her territory, Russia has an almost unparalleled abundance of natural navigable waterways. By developing her canal system, she could create a magnificent system of water-communications which would make up for the dearth of railways. The Soviet Government has endeavoured to form a river-fleet. It has undertaken the construction of new canals, the most important being the one which is to link up the Don and the Volga.

The sea-ports of Russia, before the War, forwarded 79·2 per cent. of the total goods exported and received 61·4 of all goods imported. In losing her Baltic provinces, she has also lost such excellent ports as Reval, Riga, Windau, Libau and, in Finland, Helsingfors. The only port that the U.S.S.R. now possesses on the Baltic is Leningrad.

Her other principal ports are: Odessa, Sebastopol, Rostov, Novossisk and Batoum on the Black Sea (the last two are never ice-bound); Archangel on the White Sea, and Murmansk (always ice-free because of the Gulf Stream), which has been connected by railway since 1915 with Central Russia and which, having hurriedly been put in order, has now a great future before it, particularly as, in the course of time, it will be linked up with Kotlas, the present terminus of the Siberian railway. Vladivostok, the terminus of the Trans-Siberian railway, lies on the Pacific Ocean.

Finally, the Soviet Government has undertaken the construction of a port in the extreme north of Siberia on the Arctic Ocean—Igarka.

II. Administrative Geography

THE CONSTITUTIONS

The political and economic doctrines of Communism are sanctioned by the Constitutions.

The first Soviet Constitution dates from 10 July, 1918. Afterwards modified, it became the Constitution of the R.S.F.S.R. (Russian Socialist Federal Soviet Republic) on 11 May, 1925.

The first Constitution of 1918 served as a model for the Constitutions of the other Republics of the U.S.S.R. (Union of Socialist Soviet Republics).

But between 1918 and 1925 the Soviet Republics were federated and endowed with a Federal Constitution which dated from 7 July, 1923, and in which the duties of the various organs of government were defined.

Before all these constitutional measures were adopted, on 16 January, 1918, appeared a *Declaration of the Exploited Working People*, which formed the first half of the Constitution. Drawn up by Lenin, this document is considered in Soviet literature as the political credo of the first period of the Revolution.

"The Declaration has an enormous revolutionary value." According to an official commentator, its importance exceeds anything of the type since the French *Declaration of the Rights of Man and the Citizen.* Socialism's rejoinder, this document remains the *exposé* of the principles and rules of the civilisation which it is intended shall be established by triumphant Communism.

ADMINISTRATIVE STRUCTURE

The Union of the Soviet Socialist Republics is now formed by the six following States: the *Russian* Socialist Federal Soviet Republic (R.S.F.S.R.); the *Ukrainian* Socialist Soviet Republic; the *Transcaucasian* Socialist Federal Soviet Republic; the *White Russian* Socialist Soviet Republic; the *Uzbek* Socialist Soviet Republic and the *Turcoman* Socialist Soviet Republic. The Transcaucasian Federation is composed of the Armenian, Azerbaidjan and Georgian Republics, which before its formation were independent. Peoples whose political and economical development is not advanced form autonomous Republics within the Soviet Union. Other peoples, whose national development is merely beginning, enjoy a more limited autonomy and are classed as autonomous territories. The majority of these autonomous units are found on the territory of the R.S.F.S.R., which comprises eleven Republics and eleven autonomous Republics.

The problem of nationalities has been solved by the grant of autonomy to the various peoples and by their free union with the U.S.S.R. Any nation may become a member of this Union whose frontiers can always be extended. "The Union is bound to no State, to no definite nation; it is as vast as the different parts of the world to which it stretches; it is destined to embrace the whole universe" (Maguerovsky).

Its federal formation allows the admission to membership of new countries. But if entry into the Union is free, so is withdrawal. The right to withdraw from the Union is guaranteed to each Republic (Constitution of 7 July, 1923).

ELECTORAL LAWS

The Soviets are bodies representative of workers. The right to elect and to stand for election belongs, without distinction of sex, creed, race or nationality, to citizens eighteen years old and upwards who gain their livelihood by labour; to soldiers and sailors in the Red armies and fleet, as well as to citizens of these last two categories who are no longer able to work (Art. 68 of the Constitution of the R.S.F.S.R. of 1925).

Those ineligible for the vote or for election are the following: individuals who rely on the work of others to make a profit; those who live on an income which is not brought in by their work; shopkeepers; monks and priests; insane people and offenders against the common law (Art. 69).

Tsarist Russia was, as regards administration, divided up into communes, cantons (*volost*), districts (*uezd*) and provinces (*gubernia*). The new administrative system of Soviet territories which is to replace the old divisions is established in order to serve all economic interests and according to the arrangement of the railway systems, and it leaves untouched the hierarchical division of the country into provinces, districts, cantons and communes.

THE SOVIET HIERARCHY

The system in operation is intended to be a democratic system, each local unit being administered by annually elected assemblies without intervention from the central power or the presence of its representatives. These assemblies, however, only meet occasionally, being content to appoint their executive organ (*ispolkom*) which exercises power in their name. Each assembly nominates its representatives to the body immediately above it.

At the base of this administrative system are the Soviets of the rural communes, which are elected by almost universal suffrage (one member for every hundred inhabitants). These village Soviets send their delegates (one delegate for every three hundred inhabitants, without the number of members in the Volost Assembly being allowed to exceed fifty) to the cantonal Soviet.

The cantonal Soviets send their delegates to the district Soviet.

At the base of the system, running parallel with the communal and cantonal Soviets, are the town Soviets and those elected by extra-urban groups such as factories and mills. The town Soviets have one representative for every fifteen electors in towns where the population does not exceed 10,000, and in Moscow and Leningrad there is one representative for every 400 electors.

The district Soviets, therefore, are attended by representatives from the cantonal and town Soviets. The cantonal Soviets send one representative for every 1,000 inhabitants and the town Soviets one for every 200. The predominance of the town over the country and the working classes over the peasants is ensured by this system.

The district Soviets send delegates to the provincial Soviet. The provincial Soviet is composed of district delegates (on the basis of one delegate to every 10,000 electors) and delegates from the town Soviets (one delegate for every 2,000 electors). Here again the towns have the advantage in numbers. The town Soviets, moreover, benefit by being doubly represented, since they send delegates both to the district and the provincial Soviets.

The provincial Soviets send their delegates to the Pan-Russian Congress of Soviets, which exercises constitutional, legislative, executive and judicial powers. It meets but once every two years to carry out tasks of extreme importance and to proceed to the election of the Central Executive Committee.

The Central Executive Committee (Tsik) has been called by Lenin "the proletarian Parliament." Outwardly, it has the appearance of a Parliament with two Chambers: the Soviet of the Union, composed of 371 members (the organ of class representation), and the Soviet of Nationalities (five delegates from each Republic). The Soviet of Nationalities has no power apart from the Soviet of the Union.

In the period between the sessions of the Central Executive Committee, the supreme organs of authority are the Presidium of the Executive Committee, composed of twenty-one members, and the Council of People's Commissars, composed of a president, a vice-president and ten commissars. The Council of People's Commissars and the Presidium are nominated by the Central Executive Council.

Such is the administrative cycle, which, beginning with the Soviet of the Rural Commune, ends with the Council of People's Commissars.

"The Government administration of former times in Russia may be compared to a pyramid of which the Tsar was the apex; all the officials, who were appointed or dismissed by the sole existing autocratic power, were drawn up in an ever-narrowing echelon formation which covered the entire country. When this pyramid was cast down, concentric circles were substituted, and these—from the smallest to the largest—fit into each other, from the town and village Soviet up to the Assembly of all the Soviets of Russia" (Jacques Lyon, *La Russie Sovietique*).

THE DISTRIBUTION OF POWERS

In the Soviet regime, legislative, executive and judicial powers (the famous "Trinity" of which Kant speaks) are not divided. Every administrative organ has legislative and administrative competence. The Soviets of every rank and their executive committees have sovereign power within their territories, and within their jurisdiction, and their powers (which are always considerable) embrace administrative, political and economic spheres. These prerogatives become wider as the hierarchical scale is climbed: the provincial Soviets are endowed with veritable ministerial authority. The Executive Committees of the provincial Soviets may suspend the execution of decrees and orders emanating from the People's Commissariat.

The right of adoption and modification of the Soviet Constitution is exclusively reserved to the Pan-Russian Congress of the Soviets. In practice it enacts no law, but traces in outline the policy to be followed in the various spheres of public life. The application of the principles adopted by the Congress is the duty of the Central Executive Committee.

The Central Executive Committee, the supreme organ of authority between the sessions of the Congress, and, moreover, responsible to the Congress, therefore comprises the Soviet of the Union and the Soviet of Nationalities. The Soviet of the Union, composed of 400 members elected by the Congress of Soviets, in proportion to the population of each Republic, would confer the supreme power upon the R.S.F.S.R., which comprises 74 per cent. of the total population of the Union, if this superiority in numbers was not counter-balanced by the Council of Nationalities, to which each united or autonomous Republic sends five representatives (131 in all). This arrangement gives the various nationalities a great majority over the five representatives of the R.S.F.S.R. The Council of Nationalities is not, therefore, elected in proportion to the population; it is a body entrusted with watching over the individual interests of the peoples of the Soviet Union, while the Council of the Union represents the population as a whole.

The Central Committee legislates, publishes decrees and ordinances, enacts the legal codes and regulates the economic life of the country.

The Presidium of the Central Executive Committee also legislates and is at the same time a court of law; it ratifies the verdicts of the supreme tribunals of the Republics.

The Council of the People's Commissars legislates as well as governs.

Each Commissar has the assistance of a consulting body of several members. Certain Commissariats perform duties which are exclusively within the competence of the central power, and therefore manage the affairs of the whole Union. They are the five Commissariats for Foreign Affairs, War and the Navy, Foreign Trade, Communications and Posts and Telegraphs. They are called Commissariats of the Union. In each Federal Republic the ten following Commissariats are found: Interior, Justice, Education, Agriculture, Health, Social Conjuncture, Finance, Labour, National Economy, Workers' and Peasants' Inspection. These Commissariats exist in every autonomous Republic, but they must conform to the directions and ordinances issued by the Union of Commissariats. The Commissariat for the Direction of General State Policy (abbreviated in Russian to O.G.P.U.), which combats counter-revolution, espionage and banditism, may be considered as being a Union Commissariat.

The Commissariats of each Federal Republic are controlled by their own Republic, the Soviet Congress, the Central Executive Committee and the Presidium.

The division into provinces of the old Empire of the Tsars was artificial; it answered the needs of a centralised bureaucracy and was the work of chance. The Soviet Government inherited this division of the land and utilised it for a time, but the development of national economy and the advent of new conditions necessitated a vast administrative reform.

This reform consisted in dividing the country up into districts, not in an arbitrarily administrative manner, but according to geographical and economic conditions. The regions are divided up into districts smaller than the old provinces. Provinces and districts have been suppressed. But this reform in administration has been carried out without any modification whatsoever of the fundamental hierarchy of the Soviets.

THE THIRD INTERNATIONALE

In March, 1919, the delegates of the Communist parties met at the Kremlin and set up the Third Internationale (the alleged heir to the Second Internationale), which, since that time, has shown no sign of coming to an end, but, on the contrary, tends to become re-established.

Between 1919 and 1930 the Third Internationale has held six congresses at Moscow:

The First, 4–7 March, 1919.
(Constitution set up.)

The Second, 19 July to 10 August, 1920.
(Elaboration of the twenty-one conditions of admission which caused a division in the French Socialist Party at the Congress at Tours in December, 1920.)

The Third, from 22 June to 12 July, 1921.
(The fight for the victory of the masses—a slogan which was coined to support the Trades Union movement.)

The Fourth, from 5 November to 4 December, 1922.
("Down with Fascism!"; that movement had just been successful in Italy.)

The Fifth, from 17 June to 8 July, 1924.
(The slogan was: "A united front on the lower side!" The revolutionary period was declared closed.)

The Sixth, from 17 July to 1 September, 1928.
(Slogan: "Recrudescence of inter-Capitalist contradictions"; the denunciation of the dangers of war.)

Since 1919 the number of Communist parties, which vary very much in strength, has grown to 53, but the Russian Communist Party remains the central section, the mother of the Third Internationale, whose ideas it continues to mould, and which can always be sure of finding accommodation for its Congresses amid the architectural glories of the Kremlin.

For this reason, and because the rulers of the U.S.S.R. also control the Third Internationale, there has been continual confusion between the deeds of Communists who are inspired by Moscow and the measures which are directly imputable to the Government in Moscow: the subsidies to the English miners during the strike of 1926, the support given to the Chinese of the Kuomingtang, and the grants of money made to the Red press in Germany, France and England—admitted by Ioffe on his departure from Germany (1920) and denied by Krassin while Ambassador to France (1925). Repeated attempts have been made to tack on to the non-intervention agreements a pact of moral non-aggression, limiting propaganda, or, in other words, the clandestine exportation of governmental doctrines: the intention was to prevail upon the leaders of the Red Revolution to declare, as Danton did during the French Revolution in his unforgotten pronouncement, that nations would be permitted to follow their own destinies without being disturbed by foreign-imported theories. M. Chicherin and the Soviet Government, while protesting that there was nothing in common in law between the U.S.S.R. and the Third Internationale, and precisely because these protests were raised, have always refused to give guarantees to the States with which they are in treaty that they will be free from the subversive ideas as represented by the Communism of Soviet institutions and the Bolshevist association with the movement.

This refusal has been aggravated by individual incidents of great gravity—the escape of Bessedovsky, the councillor attached to the Soviet Embassy in Paris, the disappearance in broad daylight and from central Paris of General Koutepov, formerly one of Wrangel's right-hand men, and the sensational revelations made by certain Soviet diplomats or Cheka agents in Europe—these were the reasons for the revival of suspicion among democratic States towards the hybrid character of the U.S.S.R., towards the control by a party and a political coterie of a world-wide revolutionary movement.

Inversely, the Trotskyists reproached Stalin and his closest collaborators (whom Trotsky dubbed "epigones") for having sacrificed the future of world revolution to a certain national opportunism.

Finally, it is important to note that there are several repentant Communists—M. Paul Marion, author of *Les Russies,* for example—who have turned against the dictatorship of the proletariat and now rise to champion the hitherto unrecognised rights of democracy, proposing to entrust to the Second Internationale the task of rectifying the errors of the Third.

But these are mere quibbles which do not alter the main fact that there exists a Communist system of government by force which, having overcome the disorders and confusion of its opening days, the dangers of civil war lasting four years, lives on—maybe scandalously—but nevertheless lives, without being shaken in its convictions, without wavering under the weight of doctrinal maledictions. This Government has lasted—that is what has given prestige and authority to the regime which Lenin built up amidst the tumult of October, 1917, the fiery speeches of Smolny, and while the blood of martyrs, victims and heroes—Whites, Greens and Reds alike—was being shed; for men went to suffer martyrdom and torture and to die the deaths of heroes in this modern hell wearing colours that marked their different beliefs.

THE COMMUNIST PARTY

Federalism, the inconsistencies of the local autonomy systems, and the confused distribution of power which hampers the activity of the U.S.S.R. Government, have not had the paralysing effect that might be logically feared, because this machinery, so formidable, so complex, is under the control of the motive force—the Communist Party. The organisation of the Communist Party is not part of the State apparatus, but all the "controls," at every stage, from the top of the system to the bottom, are held by the party. In that respect, Bolshevism and Fascism are of the same social type and the fruit of the same invention—dictatorship and the party system.

In every individual establishment, in every form of administration, there is a party cell or nucleus. The nuclei of any given territory are incorporated in a district, the districts in regions, the regions in the party of each republic, and the republican parties in the central party of the U.S.S.R. At every rung in the administrative ladder there is a committee, in every committee a secretariat. And the secretariat is the main-spring of the regime. "There are three stages of humanity which bear relation to one another—matriarchate, patriarchate and secretariat," Bukharin once grumbled. This institution flourishes in other lands and in other parties. In Russia it ensures the transmission of the watchwords—the "theses," to use the Bolshevist expression—from the Political Bureau (Politbureau) to the Central Committee and from the Central Committee to regions, districts and nuclei.

The Politbureau, therefore, which had nine members till December, 1927, and since then has been composed of five, may be said to have indisputable prerogatives and powers in the interval between the annual congresses. For the Politbureau is appointed by the Central Committee: in fact, it itself draws up the lists by which the election of the Central Committee is carried out. A "*feudal hierarchy!*" and a "democratic centralism" (Lenin), this apparatus works with the minimum of friction, thanks to the preliminary work done by the "*fractions*"—bodies of the élite within the élite who carry through the decisions in all the stages where opposition is likely to be met.

What is the numerical strength of the Communist Party in Russia? According to Trotsky, Molotov, one of the "epigones," calculated that there were 1,400,000 followers of Russian Communism: it is important to note that the above figure does not include the members of Communist Youth parties (*Comsomols*)—the "wolf-cubs" —and the *active sympathisers* who are generally recruited from amongst the officials of the regime. The party does not seek to increase its numbers; it proceeds of its own accord to carry out periodical purges or, in other words, wholesale expulsions and temporary deprivation of membership.

"The party also represents the spirit of sacrifice. And in this respect it can only be properly compared with the bodies of monks who in early times prepared the lands in Gaul for cultivation and led or even dominated the people" (Pierre Dominique, *Oui, mais Moscou*).

For, theoretically at least, the party possesses a code of ethics; it cherishes a desire to consolidate the reign of virtue—and this may have been inherited from Scotch Puritans or, more probable still, from the French Jacobins. It enforces discipline even to the extent of controlling the private lives of its members and of fixing their monthly salaries at a cut-and-dried figure (300 roubles *per mensem* at the maximum). These rules are sometimes transgressed, but never by the men of the *Summit*. The Summit is the body of men holding high office and *responsible appointments*. Madame Litvinov, the wife of the Commissar for Foreign Affairs, still gives lessons in order to earn a livelihood: she toes the line. . . . It is a strict line for the leaders. The fact that the scandals which are discovered from time to time and are repressed with much publicity, brings the conviction that those at the Summit enjoy no immunities but, on the contrary, run great risks. It should be noted, however, that the guillotine and the firing-party have not operated among the leaders of the party—a great contrast to what occurred during the French Reign of Terror. Excommunication from the party, supplemented by banishment, has hitherto been sufficient to remedy the worst cases of discord within it.

Bolshevism's international credo consists of "conformity to the revolutionary aims." These revolutionary aims are determined by the Congress of the party and, in the interval between the Congresses, by the Conference of the party.

Between 1917 and 1930 the Bolshevist Party held eleven Congresses. The first, after the overthrow of Tsarism (that is, the sixth of the series which had been held since 1898), met in August, 1917, at Petrograd, and the succeeding ones in Moscow:

Seventh, in March, 1918.
Eighth, in March, 1919.
Ninth, in April, 1920.
Tenth, in April, 1921.
Eleventh, in March, 1922.
Twelfth, in April, 1923 (for the first time Lenin, who was ill, was not present at the Congress).
Thirteenth, in May, 1924.
Fourteenth, in January, 1926 (when the struggle against Trotskyism began).
Fifteenth, in December, 1927 (when it became evident that Stalin had triumphed over the Trotskyist opposition).
Sixteenth, in May, 1930 (when the Five-Year plan was solemnly inaugurated in face of opposition from the Right).

It seems that at this date executive and legislative powers were fully concentrated in the hands of the Secretary-General of the party; the party does not control the Government, it governs.

CHAPTER VII

SOCIAL AND ECONOMIC ORGANISATIONS

Industrial organisation—Trusts—Syndicates—Factories—Trades Unions—Protection of workers—Rural economy—Co-operation—Contracts between State and peasants—Internal trade—The monetary system—The budgets—Taxes—The banking system—Loans—Apportionment of the national revenue—The Plan and the open market.

According to the classification which is so familiar to the doctrinaires of Moscow, revolutionary history should properly be divided up into three periods:

1. War Communism.
2. The period of restoration or the endeavours made to bring production to the pre-war level (this second period ended for industry in 1926, and for agriculture in 1927–1928).
3. Finally, the period which saw the building-up of Socialism, and which was characterised by the application of the Five-Year plan.

INDUSTRIAL ORGANISATION

The adoption of the new political economy in 1921 produced a profound transformation in industry. The organisation employed during the period of War Communism was abandoned and replaced by State Trusts.

Nationalised industry was placed under the control of the Supreme Economic Council. As laid down by the Constitution, there is one Supreme Economic Council for the whole Union. There are also similar councils in each republic belonging to the Soviet Union; below them are local councils. All nationalised industries are divided according to their importance into three groups: industry in general within the Union, industry in the republics and, finally, local industry, which is supervised by the local organs of the Supreme Economic Council. Two-thirds of nationalised industry is directly dependent on the Supreme Economic Council of the Union and one-third represents industries carried on in the republics or local industry.

The Supreme Economic Council of the Union supervises almost all the branches of basic industry: metallurgical, textile, chemical and electrical industries, coal-mines and the production of sugar and naphtha, etc. Industries of local interest chiefly comprise enterprises of medium importance, as well as several belonging mainly to the food supply, the lumber and chemical industries.

The Supreme Economic Council is divided into two principal sections: State industry and State economy. The first manages industry; the second is concerned with all economic questions (regulation of wages, industry in relation to the State budget, taxes on industry and the organisation of labour).

Every branch of industry without exception is controlled by a trust, that is to say, by an organised body composed of a certain number of factories and workshops belonging to the same industry in the same territorial zone.

The trusts are grouped together in syndicates which are intended to regulate the distribution of manufactured products and of raw materials.

The activities of these trusts, their rights and obligations, have been regulated by a decree issued in April, 1923. Soviet trusts are bodies with a proper legal standing and are managed by an administrative Council which is nominated by the Supreme Economic Council or by a local Commission set up by it.

The trusts function on a commercial basis as independent undertakings, and as laid down by the statutes approved by the Council of Labour and Defence. Their duty is to make profits in commerce.

Theoretically and legally, trusts are not Government organs. The Treasury is not responsible for debts contracted by the trusts.

The trust possesses certain funds and property as enumerated in their statutes and this constitutes their main capital. The property of the trust may be seized by the State as owner, except in the case of the liquidation of the trust. The State is entitled to receive the net profits of the trust, with the exception of sums set apart for paying off capital or put aside as reserve capital, or devoted to the betterment of workmen and employees' living conditions.

The property belonging to the trusts is divided into fixed or basic capital and floating capital. Fixed capital is composed of buildings, fixtures, machinery and everything required in production (forests and land itself form no part of this capital and are not shown on the balance-sheets).

This classification is of great importance to the masses, for the machinery and equipment, since they form the main capital of the trusts, are thus removed from private ownership, as laid down by Article 22 of the Civil Code, and can neither be alienated nor mortgaged. On the other hand, other items of main capital (instruments, live-stock, immovable property, etc.), are not withdrawn from private circulation. Floating capital may be claimed by creditors: the decree relating to the trust laid down that claims on floating capital may be made in the same way as on private funds.

At the head of each trust there is a president, who is either a workman or a technical expert: he has the assistance of Communists. The president is chosen by the

Central Power as well as by the Council of Administration; if a comparison may be made to a Western institution, the trust resembles the French administrative body of the Azote, which manages the old powder-factory in Toulouse.

During the period of War Communism, industrial returns were entered in the budget; industry delivered up all its production to the State and received in return all the raw materials, fuel, money and provisions that it required. Unprofitable industries were a heavy burden on the State budget. With the application of the NEP, and after being reorganised on a commercial basis, industry was removed from the State budget. In order to obtain the necessary capital, it fell back on bank credits, or sometimes availed itself of short- or long-term loans with the consent of the State.

Some particularly important branches of industry, however, such as heavy industry and war supplies, remained directly under State control.

But on the whole, nationalised industry no longer appeared in the budget except as regards its profits.

Profits made by the trusts are divided up as follows: one part goes towards upkeep, repairs, extension of plant and to the social insurance funds (ordinarily 13 to 16 per cent. of salaries paid); another goes to improve the lot of factory employees (men and women), to build houses for the workers, dispensaries, crèches, etc., the remainder is paid over to the State.

The average Soviet trust combines three or four industrial concerns each employing 150 to 200 workers. Of the 35 trusts dependent on the Supreme Economic Council and of the 157 local trusts, 14 great trusts alone comprised 114,000 workers, employed in 91 factories.

The reform in industrial organisation which has been set in motion aims at a greater concentration of resources. This concentration tends to cut down expenses, to put an end to bureaucratic, red-tape methods and to reduce to a minimum the loss in time and energy.

The syndicates may be defined as societies co-operating with the trusts as regards the disposal of their products and the purchase of raw materials. As a general rule, the syndicates are voluntarily formed associations and commercial in character. The most important are the textile, naphtha, skins and leather, and salt syndicates which operate throughout the country.

The syndicates exercise a monopoly. They can arbitrarily raise prices if they so desire, and were doubtless responsible for the rise of prices in 1923 and its resultant crisis. But since then their activities have been controlled and they have been guided towards a policy of cutting down prices which, if applied to exports, would suspiciously resemble dumping.

Above the trust is the syndicate; below the trust is the factory. The management committee of the factory is composed of a workman president, appointed and liable to dismissal by the trust, and employees' representatives, who are assisted by delegates from the administrative council of the trust.

Working in conjunction with the management committee of the factory, there is a board of directors—elected annually or given long-term contracts—who deal with technical matters; and to supervise internal management there is the factory committee.

The factory committee is not at present, nor ever will be, concerned with production, but it watches over the workers' interests and sees that the rules of health are observed.

TRADES UNIONS

On the other hand, the Trades Unions are concerned with the methods of production. They are represented on the managing-board of the various factories just as they are in the Supreme Economic Council.

During the period of War Communism the Trades Unions had general control of the administration of industrial establishments. In 1920–1921 Trotsky proposed to transform them into official organs of the State and entrusted them with the management of the trusts. But this idea was not carried out. With the coming of the NEP and the appearance of private capital, the safeguarding of the workers' interests has become one of the principal tasks of the Unions. Even in national industrial enterprises, the Unions undertake the responsibility of watching over the workers' welfare.

The Trades Unions are grouped according to industries. All the workers engaged in one branch of industry belong to the same Trades Union, whatever the nature of their employment: therefore, all those engaged in the metallurgical industry are made members of the metal-workers' Union whether they are miners, machine-hands, engineers, employees or directors.

Membership of the Union is optional. The factory committee (mestkom), elected by the whole body of factory workers, is the basic organisation of the Trades Union system. Immediately above it comes the Trades Union Federation or the Central Trades Union, in which the Trades Unions of one particular branch of industry are grouped together.

All Trades Unions of a territorial administrative division are grouped together in professional Union Councils, which are district, provincial or republican councils.

The supreme body is the Congress of Trades Unions of the U.S.S.R., and between its sessions the Central Council of Trades Unions, which is elected by the Congress. This Central Council is the strongest section in the Trades

Union Internationale, and rivals the Amsterdam Internationale.

The Trades Unions have their own Press, their own clubs, which are intended to develop intellectual culture, and their own rest-houses. In every town the most spacious houses have been reserved for their use and are called "Labour Palaces"; at Moscow, the former "house of the nobility" has become "Trades Union House."

The elections of workers' delegates to the Soviet are organised in the factories by the Trades Unions. They have their say in the technical organisation of production, and in rationalisation. The Central Labour Institute, which they maintain at Moscow, studies the best production methods in industry.

The factory committees, which form the base of the Trades Union system, operate in every industrial establishment employing at least twenty-five workers; if there are less than this number delegates are elected.

Strikes occur, but they are generally of short duration. They can only be set in motion to gain redress for personal injustices, for a decree of March, 1920, gave factory managers a somewhat Draconian power, conferring on them "the right to inflict all the pains and penalties as laid down in the regulations concerning punishments." "Engineers and technical experts who do not exercise this power will be considered as disorganisers of production." Tomsky, the Soviet Jouhaux, was disgraced for having opposed the severe punishments meted out to workers in accordance with the regulations—punishments which showed the iron will of "the dictatorship of the proletariat" in opposition to the easy-going attitude of the proletarians.

PROTECTION FOR THE WORKERS

No industrial establishment may commence operations without the permission of labour inspectors. This service of inspection watches over the safety of the workers and sees that the health regulations are observed; it insists on the protection of workers from dangerous machinery, the distribution of special working-clothes and the use of neutralising acids, etc., and masks in unhealthy occupations.

Labour inspectors are elected by the Trades Union councils. The observation of the regulations concerning safe working-conditions is enforced by commissions appointed by factory committees.

Any worker who has worked for 5½ months is entitled to a two weeks' holiday, and in dangerous occupations, to two months' leave of absence a year.

The working-day was fixed at seven hours by the manifesto issued on the tenth anniversary of the October Revolution. By 1933 the seven-hour working-day should have been introduced into all industries. In the mines there is a six-hour working-day.

The regulations concerning safe working-conditions, as laid down by the Labour Code, represent the minimum of precautions that must be taken. But when concluding collective contracts, the Trades Unions endeavour to procure working conditions which are an improvement—at any rate, to some extent—on the official standard.

Without any exception, the workers are covered by social insurance. In no case is the wage-earner made responsible for the cost of the scheme and all expenses fall on the contractors or on the State.

The necessary funds are furnished by the State and the contractors, who pay in for each worker 16–22 per cent. of his monthly earnings.

Insurance funds are applied as follows:

1. Assistance in cases of temporary incapacity.
2. Pensions for those disabled while at work and for widows and orphans.
3. Strike funds.
4. Medical relief.

RURAL ECONOMY.

If the October Revolution, which gave the land to the peasants, was to carry out its plan, the principles of collectivisation in an appropriate form had to come foremost in the domain of rural economy.

The agricultural artel is the simplest form of these collective organisations. Labour, land, machines, cattle and farms were all Socialised; vegetable-gardens, dwellings, lesser live-stock and farmyard animals were not Socialised.

The kolkhozy, or collective agricultural undertakings, are a more advanced type of Socialist enterprise. Here everything is Socialised, all resources of production are pooled and products equally distributed. The small cultivator is faced with radical changes in the methods of production to which he is accustomed and in living-conditions when he takes up work on these collectivised agricultural undertakings. In place of millions of peasants who live isolated on their plots of land, the kolkhoz produces a new type of agricultural worker who has entered these collectivised farms of his own free-will and recognises the advantages of large- over small-scale farming and of Communised over isolated labour.

The sovkhozy, or Soviet agricultural farms, are Socialist rural undertakings which offer the advantages of large-scale farming.

The largest of these State farms is the "Giant" sovkhoz in the steppes of the Northern Caucasus. Over an immense area of 130,000 hectares, of which half is already cultivated, wheat is produced by mechanical means. At the end of 1922 approximately 700 up-to-date tractors were employed in this sovkhoz, and this number will increase as cultivation extends. It is no exaggeration to call it a *wheat factory*. Workers who are employed as mechanics, tractor-drivers, etc., work in seven- or eight-hour shifts. A correspondent belonging to the staff of the *Frankfurt Gazette* who visited the "Giant" sovkhoz described it as follows:

"I visited this wheat factory in early summer when the crops were still standing. For hour upon hour we motored through fields where the waving corn was still green, through fields which went rolling away to the horizon. Hour after hour not a house, not even a tree broke the monotony of this carpet of verdure which covered the plain as far as the eye could see. For hour upon hour, no houses, no trees—not a soul to be seen. At the headquarters there were a few small, unpretentious buildings which housed the management, and all around were plainly-built, giant hangars for the tractors—hangars which, moreover, still awaited the greater part of the machines necessary for harvesting operations. Apart from those in charge, there were only a few small groups of mechanics, men and women tractor-drivers who lived a little further away in caravans and who were occupied in preparing the virgin soil for the next season's campaign. Otherwise, there was nothing, nobody. In the spring they had broken up, rolled and harrowed the land with 400 tractors, all of which were worked sixteen hours a day in two shifts of eight hours each. They had set about sowing this vast area of 62,000 hectares, employing mechanical means. And to carry out this work, the director told us, it had only been necessary to employ 2,500 workers for nine working-days. At the end of the summer, when harvest-time comes, the process will be repeated. It is estimated that it will take 6,000 men, aided by this immense park of the most modern machines, to harvest the crops of this vast region in two or three weeks."

CO-OPERATION

A special characteristic of Soviet life is the development of Co-operation. By his life's work Lenin had shown that, under given conditions, Co-operation would suffice to introduce Socialism into the Soviet Republic. This was Lenin's "Co-operative plan."

A State in which the manufacture of goods and the consumption of manufactured products is Co-operative, is a Socialist State, since it has in this manner effected the Socialisation of means of production and exchange.

The Co-operatives have introduced Socialism into the vast domain of exchange. They eliminate private trade and by nationalising industry prepare the way for Socialism.

The urban Co-operatives are continually being amalgamated under pressure from the Centrosoyus of Moscow. Ordinary shops, on the other hand, are increasing in number.

According to statistics, workers or employees buy more than half their supplies and three-quarters of the manufactured goods they require at the Co-operatives. Prices in the urban Co-operatives are 12 to 15 per cent. lower than in private commerce, and added to the advantage in price there is the bonus which shareholders receive at the end of the year.

Besides shops, there are bakeries, laundries and Co-operative restaurants. Through Co-operation the Government endeavours to put an end to the individual character of domestic life and to Socialise to an increasing extent the people's daily activities. There has been a considerable development in rural Co-operatives. Between 1922 and 1928 there has been an increase from 22,000 to 130,000 (F. Corcos, *Une visite à la Russie Nouvelle*).

Co-operative production societies exist together with Co-operative supply societies. There are tens of thousands of these producing cereals, flax and tobacco, and engaged in cattle-rearing and dairy-farming. These Co-operatives are federated under the management of central organising bodies such as the Pan-Russian Union of Co-operative dairies, of cotton-growing, etc.

Co-operative policy governs the supply of agricultural machines, up-to-date ploughs and tractors, etc. Approximately three-quarters of the tractors in use are part of Co-operative equipment.

The turnover for rural production and supply Co-operatives reached nearly 60 milliards of francs in 1928.

CONTRACTS BETWEEN STATE AND PEASANTS

The agricultural Co-operatives play an important rôle in the system of preliminary contracts drawn up between the State and the peasants, for the purchase of their crops. This policy, inaugurated in 1928, has since then been considerably developed.

The contracts are concluded by the State, through the medium of the agricultural Co-operatives, with the cultivators of entire rural districts or with peasant groups who undertake to trade, on the conditions laid down in the agreements, a portion of their crops which they do not require for their personal use. Further, the contracts provide for certain improvements of their lands—called the "agricultural minimum," which the peasants are obliged to carry out, also for the sorting of grains, the intensive sowing of selected kinds and, in many cases when the contract is drawn up for a long period, the complete reorganisation of the layout of lands, the application of a system of multiple crop-rotation and the establishment of labour and harvesting arrangements on a collectivised basis.

The advantage of this system lies in the fact that it stabilises prices, fixes them equitably and gives all commercial transactions a stable foundation.

In 1928 these contracts involved eight million hectares or approximately one-tenth of the whole area sown. In 1929 the contracts affected 15 million hectares, which meant that almost one-third of the cereals sold by the peasants was placed directly at the disposal of the State.

The system of contracts should accelerate the growth of production while securing markets for it. This has been proved by the rapid extension of lands given up to the cultivation of industrial plants such as cotton and sugar-beet, etc.—branches of farming which have been the most rapidly developed of all. These contracts, which are based on the system of sugar-beet culture in Northern France, contribute to the recovery in agriculture, for the terms of the commercial clauses provide for the employment of efficient methods in cultivation, the use of suitable manures and the sowing of carefully selected seed. Finally, they accustom the small-holder to living as a member of a peasant group and bring him under State influence: this helps to direct small-scale farming towards the channels of Co-operative production and distribution.

INTERNAL TRADE

The NEP gave fresh life to trade, as in a similar manner it brought about a recovery in industry and agriculture. The rhythm of commercial development is very rapid; it exceeds the progress made in Soviet economy, taking it as a whole.

In the period of War Communism, the country districts had gone back to the natural forms of economy, to the primitive system of barter. When industry revived, State trusts were created to deal with the question of trade. Several trusts established their own commercial departments in order to place their goods. Commercial companies made their appearance and in these State institutions were shareholders. So it was that the State succeeded in restricting and ousting private wholesale trade which, immediately following the application of the NEP in 1921 and again in 1922, seemed to have a prosperous future before it.

As regards retail trade, the private trader was gradually driven out by the Co-operatives. To-day, 75 per cent. of trade capital is held by the State and the Co-operatives, which carry out three-quarters of all commercial operations. The advance of State and Co-operative trading to the detriment of private trade is increasingly marked. Thanks to the Socialisation of commerce, the State is now enabled to influence prices in a very marked degree.

THE MONETARY SYSTEM

In 1920 paper money had become valueless, and, moreover, as a means of exchange, it was then only but of secondary importance. The State's industrial products were not sold but distributed to the people. State revenues were raised by imposts in kind, and by requisitions on agricultural produce. Wages were likewise paid in kind. Only in the towns where private trade had held its ground was paper money still in circulation. For six years the Soviet Government was forced to fall back on inflation. The mass of paper money reached stupendous proportions, only equalled in Germany in 1923. In 1921 the real value of this mass of paper was no more than 60 million pre-war roubles.

The adoption of the new political economy rendered necessary the purification of the monetary system. The re-establishment of trade, the need for balanced budgets, and the requirements of credit transactions made the question of a stable currency a vital one. First of all, the plan was followed of putting simultaneously into circulation two separate currencies, the one stable, the other liable to depreciate in value. The stable currency took the form of notes issued by the State Bank and covered by precious metals, stable foreign securities and bills of exchange. It was put into circulation in December, 1922. For purely technical reasons, these bank-notes were not given a rouble value but were issued in denominations of 1, 3, 5, 10, 25 and 50 *chervontzi* (the chervonetz was the name of an old coin worth ten roubles). These notes, which ever since have formed the basis of the monetary system, are not yet exchangeable for gold, but in relation to foreign securities are completely stable—in theory, at least. This stability is explained by the fact that the emission was prudently controlled, being hardly one-third of the pre-war issue, and that the State Bank was active in accumulating reserves and its stock of foreign securities, which continually increased as a result of the favourable balance in foreign trade. The State Bank notes gradually drove out of circulation the paper money, which had continually depreciated in value and was only employed as "small change" money, no note being inferior in value to one chervonetz.

"At the beginning of 1924 various currencies existed side by side in Russia; there was, on the one hand, the 1923 rouble, a State paper-issue which continually depreciated; on the other there was a note, the chervonetz, which was issued by the State Bank, a body independent of the Commissariat for Finance: finally there were certificates issued by the Commissariat for Transport quoted against gold. The two last money tokens were stable; the chervonetz issue, in which notes were worth ten gold roubles each, were given security, up to one half, by a cash reserve in dollars and, for the other half, by bills of exchange, which were actually without great monetary value. Another curious money token was the commodity rouble.

"Depreciation became very rapid: in February, 1924, 15,000 and in March 50,000 paper roubles were required to equal one gold rouble. . . . On 10 March, 1924, while carrying out vast general reforms, the Government undertook a reform of the monetary system which had been suggested by the example of Latvia, Lithuania and Germany; it fixed the value of the gold rouble in relation to the paper rouble at 50,000 for one month, and withdrew old note-issues from circulation after 10 April. At the same time it launched a new note-issue in roubles and kopecks on a gold basis, together with silver coins bearing the Soviet arms" (Jules Moch, deputy for La Drôme).

The currency of the U.S.S.R., therefore, is on the gold standard though it cannot be converted into gold. The value of the chervonetz, in relation to gold and other money tokens quoted at par against gold, remains stable and does not exceed the normal fluctuations of exchange. Par exchange values of the rouble cannot, of course, be quoted since the export of gold is forbidden: but the issue of the chervonetz with an adequate gold cover and guaranteed by foreign securities and bills of exchange of unquestionable value, all give stability to the currency. Despite its continual increase, money in circulation is yet insufficient to meet all demands.

In the first year of the Five Year plan (1928–1929) an emission three times greater than was anticipated was found to be necessary. According to Professor Bernatzky, an *émigré,* the real cover was only in the neighbourhood of 13 per cent.

It certainly seems that inflation became very marked during the year 1930. Brukhanov, the Commissar for Finance, declared: "A stable currency is an important lever for the Five-Year plan."

The reform of the credit system which was secured by the decree of 30 January, 1930, gave the control of credit transactions to the State Bank, which alone has the right to grant credits to State industrial concerns: these last may not carry out credit transactions with each other. The form of drafts which was introduced into Russia two centuries before (1729) has been abolished.

But it seems as if this suppression of commercial credits and the issue of State bonds create "a temptation to follow the line of least resistance, to adopt a course of unlimited emission, and to make State bonds a supplementary, unlimited source of wealth for financing Soviet economy" (*Vie Economique*, March, 1930).

THE BUDGET

During the first seven years of the Revolution there was no regular annual budget. Money supplies were granted on the presentation of special Government orders. Budgets were balanced at the end of the financial year after money-grants had been made according to these instructions. Soon the stabilisation of currency, of prices and of wages made it possible to forecast the budget. The budget for the financial year 1924–1925 (October to October) inaugurated the era of regular budgets. In this first budget, revenue and expenditure were balanced without having recourse to emission.

The external structure of the budget is of a somewhat complicated nature by reason of the peculiarities of the federal regime of the Soviet Union. The State budget of the Soviet Union is called the "unified Budget of the Union of Socialist Soviet Republics." It includes the budget of the Federal Government (revenue and expenditure of the Federal Government of the Soviet Union) and the budgets of the independent States which are members of the Union (revenue and expenditure of each of the Soviet Republics).

The State Budget of the Soviet Government is prepared by the People's Commissars of the Federation; after being approved by the above Council, the budget estimates are submitted for ratification by the Central Executive Committee of the Soviet Union (of the Federation). The State budgets of the different Republics are, in their turn, prepared by the People's Commissariat for Finance in these republics, examined by the People's Council of Commissars and confirmed by the Central Executive Committee of the Republic; then, after being approved, they are submitted to the Council of People's Commissars of the Union and confirmed by the Central Executive Committee of the Union.

Expenditure on national economy is the most important item in the budget of the Soviet Union. Together with expenditure on transport, it amounts to more than half the budget. Next to it come, in order, administration, the army, public welfare (education, health, etc.). The army and navy only represent 14 per cent. of the total expenditure. On the other hand, expenditure on education and health increases with every budget, likewise the subsidies granted to agriculture.

TAXES

Taxes cover 14 per cent. of the total budget receipts. Revenues from transport, posts and telegraphs are of foremost importance; industry, trade and the banks, unlike transport, do not show their revenues and expenditure in the budget but pay over to the State part of the profits of their undertakings. Owing to the recovery of these economic branches and the regularisation of their activities, they are becoming increasingly productive. This is the explanation of the rapid increase in budget receipts. The exploitation of forests is another important source of revenue.

On the outbreak of the October Revolution the old taxes, which weighed heavily upon the working classes of the community in particular, were removed and for them was substituted an income tax on a progressive scale, which yielded ten milliards of roubles. Afterwards, during the whole period of Militant Communism, taxes played but a minor part. The State's sole source of revenue, apart from the emission of paper money, was the requisitioning of the surplus production in agriculture.

At the time of the introduction of the new political economy, and when requisitions were abolished and replaced by a tax in kind which enabled the peasants to keep their surplus goods for their own use, the idea of establishing a general taxation system was sceptically received. It was thought that in the conditions of the period, the re-imposition of taxes was an impossible task. In a very short space of time, however, the results exceeded the most optimistic of forecasts.

With the introduction of a stable currency, taxes were paid in money.

The greatest proportion of the revenues was raised by the single tax on agriculture, by the income tax and by the tax on the turnovers of industrial concerns. More revenue was produced by direct than indirect taxation, the tendency of the Soviet Government being to transfer financial burdens on to direct taxation, since indirect taxation works blindly and strikes at the working classes.

The most important indirect taxes are excise duties on sugar, tobacco, textile goods, salt, naphtha, matches, tea, coffee, etc., and the tax on alcoholic drinks.

BANKING SYSTEM

By the decree of 14 December, 1917, the former State Bank and all private banks were incorporated in one organisation, the *People's Bank of the R.S.F.S.R.* The U.S.S.R. being as yet non-existent, Lenin took up Marx's theory that the banking system in Capitalist States was a forerunner of the Socialist centralised supply organisation, and it was in this way that the amalgamation came about.

During the period of Militant Communism it was considered unnecessary to maintain this credit institute as an independent body and it was incorporated in the Commissariat for Finance, of which it formed a special department. This was the time when it was debated whether to withdraw money from circulation and to rob it of its economic rôle.

But with the NEP came great changes. A decree issued in October, 1921, created the State Bank of the R.S.F.S.R., which later became the State Bank of the U.S.S.R. In 1924, after the reform carried out by Sokolnikov (with the assistance of Kutler, who died in 1925, and of Yurovsky, recently found guilty of sabotage and conspiracy), the State Bank became the central issuing house in Russia. As we have seen, it was a question of withdrawing all old currencies and substituting for them the chervonetz, whose stability was assured up to 25 per cent. by a reserve of precious metals and foreign bills of exchange. (The chervonetz was approximately equal to the pound sterling in value—9 roubles 92 kopecks; the dollar equivalent was 1 rouble 94½ kopecks.

In course of time banks sprang up everywhere: the Bank of Commerce and Industry (Prombank), the Russian Bank for Trade founded with the assistance of a Swedish financier, Achberg, and which was later absorbed in the Bank for Foreign Trade; the Bank for Electrification (1924); the Moscow Municipal Bank; the Municipalities Central Bank; the Co-operative Bank of the Union; the Ukrainian Co-operative Bank; the Central Agricultural Bank, not forgetting the Societies of Mutual Credit and the Co-operatives of Agricultural Credit which were to supply the needs of Co-operative members and peasants. But private customers never exceeded 2 per cent. of the whole. There was a widespread search after capital. The bank rate, which in the State Bank has never gone below

6 per cent., rose to 11 per cent. at the Prombank, and in the Societies of Mutual Credit to 18 per cent.

In 1927 there was a sudden change: a decree issued on 27 June dealing with the principles of the credit system gave the Soviet Bank right of control over all other credit institutions. People were no longer free to choose their banker.

In 1928 there were further revolutionary changes. Bills of exchange and drafts were abolished in 1930; at various stages the banks became the distributors of credit facilities in conformity with the general plan. The State became a central clearing-house.

Ever since its foundation, the State Bank has had power of emission. Since 1924, the Commissariat for Finance has been authorised to issue Treasury notes in denominations of one, three and five roubles. But each issue of Treasury notes must coincide with the withdrawal of an equal number of banknotes. In fact, there is no longer a corresponding cancellation of the chervonetz.

The table on p. 270 shows the various currencies in circulation since 1924.

LOANS

One of the first actions of the Soviet Government was the cancellation of State debts. Civil war, the poverty-stricken state of the country and the total lack of banking organisation prevented credit transactions.

State loans contracted by the Soviet State began in the form of short-term loans in kind. It could not be otherwise at this time when money was depreciating rapidly, commerce was disorganised and national economy reduced to a primitive condition. The first loan contracted by the Soviet Government was a corn loan, issued in July, 1922, and redeemed in January, 1923.

VARIOUS CURRENCIES IN CIRCULATION

(In millions of roubles)

	1924	1925	1926	1927	1928	1929	1930
Banknotes	346·5	652·0	780·6	1003·4	1063·7	1428·2	2145·6
Treasury Notes ..	280·7	490·9	562·5	667·4	907·7	983·4	1859·1
Total	627·2	1142·9	1343·1	1670·8	1971·4	2411·6	4004·7
Gold	131·4	184·7	153·3	173·6	148·1		
Platinum	7·4	31·8	30·5	20·7	47·0	397·8	557·8
Securities	103·6	48·4	53·1	77·1	87·0		
Ratio of cover (in %)	38·8	42·6	33·9	28·9	27·1	26·8	26·0

The bonds which represented 10 million pouds realised 6,200,000 roubles.

The success of this loan encouraged the Soviet Government to carry out a similar operation but on a larger scale. The second corn loan was issued during the summer and autumn of 1923 for a quantity of 99,600,000 pouds and brought in 44,600,000 roubles. These two loans actually represented only the anticipated agricultural returns.

The first long-term operation was the issue (as authorised by the decree of 31 October, 1922) of the First 6 per cent. Lottery Loan for a total of 100 million roubles. The redemption of this loan should be complete in 1933.

This loan was too great a strain on the market, which lacked capital, and the Commissariat for Finance had recourse to forced allotment of the shares.

But following the re-arrangement of the budget and the creation of a State currency, it was not necessary to have recourse to forced loans.

The Peasant Loan of 1924 marked the transition from short- to long-term loans.

In 1927, the Industrialisation Loan helped to finance the construction and refitment of the factories. Since that time, and in 1930 in particular, it has been by no means an easy matter to dispose of the loan vouchers.

The malignity of public opinion in Russia is emphasised by those amusing anecdotes of Soviet life which are retailed over there in the same way as we relate stories about the Marseillais. Here is one about the forced loan:

"The body of a drowned person has been recovered from the Moskva. It bore no trace of violence except two bonds of the last Soviet loan."

NATIONAL REVENUE

National revenue is made up as follows: 66·6 per cent. from the peasant populations, 16·6 per cent. from manual workers and intellectuals of the proletariat, 10 per cent. from artisans and out-workers, and 6 per cent. from people who pay the progressive scale income-tax and represent the well-to-do class in the Soviet Union.

The chief characteristics of the composition of the national revenue in the U.S.S.R. are the predominance of agricultural revenues and the very modest position in the taxation scale of the well-to-do class.

The proportion in which revenue is raised from the different classes varies from year to year. As the country becomes industrialised and the Five-Year plan is carried out, the position of proletarian manual and intellectual workers will improve both in itself and in comparison with the revenue raised from other classes in the population.

THE PLAN AND THE OPEN MARKET

Such is the picture which the Soviet Union presents: two sectors are struggling against each other, the Socialist sector, which embraces nationalised industry, collectivised agriculture, Co-operatives, banks and credits, transport, foreign trade; and the other, the private sector, which embraces small-scale private industry and individual peasant undertakings. The Socialist sector works according to the Plan, the private sector obeys the laws of the market.

The Socialist sector weighs heavily upon the private sector, encircling and dominating it. It robs it of wide strips of its territory, thereby diminishing its area and importance. Even when it does not materially weaken the resources of the private sector, the Socialist sector forces its opponent into a price-war in the open market.

The Plan provides for free production and uses it to further the ends of the Socialist movement.

Soviet economy is the first attempt made by mankind to find a controlled economy. Where confusion reigned before in production and where—to quote Vico's phrase—"the furies of private interests" once reigned unrestrained, Soviet Russia now attempts to introduce the rational principles of the Plan.

"The masses of politically conscious workers and peasants must be won over by drawing up a vast programme for ten or twenty years ahead, by giving the plans a scientific basis and making them clear and definite." This statement of Lenin's is one of the articles of faith of the Soviet Union.

To set up such an organisation may seem a Utopian idea in countries which have decided to respect economic liberty and individual initiative. When the nations were at war, however, they were obliged by circumstances to establish a system of distributing and regulating production and supply. These organisations have not outlived the hostilities.

But, on the other hand, ever since its formation, the Soviet Union has attempted to guide its national economy, to regulate it according to a plan which aims at the establishment of a Socialist society. The efforts made by Soviet Russia to introduce nationalisation into a domain where chance and individual caprice reigned supreme form a still unchronicled chapter in the history of humanity.

CHAPTER VIII

FOREIGN RELATIONS

Foreign relations maintained—First treaties concluded with Soviet Government—Lausanne—Trade agreements—Treaties of neutrality and non-aggression—The U.S.S.R. at Geneva—The U.S.S.R. and the International Labour Office—Franco-Soviet negotiations—Organisation of foreign trade—Commercial balance—Petroleum is King.

FOREIGN RELATIONS MAINTAINED

When the Russian Revolution broke out it did not deserve the definition which Prince Albert de Broglie gave to all revolutionary movements: "A formal declaration in which a nation announces to all concerned its intention of ceasing to pay its debts."

When the Soviets seized the power they confined themselves to repudiating by the decrees of 28 October to 10 November, 1919, the secret treaties concluded between February and October, 1917 (that is to say, during the period in which the Provisional Government was in power), since these treaties benefited Russian Capitalists. But before the October Revolution, the Provisional Government had itself refused to recognise all trade treaties concluded by the Tsarist Government.

There remained other treaties which had escaped repudiation on these two occasions. They appeared to be still in force—at any rate, that was the general impression when negotiations were being carried on with England in 1924 and with France in 1926. It was in virtue of such an interpretation of international law that Russia, as signatory to the Treaty of Berlin in 1878, was invited in 1923 to sign the Convention of Lausanne relating to the control over the Straits, and that the treaty of 1907 guaranteeing the neutrality of Norway was notified to the U.S.S.R. as acting for Russia, a signatory to that treaty. Finally, in virtue of the same interpretation of international law, the annexe made in 1925 to the Russo-Japanese Treaty was submitted for the approval of the Soviets.

As regards administrative agreements, such as postal, telegraphic and sanitary conventions signed before October, 1917, a certain number have been ratified by the new State of the U.S.S.R.

But as the new State became consolidated, new conventions brought it into proper touch with international affairs.

THE FIRST TREATIES CONCLUDED BY THE SOVIET GOVERNMENT

The first treaty which bore the signature of the Soviet Government was the terrible Treaty of Brest-Litovsk (3 March, 1918), which terminated the war between Russia and Germany, but which became null and void on 13 November, 1918, forty-eight hours after the defeat of the Central Empires.

Treaties were next signed, as was only proper, with the Soviets' immediate neighbours: with Esthonia, 2 February, 1920; with Lithuania, 12 July, 1920; with Latvia, 14 August, 1920; with Finland, 14 October, 1920; with Poland, 18 March, 1921; with Persia, 26 February, 1921; with Afghanistan, 28 February, 1921; with Turkey, 16 March, 1921.

All these treaties implied the recognition *de jure* of the U.S.S.R. which the Allied Powers were unanimous in their refusal to acknowledge in 1920 and 1921. In order to ensure, despite this doctrinal refusal, a minimum of protection for French subjects' interests, M. Duchesne, the French Consul, signed an agreement on 20 April,

1920, with Maxim Litvinov who was acting, not on behalf of Russia, but of the People's Commissars. "It was not the Soviet Government but the People's Commissars who were the signatories; the agreement was drawn up rather in the form of a contract in private law than a document of international law" (Ernest Lagarde, *The Recognition of the Soviet Government*). On 26 April, the negotiations opened between representatives of the Allies and a Russian commercial delegation bore fruit. On 15 May, 1920, Krassin signed a contract with the Union of Swedish Manufacturers which was supported by the guarantee of the Swedish authorities, who gave an undertaking that the gold exported from Russia by way of Reval would not be subject to seizure by them. On 30 May, 1921, Krassin met delegates of the Supreme Economic Council in London. England was represented by Mr. Wise, France by MM. du Halgouet and Avenal, Italy by Signor Giannini, Belgium by Baron de l'Escaille. On this occasion Krassin spoke *in the name and with the authority of the Soviet Government,* and Lloyd George made a statement to this effect in the House of Commons on 7 June, 1920. The Allies were unwilling to accept the situation as England had done. France stood aloof. In the Chamber of Deputies, on 24 June, 1920, M. Millerand defined the French attitude which was later shown in practice by the publication of a decree establishing a Commission of Russian Liquidation charged with drawing up a schedule of the assets and liabilities of the Russian State *vis-à-vis* the French Republic.

Owing to these circumstances the Trade Agreement between Russia and Great Britain was postponed until 16 March, 1921. A similar agreement with Germany was drawn up on 23 April, 1921; with Denmark, 2 September, 1921; with Austria, 6 December, 1921; with Italy, 26 December, 1921; with Czechoslovakia, 5 June, 1922.

The *provisional conventions* caused the establishment of relations which implied the recognition *de facto* of the U.S.S.R. and necessitated the exchange of official representatives of some importance.

Only one country—Czechslovakia—has maintained no more than provisional relations with Russia.

LAUSANNE

In 1921, Russia obtained the right to trade in France in the form of a company, Arcos Limited, managed by M. Skobelev. It was strictly controlled by the Soviet Government but, since it was outwardly a free trade organisation, French merchants were able to treat with it without their Government being called upon to recognise the Soviet regime. An ill-defined—and therefore provisional—statute governed Franco-Soviet relations during 1921 and they were unchanged by the conferences at Geneva and The Hague. But the two countries entered into negotiations after Turkey's victory over Greece in September, 1922. France, Great Britain and Italy conferred together in order to find a formula on which to base a treaty between the Allied Powers and the Government of the Grand National Assembly at Angora. In a Note despatched on 23 September, 1922, Turkey was sounded as to her views concerning a general conference. On 24 October, in answer to this Note, the Angora Government expressed its surprise that the Allied Powers had not envisaged the attendance of a Russian delegation at the conference in prospect on the pretext that there was no occasion to invite representatives of that country since she was not at war with Turkey. Nevertheless, as the programme of the proposed conference was to include, among other problems submitted to its examination, the question of the Straits, it was finally admitted as a compromise that the Powers whose territories bordered on the Black Sea should be able to take part in all negotiations concerning the Straits even if they were not at war with Turkey. Thus, thanks to this doctrinal subterfuge, the Soviet Government received an invitation on 26 October to send representatives to the Lausanne Conference.

All formal precautions were further taken to preclude the possibility of the invitation to the Soviet Government being interpreted as an implicit recognition of that Government. Russia would only be present to take part in certain discussions—those only which concerned the Straits. Great Britain, France and Italy made it clear in the despatch of 14 November to Chicherin that the Soviet Government was at liberty to include Georgian and Ukrainian representatives in its delegation, just as representatives of these republics had been already included in the Soviet delegation to the Geneva Conference.

Despite all these subtle expedients which were the fruit of the fertile imaginations of the Right, the fact of having invited the Soviet Government's attendance at Lausanne implied henceforth, directly or indirectly, the recognition *de facto*, if not *de jure*, of this same Government. It is impossible to invite someone whose existence is denied; invitation is tantamount to recognition.

The first Conference at Lausanne broke down in February. It was decided to hold another meeting in the near future but in strictest privacy, and to exclude from its deliberations the Russian delegates, whose interruptions had been too frequent and their claims too embarrassing. Chicherin and Rakovsky returned to Moscow, a few members only of the delegation remaining to await further developments in the negotiations. It was at this juncture (13 May, 1923) that the Russian plenipotentiary Vorovsky was murdered, done to death in a hotel entrance-hall by Conradi, a Russian *émigré* of Swiss extraction and a former officer of the Imperial army. Vorovsky was killed by a revolver-shot in the back; his chief-of-staff, Arens, later councillor at the Soviet Embassy in Paris, was seriously wounded. A violent Press campaign had preceded this outrage and caused public opinion in the Vaudois to be ill-disposed towards the Soviet delegation. "The Swiss authorities," wrote M. Chicherin on 18 May, 1923, "have, by their attitude, plainly condoned a crime of extremest gravity." And the People's Commissar for Foreign Affairs demanded that official action should be taken, but the Swiss Government refused to comply. In consequence, a rupture occurred on 30 June, 1923, between the U.S.S.R. and Switzerland.

The affair came up for trial at Lausanne on 5 November, 1923. The U.S.S.R. was virtually the defendant; Conradi and his accomplices Polunin and Koverda were acquitted—the usual lot of those who commit crimes of passion in France. The violent controversies raised by this verdict, the resistance to or feeling of Puritan repugnance for the U.S.S.R., which was shown by the jury's decision, postponed the recognition of the Soviets in most States, which were doubtless tempted at about this time (1923) to imitate the example given by Germany.

For Germany had changed her recognition *de facto* into recognition *de jure* by the unexpected Treaty of Rapallo (16 April, 1922). As a result of her *de facto* recognition of the U.S.S.R., Italy benefited by a trade agreement (7 February, 1924): this was in accordance with her usual methods. China followed her example on 21 May, 1924; a treaty was signed relating to the principles governing the relations of the U.S.S.R. with the Chinese Republic. Japan adopted a similar course (20 January, 1925).

In the meantime, France, having overcome the scruples of the Right extremists, had proceeded to grant recognition to the U.S.S.R. by the telegram of 28 October, 1924.

Austria, Denmark, Great Britain, Greece, the Hedjaz, Mexico, Norway and Sweden notified their recognition in diplomatic notes.

TRADE AGREEMENTS

Italy had envisaged the resumption of commercial relations on a general basis. This was a wise policy.

Germany adopted this method, and on 12 October, 1925, incorporated seven conventions in the same agreement. They dealt with:

1. Establishment of general relations.
2. Economic relations.
3. Navigation.
4. Taxes.
5. Arbitration.
6. Industrial property.
7. Consular establishments and administration of estates.

These conventions were afterwards completed by a protocol, signed on 21 December, 1928.

Six other trade agreements were signed in the same sense:

1. With Sweden—the treaty being signed on 15 March, 1924, and completed by the convention of 8 October, 1927;
2. with Norway—the treaty of 15 December, 1925;
3. with Latvia—the treaty of 2 June, 1927;
4. with Turkey—treaty of 11 March, 1927;
5. with Persia—treaty of 1 October, 1927;
6. with Esthonia—treaty of 9 February, 1929.

Apart from these eight treaties which are in force at the present time, mention must be made of the trade agreement between England and the U.S.S.R., signed by Mr. MacDonald's Government in 1924 but afterwards repudiated, together with the agreement concerning the debts, by the Conservative Government under Mr. Baldwin.

In the sphere of commercial relations between the U.S.S.R. and other States, a great number of conventions must be mentioned, those concerning the Mutual Recognition of Trade Marks, Legal Assistance in Civil Cases, Commercial Treaty Courts, Customs Dues, Postal, Railway, River and Aerial Communications, etc.

Some of these conventions are, however, too important to be omitted. They are:

1. The convention with Japan (25 January, 1928) relating to fishing on the Pacific coasts of Russia—an agreement which was particularly advantageous to Japan.
2. The agreement with China (31 May, 1924) concerning the temporary administration of the Chinese Eastern Railway; this agreement was violated by the Chinese in the spring of 1929 and after the defeat of the Chinese army in August, 1929, was once more confirmed, by the agreement of 22 December, 1929.
3. The Customs Convention with Persia (10 March, 1929).
4. The Fishery Convention with Great Britain (22 May, 1930).

A whole series of agreements has been signed by the U.S.S.R. at Geneva under the auspices of the League of Nations. Soviet delegates took part in the Economic Conference of 1927, the Disarmament Conference of 1928, likewise the Statistical Conference of the same year. They attended the Conference on the Treatment of Foreigners in 1929 and the Conference on the Codification of International Law.

The U.S.S.R. signed at Paris in 1928 a Convention relative to international exhibitions and in London in 1929 a convention concerning the protection of life at sea.

Special mention must be made of the temporary trade agreement signed in England on 16 April, 1930, and which replaced the commercial treaty of 1924, repudiated in the interval by the Baldwin Government.

TREATIES OF NEUTRALITY AND NON-AGGRESSION. THE U.S.S.R AT GENEVA

The policy of peace which was resolutely followed by the Soviet Union found expression in the signing of the treaties of "neutrality and non-aggression," by which each of the parties undertook to remain neutral in case of non-provoked aggression of which the other party was a victim.

Treaties of this nature were concluded with

Germany, on 24 April, 1926;
Lithuania, on 28 September, 1926;
Turkey, on 27 December, 1925;
Afghanistan, on 31 August, 1926;
Persia, on 1 October, 1927.

Turkey, Persia and Afghanistan were bound together by similar treaties, which combined to form a system of peace-guarantees in that part of Asia.

The treaty of 1926 with Germany was completed on 25 January, 1929, by the signing of a convention providing for the settlement of all differences arising in the future by conciliatory procedure.

But previously, while maintaining in principle a hostile attitude towards the League of Nations—a consortium of bourgeois or Capitalist States—the Government of the U.S.S.R. had, in fact, repeatedly taken part in its activities, notably in the work of the *Consultative and Technical Commission for International Communications and Transit* and *Questions of Internal Navigation* (1925.) It was at the suggestion of the Soviet representative that this Commission decided to organise an international enquiry into the conditions governing the engagement of ferrymen —an enquiry which was entrusted to the International Labour Office.

In 1927 the Government of the U.S.S.R. first refused to send delegates to the International Economic Conference and to the Manufacture of Arms and Munitions Committee on the ground that the meetings of these organisations were held in Switzerland and that Vorovsky's assassination made it impossible for the Russian delegates to stay in that country. The agreement signed on 14 April, 1927, at Berlin, between the U.S.S.R. and Switzerland removed "this obstacle of a geographical nature," as Rykov described it. The U.S.S.R., therefore, sent a delegate to the International Economic Conference in May, 1927.

In August of the same year, the U.S.S.R. was represented by two "observers," MM. Basil Antonov of *Izvestia* and Maurice Menkes of the Tass Agency, at the Conference of Experts of the Press organised at Geneva under the auspices of the League of Nations.

Since November, 1927, the U.S.S.R. has taken a very important part in the labours of the Preparatory Disarmament Commission (Sessions of 1927, 1928, 1929, 1930).

In December, 1927, Litvinov, who had come to Geneva for the meeting of this Commission, signed, in the name of his Government, the protocol of 17 June, 1925, relative to the use of gas and bacteria in war.

In 1928 and 1929, the U.S.S.R. sent an observer, M. Boris Stein, to the sessions of the *Committee of Arbitration and Safety*.

In April, 1929, she attended the *Conference on the Suppression of Coining*.

She took part in the Conference for the Limitation of the Manufacture of Narcotic Drugs which met in May, 1931.

Of these various conferences, those in which the participation of the Soviets was invested with greatest importance were unquestionably the *International Economic Conference* and the sessions of the *Preparatory Disarmament Commission*.

It was at the International Economic Conference of May, 1927, that M. Sokolnikov declared: "Notwithstanding the differences between the political and economic systems of the U.S.S.R. and Capitalist countries, collaboration between them is quite possible. The U.S.S.R. has no doubts whatever of the possibility of organising the co-existence of the two different systems" (Session of 7 May).

In the same way, M. Ossinsky, president of the Soviet delegation, having contrasted the systems existing in the U.S.S.R. and Capitalist countries, arrived at the following conclusions: The fact that differences exist does not alone signify that an active struggle between the two parties should be in any way necessary. The contrast between the two economic systems, which will inevitably exist side by side for a certain period in history, is far from precluding the possibility of an agreement in practice: on the contrary, it makes this agreement perfectly possible."

And so the representatives of the U.S.S.R. had the satisfaction of witnessing the adoption by the Conference of their resolution "concerning practical commercial co-operation between all nations." The Conference declared that, "recognising the importance of the resumption of world trade and abstaining entirely from any encroachment on the political sphere, it considered the participation of the representatives of all countries concurring in this resolution—independently of all differences in their economic systems—was a happy omen for practical commercial co-operation between all nations."

The U.S.S.R. sent a delegation for the first time to the *Preparatory Disarmament Commission*, to the session of November, 1927. Since then there have been but few changes in the composition of this delegation—Litvinov, People's Commissar for Foreign Affairs, and Lunacharsky, People's Commissar for Education, remaining the two chief members. Soon after his arrival in November, 1927, Litvinov read a declaration criticising the efforts made hitherto by the League of Nations to secure world disarmament, and he proposed the wholesale abolition of land, naval and sea forces. For this purpose, he enumerated in fourteen points the general measures by which it was intended to bring about complete and universal disarmament within four years at the most. The Commission postponed its examination of this question to the following session, which was held in March, 1928. In the meanwhile, Litvinov had drawn up his proposals in the form of a treaty measure. After some debate, except for the votes of the German and Soviet delegates, the scheme was unanimously rejected.

Litvinov then presented a new draft for the progressive reduction of armaments. The Commission decided to bring it to the notice of various Governments, while postponing its own examination of the plan to the following session.

At the new session (April, 1929), it was finally rejected. The German delegate, Count Bernstorf, and the Turk, Rushdy Bey, however, declared that in the second Soviet scheme some very interesting ideas were embodied which were of a kind to give inspiration to the labours of the Commission.

The Soviet delegation continued, none the less, to play an active part in the work of the Preparatory Disarmament Commission. In the course of the session held in November, 1930, it presented a great number of amendments which invariably aimed at more effective, more complete disarmament but which were at the same time within the scope of the plan under discussion. It succeeded in securing the adoption of an amendment introducing into the naval clauses, beside the principle of the "limitation" of armaments, the principle of "reduction," which was afterwards extended by common agreement to all categories of armaments.

THE U.S.S.R. AND THE INTERNATIONAL LABOUR OFFICE

The U.S.S.R. naturally adopted the same attitude towards the International Labour Office as it had done towards the League of Nations. Chicherin declared at the Geneva Conference in 1922: "The Russian Government, which does not recognise the League of Nations, neither can recognise its International Labour Office."

Nevertheless, at this same Geneva Conference, the Soviet delegation constantly made every effort to ensure the general ratification of the conventions adopted by the International Labour Conference. With this object in view it intervened on several occasions in course of the discussion upon the report drawn up by the Committee of Labour experts, on which the U.S.S.R. was not represented.

Article 21 of this report read as follows:

"The economic restoration requires intensive production. This production depends essentially upon labour.

"There is every reason to attach the greatest importance to the assistance which labour organisations and workers, both men and women, are anxious to render and are in a position to give to the economic restoration of Europe.

"In order to obtain the fullest effort from the workers and to avoid unfortunate competition among the nations, the attention of all States is called to the significance of the agreements and recommendations passed by the International Labour Conferences, while it is fully understood that each State reserves the right as regards the ratification of one or several of the above-mentioned conventions."

When the document came to be examined by the Economic Commission of the Conference, Rakovsky, in the name of the Russian delegation, made certain observations concerning the ratification of conventions and the application of recommendations. He declared that there was a contradiction between the first part of the paragraph, "in which all States were placed on an equal footing as regards protective labour legislation," and the second part of the paragraph, "which gave the States every latitude to accept or not to accept the agreements adopted by the Washington Conference." In consequence, he proposed that the second part of the paragraph, "while it is fully understood that each State . . ." should be erased.

M. Serruys (France) showed that the phrase, "while it is fully understood . . .," which had been added to the experts' recommendation by the First Economic Sub-Commission, neither added nor subtracted anything from the system as established by the Treaty of Versailles. The Governments of each State had always thought fit to place before their parliaments within a prescribed period all legal measures with a view to the ratification of the conventions. In the parliamentary bodies lay the sovereign power to grant ratification or to withhold it; but it was in order to avoid all misunderstanding that certain States had thought fit to add the phrase, "while it is fully understood. . . ."

Rakovsky was still insistent. "If it is intended that every convention may only be given force of law if ratified by parliament, it is none the less certain that the unanimous vote of the Geneva Conference would bear some weight with those parliaments. The phrase 'while it is fully understood . . .' is in danger of accentuating the Governments' tendency to lay before their parliaments only such measures as appear inoffensive, while the most important are not submitted for ratification by the parliaments."

Notwithstanding these criticisms, the article was kept unaltered.

At the plenary session of the Conference, in course of the debate on the report presented by the Economic Commission, Chicherin made the following statement:

"I can only repeat that the Russian delegation considers it very extraordinary that the composition of the Technical Committee charged with studying labour questions should have been decided by the President of the First Sub-Commission acting alone, and that no Russian representative has been included among the members of this committee. The Russian delegation has already protested against its exclusion from the Technical Committee, an action which appears all the more extraordinary since the very constitution of the Russian Republic is based on workers' organisations. The consequences of this exclusion are evident. Chapter VI of the Economic Commission's report, which deals with labour questions, opened with a general statement showing how important a factor the workers' co-operation would be in the economic restoration of Europe. We do not find, however, a single provision for the pressing needs of workers; neither is there any proposal concerning the co-operatives, although these organisations are generally instrumental in improving the workers' welfare. But there is one further point: Article 21, which mentions the agreements drawn up by the Washington Labour Conference, robs these agreements of most of their practical value by granting the participant nations the right to withhold ratification. This procedure, which the Russian delegation has endeavoured to suppress, is explained by the unwillingness of certain Governments, such as Switzerland, to adopt the eight-hour day. The Russian delegation considers the eight-hour day to be the fundamental principle of the workers' welfare, and it raises a formal objection to the latitude expressly allowed Governments, such as Switzerland, in the matter of the non-adoption by them of the eight-hour day.

"Finally, the Russian delegation is forced to remark that the general impression gained from the Economic Commission's report is that there is a total lack of that spirit of enterprise which is indispensable if the work of general reconstruction is really to be undertaken. The application of a whole series of international legislative measures, the adoption of an entirely new political outlook—such as I outlined at the opening session of the Geneva Conference—upon these will success primarily depend.

"Having raised these objections and made these reservations, the Russian delegation accepts the report of the Economic Commission in its entirety, except as regards certain minor points."

Under cover of the Geneva and Hague Conferences in 1922, representatives of the International Labour Office and Russian industrial organisations met and conferred together.

As a result of this meeting, the delegates got into personal touch with each other.

In 1927 the chief of the Scientific Bureau of the Commissariat of Labour came to Geneva and thoroughly examined the organisation and activities of the International Labour Office.

In 1928 M. Albert Thomas, the celebrated director of the I.L.O., stayed a few days at Moscow on his way to the Far East, though this was a strictly unofficial visit. He made a tour of some of the technical commissariats, dealing with labour questions, in order to study their working and organisation.

In technical matters, relations between the U.S.S.R. and the I.L.O.—the exchange of information, publications, etc.—have not been satisfactorily maintained from time to time.

Nevertheless, since May, 1922, there has been an exchange of technical publications between the I.L.O. and the following institutions in Russia:

1.—*Government Institutions.*—The Commissariats of Labour, Justice, Finance and Trade; the Council of Labour and Defence; the Central Statistical Administration of the U.S.S.R. and the corresponding institution in the Ukraine.

2.—*Labour Organisations.*—The National Council of Professional Trades Unions of the U.S.S.R.; the Central Council of Ukrainian Trades Unions; and the Council of Professional Trades Unions of the Moscow district. Also the central committees of the following Trades Unions: textile, transport, timber, sugar-refinery, and tannery workers; agricultural and forest workers, agriculturists and agricultural engineers, printers, those engaged in fine arts, municipal service employees, and others, etc.

3.—*Co-operative Centres.*—Central Unions of agricultural Co-operatives, artisan Co-operatives, and the Pan-Russian Council of the Co-operative movement.

4.—*Scientific Institutions.*—Conjuncture Institute at Moscow; Institutes of Industrial Hygiene at Moscow and Kharkov; the Communist Academy; the Lenin Institute and Archives.

This exchange of information enables the I.L.O. to verify the reports of its own department whose special mission is to follow the evolution of labour conditions in Russia.

On their part, Soviet organisations and administrative bodies utilise to a great extent the information contained in reports published by the International Labour Office.

FRANCO-SOVIET NEGOTIATIONS

At the Conferences of San Remo, Cannes, Geneva and The Hague, the Allies had always looked upon the sums owed to them by Russia as necessarily forming one indivisible whole and upon the settlement of claims as a question that would have to be decided in due course. The debts were so different in character that Russia's creditors were bound sooner or later to seek to benefit from priority in the order of payment. Russia's indebtedness to England, which amounted in 1917 to £650,000,000, made the English State creditor of the Russian State. On the other hand, Belgium had invested private capital in Russian mineral and industrial concerns. France, Holland and Switzerland had provided most of the money for the Russian loans.

At Geneva, the Belgian delegation, supported by the French, arranged that the problem of private property or, in other words, the denationalisation of private property belonging to foreigners should be the first to be placed before the Soviet delegates. And this implied that the main feature of revolutionary legislation would be discussed. These proceedings brought the work of the Conference to a standstill and in consequence caused the employment of methods which differed according to the nature of the debts claimed by each Allied Power.

England and Italy recognised the Soviet Government without first forcing it to recognise its inherited indebtedness. France did the same in 1924, but the telegram officially announcing her recognition of the U.S.S.R. made the most definite reservations and the most detailed claims, particularly as regards the interests of French bondholders. The year 1925 was spent in deciding what questions were to be raised when Franco-Soviet negotiations were reopened. An advisory committee for Russian affairs was set up under the presidency of M. de Monzie, who, on becoming Minister in the Painlevé Cabinet in April, 1925, was replaced by a Senator, M. Dalbiez. Being split up into rival parties, holders of Russian bonds could not give a direct and united expression of opinion and, consequently, an *Advisory Committee for the Russian Debt*, with M. Louis Dausset as president, was formed and, by official decree, given a mandate to represent these bondholders. This was the situation when France received in September, 1925, the first Russian proposals, which were drawn up by M. Krassin, Soviet Ambassador in Paris, and afterwards rejected as being totally inadequate by M. Caillaux, then Finance Minister.

In December, 1925, M. Chicherin came to Paris and suggested to M. Briand that negotiations should be resumed by summoning a conference in the widest possible form in order to examine all difficult problems outstanding between France and the U.S.S.R. On this basis, the Franco-Soviet Conference opened on 26 February, 1926. M. Rakovsky led the Soviet delegation, while M. de Monzie, Minister of Public Works, headed the French representatives and presided over the Conference.

"*We on our part as Frenchmen,*" declared the president in his inaugural address, "*will not fail honourably to safeguard and uphold rights which have been entrusted to the protection of our Government by a crowd of poor people who have trustingly invested their money in that Russia of which the Union of Soviet Socialist Republics is now the legal successor. Being resolved to pay closer attention to results than to the manner in which they are obtained, we are ready to discuss the elaboration of a system which will allow of the liquidation of inherited burdens while husbanding and augmenting the value of present resources.*"

On its part, the Soviet delegation declared its intention of forsaking formula and dogma and of basing its discussions on realities, on detailed figures and reciprocal guarantees. But it was precisely this notion of reciprocity which caused the opposing theses to clash. In the view of the French negotiators, if there was to be some relation between the payment of the debts claimed by them and the grant of credits claimed by the Soviets, there could be no question of subordinating French to Russian interests nor of *sine qua non* conditions being accepted.

Notwithstanding this antinomy, the conversations began on 30 March, 1926, by the presentation of a French memorandum which laid the foundations of a practical and equitable plan. "The French Government," this memorandum stated, "intervenes as the creditors' *negotiorum gestor* in order to obtain the payment of the Russian debt by the U.S.S.R., at the same time taking into account the partial dismemberment of the former Russian Empire and the percentage (yet to be settled) of the liabilities payable by the other States formerly part of the Russian Empire." The payments were to include arrears and redemption monies.

On 14 April, 1926, the Soviet delegation answered this memorandum by proposing a settlement by seventy-two annual payments, each of 40 million francs in gold—a final settlement without the issue of new securities and with the omission of the most-favoured-nation clause.

Agreement was therefore reached in April, 1926, on the following points:

1. The principle of settlement in gold francs.
2. The principle of a retributory settlement.

Points not agreed upon were as under:

1. The general or the limited character of the settlement.
2. The amount of the annual payments.
3. The duration of the arrangement.
4. The most-favoured-nation clause.

French and Soviet claims seemed irreconcilable. A drafting committee was entrusted with making an effort to reach an agreement by comparing at length statements made at the Conference. M. Labonne, now Secretary-General to the Morocco Government, and M. Chlenov, the distinguished jurisconsult from the Soviet Embassy, supported this effort which secured the removal to a considerable extent of the causes of friction, also the settlement at 25 per cent. of the "successor" States' share in the annual payments which were to effect the liquidation of the Russian debt. But the Russian delegation still persisted in its attempt to obtain credit grants for the U.S.S.R. as a condition to the signing of the agreement.

Between 10 July, 1926, and 19 March, 1927, the Conference did not meet: only formal business was transacted at the session of 19 March. The atmosphere became more and more hostile and there seemed no prospect of negotiations being effectively resumed: a rupture occurred between Russia and England: a campaign was started against the Soviet Embassy in Paris. On 30 June, M. Rakovsky wrote demanding the reopening of the Conference. M. de Monzie replied on 26 July recounting all the differences of opinion which had been revealed in course of the discussions and which stood in the way of an advantageous reconciliation. Nevertheless, it was decided that the conversations should be continued between the presidents of the two delegations. On the resumption of negotiations, fresh possibilities were revealed when the Soviet Ambassador, after a hurried visit to Moscow, presented his proposals in an amended form. By the terms of these proposals, the number of annual payments was fixed at sixty-two, the annual sum payable being 60 million gold francs: moreover, the U.S.S.R. granted France the benefits accruing to the most-favoured-nation clause.

Thus fixed at 60 million gold francs or 12 million dollars (gold), the annuity represented one-fifth of the interest paid before the War on Russian loans in France by the Imperial Treasury: this payment of one-fifth of the original sum was to be increased if the number of payees was reduced as the result of a decision to exclude those bondholders who had bought shares in Russian loans after 1918 and were thus suspected of having speculated. In 1927, and despite the decrease in trade between France and the U.S.S.R., the experts were perfectly justified in calculating that the volume of the Franco-Soviet commercial exchanges would allow the U.S.S.R. to transfer in francs the sums (as fixed by the agreement) by utilising its trade-balance. But Soviet economy being essentially subject to fluctuation, France was forced to seek a means of intensifying her trade exchanges with the Soviets, in such a way that the increase in the volume of exports reserved and set apart for her consumption might constitute an ever-strengthening guarantee for the annual payments which would benefit French bondholders.

It was in this light that the French negotiators looked upon the problem of credits based on exports. It was the crucial problem in the relations with the Soviet at this juncture (September, 1927).

After having presented a credit plan for 225 million dollars, which were to be turned to the account of the U.S.S.R. for three years and repaid in ten or fifteen years, the Soviets curtailed their demands to 120 million dollars. This sum was to be at their disposal for six years and repaid within the same period, one-third being composed of purchases of French goods and two-thirds of industrial supplies.

"No advances in specie are to be made! The State gives its guarantee, but let us on no account pay out anything" (Francis Delaisi, *How the Russian Debt will be Liquidated*). But the French delegation refused to submit to their Government any plan according to which the annual credit payments exceeded the annual debt payments. Efforts were being made to reach an agreement when, owing to the trend of events, the conference was broken off. Quite forgetful of his rôle as a diplomat in giving vent to his partisan feelings while on a visit to Moscow in August, Rakovsky had made some very hostile remarks concerning France. These remarks were reported to M. Poincaré and caused an exchange of Notes with M. Chicherin and finally the Ambassador's recall.

In the meanwhile, Rykov's somewhat premature announcement to the Ukrainian Communist Party Congress at Kharkov to the effect that the Paris Conference had been successful was contradicted by the French Government. Nevertheless, the views expressed in this speech showed the intentions of the U.S.S.R. at the end of September, 1927. The acceptance in definite treaty form of the Soviet proposals never came about, through various causes—M. Rakovsky's departure, understandable misgivings on the part of M. Poincaré, a Press campaign and the trend of public opinion in France. Thanks to M. Briand's tact and goodwill, there was no definite rupture of negotiations, but a prolonged interruption in the work of the Conference. The two Governments are, therefore, justified in reopening the doors, which were somewhat noisily closed, at any moment they may think opportune. In any case, no one can possibly carry on the task of effecting a reconciliation between France and the U.S.S.R. without taking into account the preliminary work done by the Paris Conference (February, 1926–September, 1927).

ORGANISATION OF FOREIGN TRADE

The monopoly of trade is one of the "dominating heights" held by the Soviet State. Owing to this undivided and absolute control of foreign trade, the Soviet State manages national production and consumption.

The body which exercises this monopoly is the People's Commissariat for Foreign Trade (Vneshtorg).

The chief characteristic of the system of Soviet external trade relations is the Plan by which dealings are regulated. The aim of the Plan is to control foreign trade in a rational fashion and to keep it in harmony with the general development of national economy. It is drawn up by the Vneshtorg with the co-operation of all the Commissariats concerned, then discussed by the State-Planning Commission (Gosplan) and finally approved by the Council of People's Commissars.

The trade Plan arranges the categories of goods for importation or exportation. The functions of the administrative organs are to regulate trade with foreign countries within the limits fixed by the Plan.

What are these organs? There is first of all the Commissariat for Foreign Trade, then special societies exercising this monopoly, and finally trusts and syndicates.

These societies are very unlike in structure. Some of them deal specially with foreign trade in certain kinds of goods. Take for example the joint-stock company Exportkhleb, whose business is the exportation of cereals. Its annual turnover amounts to several millions of roubles.

In certain cases, the right to trade in certain classes of goods is granted to the trusts producing these goods: this applies to timber and petroleum.

Central organisations of the Co-operatives enjoy special rights as regards foreign trade, but their activities are controlled by the Vneshtorg.

The Commissariat for Foreign Trade is divided into two sections: one is concerned with the actual administration and supervision and almost corresponds to the ordinary Trade Ministry; the other is purely commercial in character (Gostorg) and may be compared to a big business house with a vast system of branch offices.

The Foreign Trade Commissariat's organisations abroad are trade delegations (Torgpredstvo) attached to the diplomatic missions of the Soviet Union. These commercial bodies are the incarnation, so to speak, of the foreign trade monopoly exercised by the State. All transactions in foreign countries are carried out directly by the machinery of the Torgpredstvo or by those organisations which have the right to engage in foreign trade under its control.

This explains why the Soviet Government attaches so much importance to the clauses in the treaties ensuring the independence and the protection of commercial representative bodies. In the absence of diplomatic agreements, under French law the Soviet commercial organisation has been refused legal immunity. A judgment given in the Court of Appeal on 18 February, 1929 (*Gazette du Palais*, 7 March, 1929), pronounced that the principle of the sovereignty of States is foreign to the operations carried on by the trade delegation. As a result of this decision, attachments could be made on property belonging to the commercial organs of the U.S.S.R.

THE TRADE BALANCE

The trade balance has always been a vital item in balancing the State budget in Russia. The necessity for a satisfactory surplus in trade has become still more vital for the U.S.S.R., which is more than ever in need of foreign securities to offset various categories on the debit side of the budget. The Soviet Government can only procure these securities if there is a favourable trade balance, since on the credit side of the budget other ordinary revenue categories do not exist.

The chief characteristic of Soviet foreign trade during the early years of the regime was the predominance of imports over exports. The economic recovery of the country necessitated a considerable influx of foreign imports. Moreover, the resources of the country were not ample enough to permit of export.

For the first time in 1922–1923, the improvement in the food supply situation in the Union enabled the Soviets to develop their exports, to diminish the imports of foodstuffs and thus to obtain a favourable trade balance.

The fluctuations in the trade balance read as follows:

ANNUAL AVERAGE

(In millions of roubles)

Year.		Exports.	Imports.	Total.
1909–1913	..	1,501	1,140	2,641
1921–1925	..	578	723	1,301
1925–1926	..	703	756	1,459
1926–1927	..	807	714	1,521
1927–1928	..	788	946	1,734
1928–1929	..	890	837	1,727

As can be clearly seen from this table, the volume of foreign trade is still very inferior to what it was before the War. The grand total of purchases and sales abroad in 1928–1929 only represented 65 per cent. of the annual average of 1909–1913.

The nature of Soviet imports is very different to that of Russian imports before the War. There has been a considerable reduction in the importation of articles destined for private consumption and use, but, on the other hand, the importation of articles destined for industrial use and for agricultural equipment has considerably increased. The quota for articles and goods destined for private consumption which was 18 per cent. in 1909–1913 fell to 8·6 in 1928–1929, while the quota for raw materials and semi-manufactures rose from 48·7 to 54·5 per cent., and for manufactured goods from 32·2 to 35·6 per cent. The principal categories of imported merchandise are: industrial and agricultural machinery, cotton, wool, metals, motor-cars and colonial produce. France, who might easily be one of the chief purveyors of goods to the U.S.S.R., has, as regards the volume of trade, hitherto only occupied a relatively unimportant place in the list of countries having commercial dealings with the U.S.S.R.

Compared with their pre-war nature, exports in particular have undergone great changes. Cereals, which formerly represented approximately 40 per cent. of the total value of exports, have practically ceased to figure among Soviet sales abroad. In 1928–1929, the export of cereals was only 1·6 million pouds as against 600 million pouds in pre-war days (14·5 millions in 1924–1925, 10 millions in 1926–1927, 6·5 millions in 1927–1928). On the other hand, exports of naphtha, timber and manganese, as well as tissues and sugar for Oriental markets, have considerably increased. In 1928–1929, timber, naphtha and furs formed the principal categories of Soviet export merchandise. Next in order come butter, sugar, flax, tissues (for the markets of the Orient), eggs, oil-cake and minerals, etc.

The principal exports of the U.S.S.R. to France are petroleum, timber, flax, manganese and furs.

Germany continues to hold first place among those countries who trade with the U.S.S.R., both as regards imports to and exports from that country. Great Britain comes next as regards imports. France is fourth, both in exports and imports. Of the six Oriental countries whose special regime is particularly adapted for trade with the U.S.S.R., Persia holds first place. During the last few years there has been a continual increase in trade with Great Britain, the United States, France and the Orient.

The opposite table shows the imports and exports of merchandise by the Soviet Union for the year 1928–1929 from and to the various countries.

PETROLEUM IS KING

But the policy of the new Russia towards the rest of the world really hinges upon her great petroleum wealth. That king of modern products, which has become universally powerful with a rapidity never before equalled, is a vital factor in the political situation.

At the beginning of the twentieth century, Russia

(*In millions of Roubles*)

Countries.	Exports.	Imports.
Germany	208·5	188·5
England	192·5	44·3
Argentine	3·7	28·9
Australia	—	24·0
Austria	8·2	20·7
Belgium	16·0	3·8
Brazil	—	2·0
China (with the exception of Western China) ..	10·9	20·8
Denmark	14·4	2·5
Egypt	8·5	27·8
Esthonia	3·6	1·8
United States	38·5	152·9
Finland	5·5	10·5
France	43·1	30·0
Greece	4·8	0·1
Holland	26·3	1·9
Italy	30·2	8·2
Japan	14·1	7·3
Latvia	69·9	15·3
Norway	2·5	8·5
Poland	13·0	16·5
Sweden	2·4	16·8
Czechoslovakia	8·3	19·9
Other countries (except the following)	26·0	67·0
	750·9	720·0
Afghanistan	7·0	11·7
Western China	16·0	13·8
Mongolia	9·9	13·4
Persia	74·1	63·8
Tannu-Tuvas	2·3	1·1
Turkey	17·4	12·1
Total for Oriental Countries	126·7	115·9
Grand Total ..	877·6	835·9

already produced 11 million tons of petrol and was in the first rank of countries engaged in this new industry, which was as yet only on the threshold of development. Although she was shortly to lose her prominent position as a producer of petroleum, she retained control of the European market. Despite the increase in American production, the reserves of oil in the Russian oil-fields are estimated to be equal to the total reserves in the United States and in Mexico put together.

The principal oil-fields are in the Caucasus in the Baku and Grozny districts, at Emba, on the borders of the Sea of Azov, in Turkestan and at Sakhalin. Oil-fields have recently been discovered in the Urals. During the War, the capture of the oil-borings at Baku became one of the main objects of the Central Empires. General Liman von Sanders complained that too many interests were sacrificed to the seizure of Baku, which came about after the signing of the Treaty of Brest-Litovsk (3 March, 1918). The Turks occupied Batoum, a port on the Black Sea from which the petroleum is exported from the Caucasus (15 April, 1918).

The Allies endeavoured to seize these treasures from the enemy. On 16 October, 1918, English and Russian troops entered Baku by way of Persia, but by September the Turks were again in occupation of the place. On 16 November, as a result of the Armistice, the English general Thompson established his forces in Baku in order to control, in the name of the Allies and with the assistance of the Georgian authorities, the Baku-Batoum railway. In the autumn of 1919, the English gave their support to Denikin: the Soviet Government, the White armies and the independent republics in the Caucasus struggled fiercely for the possession of this marvellous underground wealth. The Bolsheviks captured it in April, 1920, and from 1921 onwards the Caucasus produced 4,100,000 tons, 40 per cent. of the pre-war output.

In the meanwhile, big companies such as the Standard and the Royal Dutch, convinced that, in view of the possibility of a Russian counter-revolution, it was advisable to start operations, bought the rights from the former Russian owners. In May, 1920, the Standard Company bought up the shares of the Nobel Company, which controlled 40 per cent. of Russian petroleum production; in July, 1920, the Baatavische Company purchased the Nantachev and Lianosov properties. Following further purchases, shares in several other concerns were taken up on the Paris Bourse.

This was the situation and the general attitude when the Conference opened at Geneva. It was said that the reports on the conversations which took place there ought to be written, not in ink, but in petrol. The point to be ascertained was, in fact, what form the demands of the Allied Powers, the champions of property rights, would take—compensation or restriction. England seemed ready to consider an offer of compensation, for this would favour the Anglo-Dutch group which held rights granted before the nationalisation of the oil-fields. But this group was even more anxious to obtain new concessions and the right to work them.

Belgium, first supported by France and later by the United States, championed the cause of the former proprietors and demanded the restoration of their property. Belgium's success was interpreted as being a victory for the Standard Oil Company.

At The Hague (15 June, 1922), Sir Henri Deterding (Royal Dutch) unsuccessfully attempted to obtain acceptance of a plan of compensation. But Litvinov regarded it as unacceptable and upheld the right of Soviets to make concessions without any regard to the claims of former owners.

After The Hague, the economic blockade. On 19 September, following a conference of petrol-producers, the International Group of Petroleum Companies was formed. Its main principle was to force all applicants for petroleum concessions in Russia to recognise the rights of the former proprietors.

In the meanwhile, the Royal Dutch had made a deal for 70,000 tons of Russian petrol. The Group admitted on 25 September, 1925, that commercial transactions might be carried out and even general relations resumed with the Soviets. In 1924 Signor Mussolini negotiated with the Soviets for his supply of fuel oil. In August, 1924, Sir Henri Deterding, the Anglo-Persian and the Standard of New York and Vacuum Oil Companies negotiated the purchase of 70,000 tons, which was increased in January, 1925, to 208,000 tons. M. Jean Herbette, the French Ambassador, and M. Lomov, president of the Russian Naphtha Company, signed on 24 March, 1925, a supply contract for the French naval service.

The main feature of Soviet policy as regards the great petrol trusts during the years 1925, 1926, 1927 was the employment of a traditional expedient, that of continually playing off the Standard and the Royal Dutch Companies against each other, and even of introducing a third ambitious competitor into the struggle—the Sinclair Company—which had been granted a concession at Sakhalin until 1925 or until the eve of the evacuation of the district by the Japanese. The greedy wrangles of these rival firms, which were continued with almost devilish persistence, when denounced, excited the fury of the unsophisticated Russian people and they were invited from time to time to burn Sir Henri Deterding in effigy, raised upon this symbolic pyre like one of their own leaders of State. In France, the French petroleum company, created on the initiative of M. Poincaré's Government in order to benefit in the future from the French

EXPORT OF OIL PRODUCTS INTO DIFFERENT COUNTRIES

(In Metric Tons)

Country of Destination	1913	1921–22	1922–23	1923–24	1924–25	1925–26	1926–27	1927–28	1928–29
England	179,000	81,800	142,100	184,000	326,000	385,000	382,000	387,000	725,400
Egypt, India ..	123,000	—	—	207,000	226,000	85,000	157,000	373,000	412,400
Denmark, Sweden, Norway ..	—	—	2,000	2,000	14,000	14,000	11,000	47,000	63,500
Germany ..	137,000	24,000	62,000	70,000	180,000	201,000	247,000	368,000	484,600
France	112,000	22,000	5,000	55,000	139,000	180,000	386,000	355,000	356,100
Belgium, Holland	116,000	—	14,000	74,000	54,000	62,000	69,000	85,000	181,300
Italy	12,000	3,500	7,000	36,000	246,000	380,000	447,000	485,000	519,100
Austria Hungary, Czechoslovakia	—	200	31,900	70,000	43,000	39,000	99,000	108,000	124,700
Turkey, Syria ..	149,000	5,000	35,000	25,000	33,000	44,000	34,000	12,000	184,300
Greece	—	—	—	—	16,000	11,000	22,000	38,000	18,500
Bulgaria	—	—	1,200	2,500	11,000	8,000	3,000	7,000	7,100
Spain, Portugal ..	—	—	—	—	—	15,000	69,000	206,000	307,900
America	—	—	—	—	—	—	—	6,000	16,400
Africa	—	—	—	—	—	—	—	19,000	85,200
Baltic States, Finland	47,000	4,000	10,000	24,000	26,000	29,000	45,000	57,000	63,400
Other Countries ..	72,000	—	16,800	27,000	39,000	41,000	42,000	60,000	60,300
As fuel for vessels	—	—	—	—	24,000	20,000	38,000	65,000	95,700
Total ..	947,000	140,500	327,000	749,500	1,377,000	1,514,000	2,051,000	2,787,000	3,625,900

share in the development of the Mosul oil-fields, turned its attention in the meantime to obtaining supplies of Russian petrol through the Petrofina syndicate. In Spain, General Primo de Rivera established a petroleum monopoly, obtaining supplies from the Russian Petroleum Syndicate, with which a three-year contract was drawn up on 27 December, 1927.

In 1928 Sir Henri Deterding declared that a crisis resulting from over-production was at hand. The need for an organised market became doubly clear; the Royal Dutch and Standard companies became reconciled; an agreement was reached between the ROP (Russian Oil Products), a semi-wholesale and retail Russian export firm, which since 1925 had been endeavouring to upset prices, and the Combine (a group of petrol-distributing companies operating in England). But this agreement, which had the effect of raising prices in Great Britain—so much so that the House of Commons showed consternation—did not influence the world market, which continued to be upset by the export of Russian petrol. Exports of petroleum were as shown on the previous page.

The Five-Year plan fixed for 1931 the extraction of oil at 22 million tons (in 1928–1929 it had been 13,700,000). Forty million tons is the estimated output for 1933. The Baku-Batoum pipe-line, which was built in 1927–1928, ensures that, with the vastly increased production, there is always an ample supply of oil ready for shipment. The Soviet Union of Oil and Gas Industries, known as Soyuzneft, which was created by the decree of 30 November, 1929, ensures the proper organisation of an industry whose importance in European economy cannot be exaggerated.

CHAPTER IX

PROGRESS AND PROSPECTS

The reasons for the Five-Year plan—Essential characteristics—Finance—The Plan in operation—Soviet dumping—Actual results of the Plan—Public works and the Plan—The Turksib railway—A new Siberian port—Magnitostroy—Electrification—Labour systems—Socialist rivalry—Education—Theatre and literature—Soviet attitude towards religion—The law and the family—Legal position of women—New forms of social life—The housing question—Urban life—The New Man.

THE REASONS FOR THE FIVE-YEAR PLAN

The Soviet economic system is based upon a plan. In 1920, on Lenin's initiative, a detailed scheme for the reorganisation of all the economic resources of the country was drawn up, whereby the electrification of industries, transport and agriculture could be effected, and the plan was adopted by the Tenth Pan-Russian Soviet Congress held at the end of 1921.

In 1924, by means of a system of estimates and regulations, the country's entire industrial activity was planned for a period of one year. Efforts were then made to calculate and include in the scheme the future economic developments within a period of five years. The actual Five-Year plan, comprising the financial years from 1928 to 1933, was the first to be submitted for approval by the Communist Party and the Soviet authority. Since October, 1928, it has been in general application.

ESSENTIAL CHARACTERISTICS

"The fundamental task of the Five-Year plan is to effect a complete upheaval of the country's entire economic system. Why and how is this to be done? If it had attempted to enforce Marxist doctrines in a country in which industry and Capitalism were the predominant forces, it would merely have proceeded to direct its adherents' activities to the organisation of industry and Capitalism in accordance with collectivist theories. But such is not the position of Russia and the countries under Soviet rule. Russia is essentially an agrarian country; ninety per cent. of its population were peasants at the outbreak of the Revolution. Apart from what might be forthcoming from the great landed estates, industry had little or no capital behind it. The Bolsheviks immediately realised that, though their Revolution might have strictly conformed to the theory of Karl Marx, it had been brought about in circumstances opposed to Marxist premises, and in a country where its message would convey no meaning. Consequently it was bound to be unreal, insecure and fraught with danger. If the projected scheme were to succeed and win over the sceptical, Russia must be converted into a vast industrial power, at least the equal of the greatest among such powers in the world. They determined that such predominance should be hers; it was to be secured by a Holy Crusade for production to the utmost capacity, with its inevitable corollary, the Holy Crusade of forced labour with all the consequences of these premises.

"This merciless decision was duly applied to the Five-Year plan, to the preparation of which the theorists and economists of the Communist Party had devoted their energies for the last three years, and to which the Gosplan gave the finishing touches. Its aim, in practice, is to create a nationalised industry by means of intensified production. Though at its inception such an industry was practically non-existent, it was started on a vast scale, without any consideration of the country's actual needs or of the resources ready for development: its aim was to imitate the system in force in the most powerful Capitalist countries, such as the United States, Germany and England. The Soviet intentions were obvious: industrial output was to be speeded up by artisans toiling at high pressure in order that it might usurp the position of agriculture as the predominant force in the country. At the same time the agricultural output was to be intensified by filching from the moujik the field which he cultivated in his old-fashioned methods and by force or persuasion instituting through the countryside the collective methods by now in force in industries. By such means that serious menace to the Plan's success, dualism, with worker opposed to peasant, factory to agriculture, would be avoided. Such is the Five-Year plan, an undertaking which some hold to be sheer madness, and others a calculated cruelty, especially if it is to be accomplished within the narrow limits of the five years imposed upon it, and possesses only the resources which its organisers can command" (J. C. Balet).

With imposing formality the Five-Year plan was presented to the delegates of the Fifteenth Soviet Congress in the spring of 1929. Krzhizhanovsky, the President of the Advisory Commission on Finance, was in the chair, with a large map of the Soviet Union hung up beside him. As he enumerated the electric power stations to be erected in the course of the following years, tiny electric lamps lit up the corresponding parts of the map. He spoke of the blast furnaces to be constructed, of factories and petrol stations—and other little lamps flashed forth. He gave a list of the future sovkhozy and kolkhozy, and far and wide the great steppes gleamed with electric light; very soon the whole map was one blaze of light and this scheme of projected construction lay exposed for all to see. And when Krzhizhanovsky, displaying the flashing map, exclaimed: "This is the aim of our struggles," his vast audience was seized by a fervour that seemed to be inspired and was quite unintelligible to the common-sense mind of the West; the very reporter checked his pen in mid-air, his heart filled with emotion.

The Soviet rule is dependent upon the artisans. Now, in the Russian Republic that class only represents a small fraction, as compared with the peasantry. In order to maintain and strengthen the Government the influence of the proletariat must be rendered more effective. If the industries were to disappear, the working classes would lose their importance and the peasantry rise up like a tidal wave and sweep away the Government.

The first aim and object of the Five-Year plan is to industrialise the whole country. Within five years, if the claims of its organisers are to be credited, the output of the Soviet coal-mines will have exceeded those of France and risen from the fifth to the fourth place in the mining countries of the world. In steel output it will overtake England, France and Italy and rise from the sixth to the third place.

The Plan anticipates a threefold increase in its industrial products. Three thousand traction engines will change life in the villages beyond all recognition. From a technical and economic point of view the Plan is summed up in the slogan: "Catch up the Capitalist countries and get ahead of them." From the social point of view the Plan aims at building up the Socialist State. The proportion of State-controlled services, which in 1929 represented 52·7 per cent. of total production, according to calculations should exceed 68·9 per cent. towards the end of the five years: it will rise from 80 per cent. to 92 per cent. in industry and from 2 per cent. to 15 per cent. in agriculture.

By the Five-Year plan it is proposed to effect far-reaching changes in rural life by increasing the number of sovkhozy and kolkhozy. An increase in the number of depots hiring out tractors and other agricultural implements will more speedily promote the collectivist spirit among the villagers. Instead of thousands of small owners there will spring up on the kolkhozy a vast reserve of workers, all imbued with the Socialist spirit. In the year 1932–1933, 25 per cent. of the peasants' savings will be invested in the kolkhozy, which will by then be equipped with the most up-to-date agricultural machinery. Thus a quarter of the peasantry, freed from the fetters of private enterprise, will speed up the output of agricultural produce and keep the proletariat in the towns in employment, while the latter's material and cultural condition will be benefited by the improvements to which both classes of workers have contributed. So great a rise as 71 per cent. in the townsmen's rate of wages has been anticipated. Towards the end of the five years a seven-hour working day will have been established in all industries, as proposed by the manifesto of 7 November, 1927, the Tenth Anniversary of the October Revolution. Many milliards of roubles will be expended in the building of workmen's dwellings.

With the universal adoption of the seven-hour working day, with the erection of new factories and the industrialisation of the whole country, strikes due to overpopulation in the countryside will cease—indeed, when Stalin refused grants to strikers, he declared that the day of strikes was over.

The Five-Year plan is also making provision for what it calls "The Cultural Revolution." Large numbers of skilled artisans will be enrolled, thousands and thousands of engineers and craftsmen called into being. Compulsory education, innumerable clubs and universities, Socialised towns built to order, national culture springing up from the soil of the self-governing Republics—all these blessings, and many more, will be the distinguishing marks of the Cultural Revolution. Such are the essential characteristics of the Five-Year plan.

FINANCE

To carry out this Plan will require the investment of capital to an amount unsurpassed in the history of the world. Its estimated cost would amount to 86 milliard gold roubles. Now the Republic cannot depend upon the National Treasury nor on foreign loans. Hence its only resource is an immense mobilisation of annual revenue. How is this to be effected? By means of a budget and the utilisation of the revenues from the Socialised sector of the country, i.e. its industries, State banks and insurance companies. The amount to be thus appropriated represents half the national revenue, as shown in the following table:

	Mil. roubles	Percentage
Inland Revenue ..	44,704	52·3
Nationalised Industries ..	18,943	22·1
Banks	6,777	7·9
Social Services	8,650	10·2
Minor Items	6,645	7·5
	85,719	100·0

Reckoned in sterling and multiplied by twelve (the nominal bank rate of the Russian State Bank), the total reached is over one billion three millions in five years. It may be noted that so colossal a sum has never yet been shown on any budget except in years of war or inflation.

Departmental expenses are budgeted as follows:

	Mil. roubles.
Agriculture	7,086
Irrigation	4,050
Forestry	550
Industries	17,905
Electrification	2,960
Transport	9,835
Post Office..	304
Trading and Co-operative Societies ..	7,637
Municipal Expenditure	2,470
Housing	3,960
Various economic projects	1,590
Short-term credits	700
	59,047

Social Services and Education:

Education	10,210
Health	4,640
Insurance	6,046
Administrative Expenses	9,915
Total	89,858

These figures show an expenditure in excess of income. Such exuberant confidence and optimism are to be explained by a belief in (*a*) the immense powers of expansion of the national revenue, (*b*) the fall in the price of raw materials.[1] They are explained by the overpowering impulse given to Russian effort ever since this mighty task to rouse the hopes of the proletarian masses was set before them. There is a spirit inherent in the Five-Year plan for which some writers have found a parallel in the single purpose that fires the hearts of nations at war or even the inspired zeal of the Crusader. This spirit of enthusiasm burns most ardently in the breasts of the younger generation, who in 1914 or 1917 were mere children, and whose zeal finds expression in a furious, diversified, all-pervading propaganda. The inevitable halts in the progress of carrying out the Plan entail much bitterness of heart, complaints and even rebellions.

THE PLAN IN OPERATION

"One may ask if the dreams of industrialisation to the utmost limits, the policy pursued by the Bolsheviks, will not meet with the same fate as befell Peter the Great and all those whom the chimera of Russian imagination has beguiled, utterly regardless of the country's strength and prospects. In a word, does not Soviet Russia on the road to industrialisation run the risk of falling by the wayside, just as Tsarist Russia fell on the road to San Sophia?" (Henri Rollin).

[1] See Grinko, *The Five-Year Plan*; he was one of its authors and People's Commissar for Finance in November, 1930.

But whoever

> "endeavoured to ignore the psychological state of the overwhelming majority of the young workers by alleging that instances of backsliding have been reported and that the aims in the contests have proved difficult of attainment, would form a completely wrong impression of the U.S.S.R. of to-day and on the chances of the Plan's success" (Roger Franck).

The Plan was from the outset confronted with serious difficulties, some indeed intensified by its exaggerated success. Such vast masses of peasants came pouring into the kolkhozy that agricultural machinery had to be purchased more extensively; hence the progress in establishing Socialist principles in rural districts was retarded, or a decrease in the export of produce would have resulted. Shortage of labour for the mines or the transference of miners to other trades, has brought about a 30 per cent. reduction in the second year's output in the Donetz coalfields and had similar adverse effects in others. These breaks in the front line, or rather these unforeseen casualties, obliged its promoters to extend a three months' grace in the second stage of the Plan, from October, 1930, to January, 1931.

On the other hand, reduction in prices of raw materials on which they had reckoned to supply their own factories had not been procured by the export of Soviet manufactured articles. Contrary to the theory, the monopoly of foreign trading has not secured for the Soviet markets complete independence of other trading countries in the world. Since prices of raw materials have still further fallen and have sunk more rapidly than those of manufactured articles, it has become vitally necessary to export wood, petroleum and furs in sufficient quantities to counterbalance the fall in value of these raw materials.

The American financial crisis, which checked the demand in the luxury trade for expensive furs, immediately held up Russian purchases of machinery, a fifth of the cost (at the very least) having been defrayed by the sale of sables.

The main result of the economic crisis was the rapid decrease in foreign trade turnovers, either because of the actual fall in prices or owing to the obstructive policy of certain purchasers who combined to keep down prices. London brokers, for instance, secured a considerable reduction in price of their purchases of Russian timber, and this involved the Republic in the loss of about two million pounds. The consequence of this enforced increase in exported goods was that the internal supply of food stuffs had to be ruthlessly cut down. The prescribed standard of living had to be still more rigidly enforced, food tickets again imposed, and under-nourishment brought its inevitable consequence, under-production. There was shortage of bread, sugar (55,000 tons were bought abroad in 1930), and meat, due to the wanton destruction of cattle by recalcitrant kulaks or by peasants who disposed of their beasts in order to be able to enter the kolkhozy. Finally, supplies of vegetables fell short through delay in tending the kitchen gardens. These various factors combined in 1930 to delay the execution of the Plan, which had been speeded up, at any rate in certain branches or sectors. Each section of the Plan being closely connected with all the others, any speeding up of some of the undertakings projected is as fatal to its achievement as the slowing down of others. Any upsetting of the balance threatens its very existence.

SOVIET DUMPING

The increased sales of Russian goods in the markets of Europe, America and North Africa, coinciding with the deflation due to the American crisis, aroused the liveliest apprehensions, even among traders, who had so far paid but scant attention to Russian economic developments. Although the percentage of Soviet goods or products imported into France has always been insignificant, the French Government was the first to take alarm and to proceed to measures of retaliation. America had already (June, 1930) put an embargo on many shiploads of goods on the grounds that such goods had been manufactured at Archangel by slave labour, justifying her action by a law of 1864 on Slavery, but after two weeks had elapsed and a lawsuit had been instituted by a private individual, the embargo was lifted.

In the *Ere Nouvelle* of 4 August and 5 October, 1930, Senator Dalbiez, a member of the Franco-Soviet Conference, took violent exception to this Soviet dumping, and called for urgent measures of retaliation. At the same time, Roumania, Czechoslovakia, Poland, Bulgaria and Hungary, finding themselves again threatened with competition from Russian cereals, called for some international measures of protection. The echo of these protests even reached Greece (Session of September, 1930).

M. Flandin, at that time the French Minister of Trade, therefore instituted, in a decree of 3 October, 1930, a system of licences, which was intended to check the import of cereals, meat, eggs, flax and wood. The same system was very soon afterwards adopted by Belgium, while the corn-growing countries of Central Europe closed their frontiers to Russian goods. According to M. Philippe Lamour, this was a "policy born of fear," and he considered the alleged Soviet dumping system to be no more than the manifestation of an economic system "in which the net price was shorn of an important factor—profit." On the other hand, Germany and Italy have specifically declined to take any action in this fight against dumping, which their experts proclaim to be non-existent or quite harmless.

Soviet imports into France do not seem to have sensibly diminished since the decree of 3 October; the only decrease has been in Soviet purchases. Such a state of affairs and the undisguised hostility which the incident has provoked have naturally added to the difficulties of the policy, which certain individuals have set themselves, to bring about an agreement between France and the Soviet Republic on conditions similar to those which the latter Power has concluded with Italy, and by which is implied a mutual engagement between the two countries—with reservations.

To take a wider view of the situation, the charge of dumping which has been brought against the Soviets has not been, and cannot be, subjected to any impartial test. Dumping pre-supposes unfair competition by an artificial reduction in prices; it seems, then, impossible to prove that the net costs of Russian cereals, wood or petroleum are higher than the prices at which these three products respectively are sold in the markets of other countries. Besides, if we imagine that with revolutionary intent the U.S.S.R. has sold at a loss considerable quantities of food stuffs or oils, we shall have to contemplate a display of violence and aggression which will be aimed at the whole world and of such intensity that any counter measure proposed or actually enforced will be doomed beforehand to failure. But all economists unanimously recognise the fact that Russian currency in these countries has no corresponding value in the money markets of other countries as a medium for normal exchange or trade.

After a violent outcry, the question of dumping has ceased to provoke discussion and is in some measure settled. Dishonest sales by the Republic have stopped and the European Reconstruction Committee, on the proposal of Mr. Henderson (Great Britain), Dr. Curtius (Germany) and Signor Grandi (Italy), has chosen as the first subject for its deliberations the drawing up of the rules of procedure (in conformity with the statute of the League of Nations), by which Russia, Turkey and Iceland would send representatives to the European Economic Council (18 January, 1931).

ACTUAL RESULTS OF THE PLAN

Nevertheless, the results obtained and widely advertised are still such as to enable Stalin to glorify the work in process of realisation. "The output of our industries," he exclaimed, on 28 May, 1930, at an Assembly of the Communist Party, "is progressing in an upward curve, the peak of which has nowhere yet been reached." On 19 December, 1930, Kuybyshev asserted that the progress of the Plan had exceeded all anticipations in the great Russian industries, whose gross production showed in 1929 an increase of 25 per cent., an excess of 5 per cent. over the figures calculated in the Plan, while in the first year the increase had been 3 per cent. more than the figure planned." In agriculture the harvest of grain increased by 21·8 per cent., rising from 71 to 87·4 million tons, while sugar beet reached a total of 151·7 million cwts. compared with 62·5 million cwts. in the preceding year. "The Russian Five-Year plan may be said to have been from 75 to 80 per cent. successful," said M. Jules Parmentier, the great authority on finance, in February, 1931.

Its most impressive feature has been the industrialisation of agriculture. On 1 March, 1930, out of 26 million peasants 14 millions had deserted their holdings and joined with the kolkhozy. Though Stalin did not share his followers' ecstasies at so outstanding a triumph, yet the "*period of widespread reaction,*" as he was pleased to term it, resounds to the credit of the uplifting force of Socialism. Other observers maintain that the peasants' exodus to work on collectivised lands is merely because they are attracted for the time being by the novelty of the system, or that it is just the individual mind asserting itself in an undertaking only Socialist on the surface. Finally, it was noted that certain kolkhozy would not surrender the amounts claimed by the State, either deliberately refusing to meet these demands made by the towns or alleging that their own requirements were a prior consideration, so that the mentality of the kulak seemed to be transformed into that of a collectivist! Such reports and interpretations of the situation cannot be checked directly. Published figures and statistics are the only means for verification, and from these it is evident that sowings and cultivations have increased to a very great extent.

The total acreage under cultivation, as organised by the Corn Trust, rose in 1929 to 150,000 hectares, in the following year to 1,060,000 hectares, and in the present year should reach 14 million. Acreage controlled by the Central Committee, which at the beginning of the enterprise amounted to 430,000 hectares, attained 860,000 hectares in 1929, and by this year will amount to 2,500,000 hectares. Thus the Corn Trust alone at the completion of the Plan will have under cultivation an acreage as vast as the whole cultivated area of the Argentine. The various Soviet economic societies on the completion of the Plan will control 1,000,000 hectares of corn more than are now cultivated in the whole of Canada.

According to the Plan, in 1933 the total area under cultivation by all the Soviet departments will have amounted to 5,000,000 hectares. Actually 3,800,000 hectares were being cultivated in 1930 through Soviet agency, while it was estimated that last year, that is to say, the third year of the Plan, the total would amount to 8,000,000 hectares.

Whereas in 1928 the kolkhozy had under cultivation 14,000,000 hectares, the acreage in 1930 exceeded 36,000,000, an area as extensive as that in France and Italy combined. Since 1930 it has been possible for the kolkhozy to hand over to the U.S.S.R. more than half the corn marketed in the country. In so far as the kolkhozy have co-operated, the Five-Year plan has been realised and exceeded within two years.

According to the official statement the budget of the Republic was made up as follows: Labour and Peasantry —working without assistance—contributed in 1928, 75·2 per cent. of the total national revenue; this figure has risen to 77·1 per cent. in the following year. The kulak's and Nepman's share, representing 8·1 per cent. in 1927, fell to 1·8 per cent. in 1930. Percentage of revenue from home industries decreased from 6·5 per cent. in 1927 to 4·4 per cent. in 1929, while that of State-controlled industries rose from 8·4 per cent. in 1927 to 15·2 per cent. in 1929. Finally, under the heading of sundry expenses, of which the main item is the cost of pensions, was a sum representing in 1928 1·8 per cent. and 1·5 per cent. in 1930.

PUBLIC WORKS AND THE PLAN

In another part of the Plan it is intended to construct vast public works which will convert the old agrarian Russia into a modern industrialised country. Far greater facilities for the conveyance of goods by rail, as well as a rise of site values in the neighbouring districts, will result from the construction of the canal which is to link the Volga to the Don, and which will join up, at Stalingrad, those two great rivers, thereabout sixty-five miles distant from each other. Direct communication between the Caspian and the Black Seas will bring about many changes in the country's economic life. The fertile district stretching along the left bank of the Lower Volga will be able to export its cereals at lower costs from the Black Sea ports. It is estimated that the reduction in freights for the transport of corn to Rostov, a port on the Sea of Azov, will be not less than 12s. a ton. Timber from the Ural forests can be transported and delivered at the Donetz coal-mines, and coal from these pits conveyed at low rates to the industrial centres rising up on the banks of the Volga, even as far as Nizhni-Novgorod. As the extension of the canal from the Rhine to the Danube, the Volga-Don Canal will complete, it is calculated, the vast system of waterways from Europe to Asia.

THE TURKSIB

In the construction of the Turkestan-Siberian Railway (Turksib), to which we have already referred, the delays anticipated at the beginning of 1930 have been overcome and the line is now completed. In conjunction with the Volga-Don Canal it will prove a powerful factor in developing the prosperity of the districts in Central Asia. An ample supply of Siberian corn for the Soviet Republics in Central Asia will prove a substitute for the corn which those countries at present import from the Lower Volga, and cereals from that district will be freed for export to markets throughout the world in greater quantities. Moreover (and this is by far the most important purpose in the scheme), when Siberian corn is conveyed by the Turksib Railway, no more rice or corn need be grown in Soviet Asia and cotton can be cultivated extensively in their place. By thus growing its own cotton supplies, the textile industry of the U.S.S.R. will be stimulated to new activities by ever-increasing supplies of raw material; expenses budgeted for such items imported from abroad will be reduced and more machinery imported.

A NEW SIBERIAN PORT

In June, 1929, the Soviets presented the South Siberian Government with a seaport on the Kara Sea. Igarka, on the right bank of the river Yenissei, has anchorage for at least fifty large vessels. The port stands about 25 miles up the river, which flows into the Arctic Ocean. The clearing of the neighbouring forests was only begun in May, 1929. Clubs, schools, hospitals, electrical, meteorological and broadcast stations—all have sprung up in this untilled, ice-bound soil. A little farther north, schemes are prepared to work extensive seams in the surface mines, in which platinum, copper, cobalt and many rare minerals are to be found. The lines for the construction of a railway over the ice have been marked out. Part of the Siberian tundra, with its unknown wealth in mines and furs, will in the near future be opened up.

MAGNITOSTROY

Mount Magnitnaya, from which the Magnitogorsk Company, under formation, derives its name, enjoys a world-wide reputation; 255 million tons of minerals lie buried in its granite mass. The Company's huge excavators will extract annually 2,300,000 tons of minerals from this gigantic mountain. The most important mining centres of Europe seem dwarf-like compared with this colossus. It will surpass the largest mines in Europe in extent and equipment. At the foot of the mountain, till recently a wide extent of steppe, a town of 30,000 inhabitants has now sprung up, where a Socialist system is in full force and the living conditions in general have been to a very large extent Socialised.

The Company's engineers have undertaken that the mine shall be completely ready for working by 1 October, 1932. It was being partly worked in October of last year.

ELECTRIFICATION

"Communism is Soviet supremacy plus electrification" is one of Lenin's aphorisms. It is true that electrification, or in other words, the widespread application of the forces that set in motion a highly developed industry, is the basis of Socialism.

Since 1920 a Government Commission for the electrification of Russia has been working out a scheme to reorganise economic life throughout the country. This scheme planned the construction of thirty local electric stations of a global force of 1½ million kilowatts in ten to fifteen years. At the beginning of 1930 fourteen such stations with a global power of 527,000 kws. had been erected and were actually in working. Fourteen stations (with a total power of 974,000 kws.) were to be erected in 1930, and the construction started in the same year of thirteen stations with a total of 983,000 kws. The total power from all the electric State stations to be in operation by the end of next year will be 5,300,000 kws.; on the first of October, 1928, it was only 573,000 kws.

The Dnieprostroy on the Dnieper will be the greatest power station of Europe, with a power of 372,000 kws., which should be extended to 558,000 kws. Very high-powered electro-metallurgic stations will be set up along the coal basin to the south of Moscow, with an electric station at Bobrikov of 350,000 kws. and at Kashira of 205,000 kws., respectively. The Volkhovstroy, on the bank of the river Volkhova which flows into Lake Onega, is the first hydro-electric high-powered station of the Republic. The decision to erect a huge station on the river was taken in 1918. This station supplies Leningrad and provides 58,000 kws.

In 1917 in all the country districts of Russia there were only 117 electric stations. This figure included the small village stations which received the current from neighbouring stations. After October, 1917, the villages dispensed with the resinous torch in favour of paraffin, discarded in its turn for electric light. Since the Revolution many new electric stations have been erected in the villages. By the end of 1929 there were already 1,100 village stations with a total power of about 350,000 kws., far exceeding the 11,000 of 1917. The kolkhozy are beginning to construct their own stations, and electric power is not only used for lighting purposes, but also for work in the factories. In the near future, when living in the rural districts has been completely collectivised, electricity will have to be developed on a very extensive scale.

LABOUR SYSTEMS

Despite Bukharin and certain Socialists who themselves hold that its estimates were exaggerated and far too optimistic, the fact remains that Soviet-planned economy has achieved undoubted success and that the Five-Year plan itself is likely to be realised. Such a result is due to a Government which could arouse the keennest enthusiasm among the masses and, while it spurred them on to toil at tasks growing daily more arduous, promoted their well-being in mind and body to an extent which compensated them for such superhuman efforts.

While fiercely denouncing rationalisation under Capitalism, Soviet economists are wont to extol the system when enforced by their own party, claiming that the former aims at a widespread exploitation of the workers, whereas a corollary to Socialist rationalisation is the improvement of working-class conditions of life. Moreover, genuine rationalisation (in the etymological sense of the word) will always be impossible under a system so hopelessly anarchic as Capitalism. The aim of Capitalism is once and for all to eradicate the pest of plunder and blunder by rationalising all enterprises, which means that all commerce must come under rationalised control. This goal can only be attained by the Socialist.

Labour under conditions of slavery is held to be compensated for by a rise in pay and shorter daily hours. The working day was fixed at seven hours by the November, 1927, manifesto. A seven-hour working day should be established in all industries by the end of the Five-Year plan. According to Soviet anticipations, a seven-hour day will be succeeded by one of six hours and from 1943 onwards by a five-hour working day.

Production without intermission is one of the chief features of rationalisation in the U.S.S.R. and, though not yet so proclaimed, an attempt on the part of the Government to improve the workers' living conditions. The Law of 27 August, 1929, introduced the system of continuous labour in all Soviet industries and institutions. This innovation, so states the Law, should not in a single instance increase the total of working hours throughout the year. Before the passing of the Law a working year included 65 rest days (Sundays, Revolutionary Holidays and Saints' Days), and 300 working days. The new decree instituted a working year of 72 weeks, each of five days, with five Revolutionary holidays when all work ceases (22 January, 1 and 2 May and 7 and 8 November). Thus every worker does his four days' work and rests on the fifth day. Employees in industries or business houses where the week without intermission is the established rule are divided into five groups. These must be composed of the same number of artisans and employees. The weekly rest day ordained by law is granted simultaneously to all the employees in each group on a fixed day in each five-day week.

Thus Soviet workers obtain in all 70 rest days compared with 65 before the decree. By means of the week of uninterrupted labour, work with tools, lathes and other implements in the workshops is carried on, not for 300 days as formerly, but for 360 days in the year. Hence it should be possible to increase industrial output by nearly 20 per cent. without the investment of any additional capital. It is estimated that the increased production thus obtained has effected a saving of nearly two milliard roubles of fresh capital. With uninterrupted work the numbers of workmen will be increased by one-sixth and unemployment in consequence will be greatly reduced.

The system also affords the working classes not only longer hours of leisure but better chances of enjoying their recreations, for these are to be arranged on a system of shifts. A statutory distribution of rest days checks overcrowding of tramways and suburban trains and the rush to the parks, museums, cinemas and theatres on Saturday afternoons and Sundays.

But the great benefit to the State lies in the vast increase of production thereby obtained. As a result of continuous work the second year of the Plan witnessed an increase of output by 31 per cent. instead of the 24 per cent. anticipated. By 1933, the week of continuous working will have been enforced in all industries.

SOCIALIST RIVALRY

A foreigner examining with all due care the Plan at its present stage in this year of grace would rightly dismiss its realisation, even in part and incomplete, as beyond the wildest dreams of fancy. Such a view fails to realise the faith which moves mountains, that is to say, the fanaticism so subtly inspired by internal Russian Communistic propaganda. The bulletins of the Five-Year plan appearing in the forms of graphs arouse the liveliest interest, and are read as eagerly as the *communiques* of July, 1918, that brought to the Allied nations the good news of fresh advances. Industrialisation stirs the hearts of the Russian masses, just as the defence of their own country was the only thought in 1914 of French and Belgians. The very poorest follow the statistics and study the figures, and the sacrifices of every day are cheerfully endured in the cause of their Ideal, just as an ascetic counts suffering and privations as the glorification of his creed. Is this some magnificent conviction, or merely a cause championed to the verge of hysteria? The true answer is to be sought in reports from the most impartial witnesses, travellers least predisposed to Soviet sympathies. Such heart-felt sentiments translated into action have evoked even from many opponents of the undertaking unanimous expressions of good will.

One of the most remarkable features of present-day life in Russia is the rivalry that stirs all Socialists alike. Voluntarily, and of their own initiative, groups combine to check shirking, to obtain a bigger output and improve quality. Factories, kolkhozy and villages compete to see whose progress shall be the fastest, who can raise the best crops; they vie with each other in self-discipline and in the reduction of net costs. An expression borrowed from the army—shock troops—shows that labour possesses, or is about to appoint, its advance guards, its leaders of manual workers. These are transformed into technicians as far as possible, or at any rate into skilled workers; for the lack of these two classes of operatives, despite German assistance (in 1931 there were 14,000 German engineers in Russia), is one of the chief obstacles in the execution of the Plan. Of the total numbers of trained artisans considered necessary only one-fifth have so far been forthcoming—hence the importance of creating a highly intelligent proletariat and the employment of the most violent measures to stir the masses from their apathy. This eagerness goes by the name of *Cultural Revolution.*

EDUCATION

In the Tsarist Empire before the Revolution the number of illiterates was slightly over 72·2 *in the country and* 40·6 *per cent. in the towns.* "When the Revolution broke out no other country was so handicapped as Russia by the impossibility of replacing its former rulers by an intelligentsia sprung from the ranks of the people" (Jacques Lyon). In the general eagerness to solve the problem of illiteracy, parents and children, who were found to be of the same degree of ignorance, were taught side by side, but the adults objected that this system of co-education was humiliating to them, and special schools were started for their benefit, where they could remain blissfully ignorant that their progress was much slower than that of their offspring" (Alfred Fabre-Luce). There was a deficiency of school buildings, of desks, books and all such requirements, of trained teachers—indeed, of any school staff whatever. A mob of innovators and faddists barred the path of progress of Soviet education. Amidst such chaos and during the long presidency of M. Lunacharsky, a Communist author, a Bill of Compulsory Education for all classes was drawn up and passed in 1929. In the previous year 10,000,000 children had attended primary schools and this total was to be raised to 15,000,000 according to the Plan.

The main principle of Russian education, "One School for All," found its inspiration in the West. A preliminary investigation was made in Germany, so as to make a system originally French practical and effective. It should be noted that this plan of establishing schools suitable for all degrees of birth and intelligence still accupies the energies of the authorities. A Statute of the U.S.S.R. Central Executive Committee (16 October, 1928) provided for free schools for all, at which attendance was to be compulsory and which were to be worked on the co-educational system. But this Statute has never been enforced.

The Statute of Universal Compulsory Education was promulgated in June, 1928. Lunacharsky still retained his position as People's Commissar for Education. The Statute was the conception of the Gosplan. It was thus an integral part of the Plan. It enacted that compulsory education should be provided in the course of 1931 for all children over eight years of age. During that year the number of pupils reached a total of approximately 10½ millions. The cost of such education for the full five years of the Plan is reckoned at over £335,000,000 sterling. The Statute limits compulsory education to schools in towns, but in 1931 the system was extended to include villages as well. It is as yet too soon to estimate the extent to which it has been enforced. The first task was to combat illiteracy. From 1897 to 1920 (24 years), the total of men who could read and write was brought up from 33·7 per cent. to 44·6 per cent. and the total of women from 11·7 per cent. to 25·8 per cent. Between 1921 and 1927 (6 years) the proportion has increased, for men from 46·6 per cent. to 58·2 per cent., and for women from 27·8 per cent. to 44·4 per cent. Thus in the first stage of its struggle against ignorance, the Soviet Republic has made vast progress and at a rate unknown before the Revolution. But in 1930 there were still 18,000,000 illiterates from fifteen to thirty-five years of age, nearly all in the rural districts.

To the output of books the U.S.S.R. has devoted much activity with very fair results. All the totals of Tsarist Russia have been far exceeded. "If the importance of printed matter," Henry Béraud wrote with some satisfaction, "were to be measured in number and bulk, Soviet journalism might be said to be one of the most important in the world. Moscow pours forth throughout the whole country vast torrents of printed matter." In the year 1928, 570 Soviet newspapers were published, a total of 250 per cent. in excess of the pre-war numbers. In 1927, 253,000,000 copies of books were printed compared with 119,000,000 in 1913. Every year sees an increase in published works and the Plan anticipates that the number of books, excluding periodicals, will have increased to twice the present number of printed sheets by the end of the five-year period. During the same period there will also be a similar increase in the number of periodicals, 960 million sheets instead of 540 millions, while the circulation of newspapers published will be practically doubled. As far as books and papers are concerned, the requirements of the U.S.S.R. are literally endless.

THEATRE AND LITERATURE

The Russian Revolution has not yet managed to dominate the theatre. "People were starving, but they went to hear Chaliapin. The new Government continued its support of the artists and, though it has had to submit periodically to be used for lectures and for the staging of political plays, the theatre has always enjoyed certain immunities" (Luc Durtain). Like the Governments set up by the bourgeois, the dictators of the Russian proletariat pays to the stage and all that it represents the timid homage that it scorns to pay to religion and all its creeds. It would be only too pleased to transform the actor into some form of priest.

But it is in the cinema that the Soviet Government has discovered the means to further its most high-flown ambitions. Indeed, according to the Argentine writer, Arturo Mon, Lenin would probably have said: "Charlie Chaplin is the only person in the whole world whom I should have liked to meet!" Film-mania is rife throughout the whole Republic. The industry was at one time nationalised, but was later successfully exploited by State Trusts and normal private enterprise. From these helter-skelter efforts has emerged an art of which *The Battleship Potemkin* or *Troops of the Line* are typical examples. These films have been repeatedly hailed with enthusiasm by the world's film-fans. "The scenes are shown and immediately shifted, as if someone had touched a spring; perspectives driven into each picture apparently with sharp, brand-new tools, every moment calculated with mathematical precision and, in order fully to enhance the effectiveness of such bold methods, throughout runs an inherent simplicity" (Luc Durtain). In the year 1928 the U.S.S.R. had installed 8,500 cinemas. By the end of the Five-Year plan, this total should amount to 35,000. A Hollywood infinitely extended, to satisfy a proletariat who cry for the circus and will be given the limelight!

The race-courses have also been reopened in Moscow Is this the "Circenses," as represented by Longchamps or the Derby? Well, not exactly. "The names of the horses entered are Manifesto, Finance, Self-Government, Dollar, Down at Heels, and their respective owners are the Cavalry Division of the Ogpu, the Communist Military Academy Club, the National Rifle Club, the Moscow Mounted Police Squad and the Soviet of the People's Commissars in the Crimea. They are all trained at the 'Orient' national racing stable. This is a sign of the times. You might expect that some slight enthusiasm would be aroused as they thunder past the winning-post. But there have been no cries of 'Rifleman's Club!' or 'Communist Schools!' like the shouts of 'Rothschild!' or 'Jennings!' such as are heard at Epsom. Sometimes the band ventures on a dance tune. A horse neighs, a little boy bursts into tears. About half a dozen citizens troop off for their winnings and hasten to the bar" (André Beucler). This completes the picture of a Russia reborn, but by no operation of force or reason can the dear old vices of drink and gambling be left out of it.

"I cannot say whether former public galleries, like the Hermitage, used to be crowded by what some called the general public, and others the art-loving few. To-day, at any rate, the museums are thronged from early in the morning, and you may see troops of thoughtful sight-seers traipsing along and lecturers holding forth" (Georges Duhamel). In this reverence for the masterpieces of the past, this organised teaching of the beautiful and the opening of art schools to all and sundry lies the Bolsheviks' chief and irrefutable claim to the gratitude of all people of culture.

The system as applied to writers is somewhat stifling. After the period of stress, when authors and poets scarcely dared breathe, and had to struggle merely to keep alive, attempts were made to conscript writers in the fight for Marxist theories. Ever since its rise to power, the Government has aimed at employing literature to further its propaganda. But even under Bolshevism Russia has had her real poets who were inspired by their frenzied love of liberty, such as Alexander Block, Essenin, Pasternak, or such flamboyant writers as Babel. Governmental poetry has so far only produced a Demian Bedny, a Red Tyrtæus, who has degenerated into a sort of poetical clown of Communism. Maïakovsky, a kind of Russian Marinetti, whose suicide was as tragic as that of Essenin, had escaped from the toils of his own futurism. So far from having been driven from the field by the fierce and fiery prose works patronised by those in authority, there has been a renaissance of artistic realism in the works of many new writers. No revolution has ever had much use for its literature. "Life is vast," writes Seifullina, "whole volumes would have to be written to do it justice. Yet all things revolve endlessly around it. There is no time to write of them or relate them. It is best to furnish fragments." We live in an age when "only two things count, life and death" (Pilniak). So "modern Russian literature is blind to the playful fancies of a Gide or the witticisms of a Giraudoux; it is ignorant of the factors that go to make the strength or weakness of French writers, ignorant of ten centuries of tradition and Rome as well" (Vladimir Pozner). Literature remains what it was formerly, "the antithesis of Latin classicism: it is still unbalanced, with a tendency towards the unhappy and so towards the humane" (Paul Hazard). But the name of Gorky still shines forth, a beacon on the hill-top.

Again, the leaders of the October Revolution have every reason to congratulate themselves on the progress made in the Pure Sciences. In this branch all evidence points to the same conclusion—appointments have been very wisely made, especially that of the famous Professor Langevin in Mathematics and Physics, and Professor Portmann for Medicine and Surgery. In the Federal School of Science at Leningrad the professorial chairs have been or are held by some of the most distinguished scholars of our age, such as the eighty-year-old Savlov, one of the greatest scholars in experimental biology, the chemist Ipatiev, and the botanist Navachin (1858–1930), whose researches in microscopic cellulation are world-famed.

The Science Academy is granted a subsidy independent of budgetary restrictions. The U.S.S.R. make it a point of honour not to stint its teachers, those of them, at any rate, whose conclusions are not likely to wound the intellectual susceptibilities of Marxism; and this exception implies that, under the new Government, History will not fare as agreeably as the Integral Calculus. Metaphysics, like History, has to proceed warily in Moscow. Freedom for religious thought is severely restricted and many people in Russia to-day, like Frenchmen of former times, find this restriction the most oppressive of all to endure.

SOVIET ATTITUDE TOWARDS RELIGION

"Holy Russia!" That inspiring cry, which to-day is so full of unutterable longing, possessed a deep historical significance. But the American writer, Maurice Hindus (*Humanity Uprooted*, 1929), finds Russia sinking to such depths of moral degradation that he has nothing to say in defence of the legend of "Holy Russia," and stigmatises it as "mawkish and insipid." Was the Cross with its seven branches, thrown down with the Tsar, the Lord's Anointed? Has the Revolution nationalised souls as well as property? What flicker of old religious fervour still glows in the hearts of millions of Russians after fifteen years of Red Dictatorship? In the riddle of Moscow there is nothing so obscure or pitiful as the answer to these questions.

The October Revolution re-affirmed the promises of the Provisional Government by proclaiming freedom of worship and respect for the churches. Grants made to the various sects had been annulled on 2 February, 1918, in a statute signed by Mme. Alexandra Kollantay. A fortnight later, another edict defined the status of the churches and proclaimed the application of a universal formula of freedom. Orthodoxy appeared to be humbled to the status of the many creeds which the minority among the Faithful embraced so indiscriminately. For in the Old Russia every belief, or almost all of them, had its place—the Great Russians, Ukrainians, White Russians and Georgians being mostly Orthodox; the Poles and Lithuanians, Roman Catholics; the Armenians, following the Greek

Armenian Church; the Letts, Esthonians and Finns being Protestants; Tartars on the Volga and in the Crimea, Kirghizians and Bashkirs, Mohammedans; and Kalmuks and Buriats being mainly Buddhists. In the West, the Uniat Church, a community midway between Catholicism and Orthodoxy, which had adopted Eastern Liturgy while acknowledging the Papal supremacy, had to endure the cross-fire of interdicts and the proselytism of rival churches.

In 1917 the Orthodox Church ceased to be under Government control and became a free association of the Faithful. An age of religious equality was inaugurated through a country still echoing with voices muttering in prayer. Following its oppression of all faiths, the official attitude towards religion suddenly became neutral. Persecutions ceased altogether after 1917. Bolsheviks justly pride themselves on having forbidden all forms of vandalism and protected all that the religious hold most dear, but their respect for the Church is merely superficial. In practice, Orthodoxy, the State religion, has been replaced by a State materialism, which has no relation whatever with materialism as defined by Karl Marx. The only logical connection between the two is to be found in a phrase, a second-rate Marxist slogan: "Religion, the dope of the masses." This fantastic aphorism was written upon the walls around Red Square, just beside the Iberian Virgin, and as they passed by most of the Red officials were punctilious in saluting it by raising their caps adorned with the badges, so typical of Soviet rule, the hammer and sickle.

During the Civil War there were whole hecatombs of priests and monks, and in 1920, in the war against Poland, an onslaught on Polish priests; but this martyrdom of a few holy men was nothing compared to the ghastly wholesale slaughter of the Bolshevist Reign of Terror.

After all, life in churches and convents still went on during the terrible days of the Commune.

The most stupendous event was the Assembly of the Pan-Russian Church Council, which sat for a whole year (August, 1917, to 1918), and whose labours were not interrupted or disturbed by the tragedies in the world without its doors. While laws, morality and life in general were shaken to their foundations, this Council, assembled at the bidding of a few laymen, was trying to effect a complete reform of church legislation and to re-establish the Russian patriarchate suppressed in 1700. On the very day that Bolshevism rose triumphant, Archbishop Tykhon was proclaimed Patriarch. It is to be regretted that Russians in exile should have greeted this event as the first step in the restoration of the monarchy and thus afforded an excuse for reprisals of which Tykhon was destined to be the victim. The Patriarch was interned in the Donskoy Monastery and only regained his liberty in 1923. Two years later he died, leaving a will drawn up on his deathbed, in which he counselled obedience to Cæsar, support of the Government and repudiation of the refractory Bishops. Such a document was undoubtedly suspect and at once detected as a forgery, which would inevitably aggravate the grave dangers threatening Orthodoxy. Tykhon had been ordered to convoke an Assembly in 1921 and actually summoned it two years later, but professed that it had no power to act. Its members wrangled fiercely among themselves and the Patriarch of Constantinople, Gregory VII, was appealed to for a decision; this prelate repudiated Tykhon's action and the final result was the appointment of a rival hierarchy, known as the Synod or Concordat.

The patriarchal throne being vacant on Tykhon's demise, a "*Protector of the Patriarchate*" was appointed in the person of Peter Krutitzky, a minor official who had served in the Religions Department under Kerensky and who, having taken Holy Orders after the Revolution, was then elected Metropolitan in less than six years. His activities were opposed by the Synodal Church, the church of the reformers, whose spokesman was a priest of remarkable courage and eloquence, Bishop Vvedensky.

A confusion worthy of the Tower of Babel was the result. There were the Living Church (a Soviet invention), the Renaissance Church (another Soviet invention), the Old Catholic Church, the Workers' Free Church, not to mention churches independent of the Patriarch, of which the Ukrainian Church was the most important. In an age which followed its creed as fancy dictated, any sentiment that was not affected, scornful, or servile met with the same fate as the worship of the Supreme Being, or the Mysteries of the Mother-God, in the daring days of the French Revolution. Such compromises, which the Baptists and other such off-shoots of Protestantism permit to their adherents in similar circumstances, had results no less limited or precarious.

In this bankruptcy of Orthodoxy would it not have been possible for the Catholic Church to have composed its age-long differences with the Eastern Church? Unhappily, since the emancipation of Poland, the sovereignty of the Roman Catholic Church was confined to two dioceses and a few parishes scattered over the vast territory of Russia. Scarcely tolerated by the Tsars, spied upon and obstructed at every turn, Christian proselytism had made no progress in winning new converts. Two French priests, Father Amaudru and Father Pius Neveu, of the College of the Assumption, held office during the Revolutionary outburst, and in the following years. Changed indeed was the status of Catholicism in Moscow when Bishop Neveu, only consecrated on the previous day by Cardinal Herbigny, officiated at the Saint Louis-des-Français, clad in full vestments and with all pontifical pomp and ceremony. Surely the presence of a French bishop in Moscow would remove any grounds for suspicion on the part of the Soviets towards Catholics, whose Church had been represented previously by bishops of Polish extraction. Such, at any rate, was the spirit which animated the conversations held in Paris between the Presidents of the Soviet and French delegations, Rakovsky and de Monzie, and which prepared the way for the fulfilment by Monseigneur d'Herbini of his mission as Papal Legate.

But only a few hours after this solemn service the new Bishop was handed a letter of recall so abrupt and unreasonable in its expression that many hold that it was the outcome of some secret application from the Orthodox authorities, ever hostile, and lately even more embittered, towards the Church of Rome.

The Vatican, indeed, claims to be the centre of all authority and upholds this right with growing insistence, even in its attitude towards the Uniats, whose creed, indeed, has always been closely allied to the Roman Faith. "The Slavs jealously guard their individualism, and in all spheres of life favour methods based on the principles of autonomy. They distrust those principles of honour and unity on which the genius of Latin races thrives" (E. Despreaux, *Le Monde Slav*). So that when Stalin speaks in terms of deference of Christian customs (Easter, 1927) or refers with regret to "certain unpardonable offences in the struggle against religious prejudices" (Ordinance of the Central Committee, 14 March, 1930), these courtly phrases are intended for the ears of the Orthodox masses, whose susceptibilities it seems politic to appease.

"The battle on the religious front," that is to say, the attacks launched against all creeds by Soviet propaganda, was first started in 1925, and was not inspired by the doctrines laid down by Lenin. In that year, the first anti-religious Congress was held and the League of Atheists inaugurated. Other similar societies were formed in 1926, the "Down-with-all-Faiths" League for the Russians, the "No-Creed" League for the Ukrainians, and that of "Science and Religion" for the Mohammedans. The societies affiliated to this semi-official atheism had a total of a million members.

The formation of these leagues and societies—a movement which was viewed with satisfaction by the Government—was inevitably followed by further meddling with Church funds and fresh persecutions in the name of the Law. The Holy See and the English Churches sounded the note of alarm throughout the Christian world. The encyclical of Pius XI (February, 1930) was opposed by a campaign of protest which was not without certain picturesque features. Its protagonists included some universities, a college of dentistry, the Patriarch Christopher of Georgia, rabbis from Minsk, and a priest, Avglo de Mohilev, all of whom showed more enthusiasm for governmental affairs than they had done for doctrinal precedent and Concordats. Funds collected for aerial defence were utilised to construct a fleet of airships to be known as "*Our Answer to the Pope of Rome.*"

This ridiculous spectacle of a whole nation behaving like children, these tracts scattered broadcast in which any Western reader would at once recognise all the old claptrap of anti-clericalism, this truceless war against the various creeds, characterised by imprisonment of Orthodox priests, Armenian bishops, Muftis, and Sionists, seems to have aroused, at any rate in the towns, a recrudescence of that Slav mysticism to which Berdiaev has given such noble expression. "The poor, those who live from hand to mouth, the employees with their scanty wages, and especially the women, have found in religion a refuge where they forget the unbearable misery of their lives. Let anyone visit the tiny rooms, each with its ikon, and take part in the Church services at Easter or at Christmas and they will be convinced of this truth. Police persecutions and Government propaganda are powerless when confronted with such determination and endurance" (Paul Marion).

The resistance of the religious sects is intensified by every act of violence, every injustice which they are called upon to endure. In 1925 the Church of the Nativity at Rostov-on-Don had to pay a fine of 70,000 chervonetz (£7,200). Since the upkeep of the Russian Churches is undertaken by the religious associations after the system introduced by M. Briand, the devotion and spirit of self-sacrifice displayed by the Faithful and those by whose efforts the services continue to be celebrated, are indeed remarkable, especially in the present period of financial depression. Moreover, this conflict arose quite fortuitously and has no logical connection with the development of the revolutionary regime, while its unprecedented intensity has proved disconcerting even to the most indulgent commentators on Soviet history. The only plausible explanation of these persecutions is, perhaps, the fierce struggle for Soviet pre-eminence in the Catholic world and their fear that their propaganda may prove powerless among the civilised Powers that surround them, and beat in vain against the rock of Holy Scripture, Gospel or Koran. Has not Herman, the Bolshevist poet, called the Kremlin the Moujik's Vatican?

Finally, when Chicherin at the Conference of Genoa, was sipping his wine with the Archbishop, he certainly had in mind some form of alliance with the Papacy and was calculating upon the prestige which New Russia would gain from such negotiations. Some discussions are said to have taken place with this purpose in view; whether sincere or merely a pretence, they aroused the liveliest indignation among orthodox Christians and resulted some few months later in the arrest of Monseigneur Cieplak, Catholic Archbishop of Petrograd, and fifteen other members of the Catholic clergy, and in their sentence to death at the tender hands of Bolshevist justice. Once again, haunted by memories of the French Revolution, Bolshevism was led astray to follow the bad example of that movement by the evil that gnawed its vitals.

THE LAW AND THE FAMILY

Except for the Code drawn up by Nicholas I and the legislation introduced by Speransky (1833) and still in force, the only legal procedure in Russia had been such laws as were enacted by the Bolsheviks during the war period (1917–1921); the fundamental principle of these legal codes, drawn up on the impulse of the moment, hurriedly inscribed in 1922 and subsequently re-drafted, is to be found in Article 1 of the Civil Code. "All civil rights, unless exercised in a manner opposed to their economic and social purposes, are under the protection of the Law." This conception of the safeguarding of public interests, developed to an unlimited extent and, according to some authorities, due to the influence of Professor Duguit, "sets up the State as arbiter of civil rights in the light of its own interests" (Baron Nolde).

The most startling innovations in Soviet legislation are those dealing with the family.

The Family Code (1918), which comprises the laws of matrimony, family relations and those governing the custody of children and civil status, "proceed boldly to establish the right that ever figured as the foremost demand in the feminist programme by instituting marriage as a union of bodies and souls, but not of incomes—a sort of partnership on an economic basis (Art. 105); by refusing the husband the right of making his wife assume his name (Art. 103); by establishing complete freedom between married couples, not only with regard to their conjugal relations, but also to the upbringing of children under age (Arts. 148 to 151); by substituting for our paternal authority the 'rights of father and mother' (Arts. 149 to 158) which both parents can exercise equally and which, in the event of disagreement between them, can only be enforced after an appeal to the Tribunal set up to compose their differences (Art. 152). Having been formerly immersed in her husband's personal status, or 'covered' by it, a married woman's own legal status had gradually lost all association with rights and justice, save for the possession of certain authority in the household which she retained only by some relaxation in her dependent position, conceded to her in some cases at her husband's express command, in others by means of some provision made in her favour with regard to the spending of their joint incomes or to the disposal of her personal property. Generally speaking, she was allowed some control over the children—a right which the law had exclusively reserved to the father. The Code of 1918 removes all these disabilities at one fell swoop. The official appointed to enter in the records such particulars as are required for a marriage at a registry office, is empowered by the Family Code, in the case of persons of twenty-one years of age and upwards (Art. 67), merely to draw up a statement which both parties must sign (Art. 44)—he does not have to obtain the permission of their respective parents—to the effect that they are entering into matrimony of their own free will and that there are no legal impediments such as the prohibited degree of consanguinity or the ties of a previous marriage

(Arts. 59, 68, 70). It permits divorce, either by mutual consent of husband and wife, which can be declared in the presence of the appointed State official (Art. 91), who is authorised to grant the petition only if assured that the consent is mutual (Art. 92)—or by a petition for dissolution on the part of either of the parties concerned which must be heard in court, the decision of the court not being bound by the grounds for divorce enumerated in the Code (Arts. 87, 90, 93, 99). Bolshevist legislation far exceeds the system of laws prevalent in other countries in its reaction against parental control, in denying to father or mother as such the right to any lucrative or beneficial interest; in their enactment (Art. 160) that 'children have no right of inheritance to their parents' estate nor parents to their children's estate'—the sole exception being the duty of providing adequate maintenance (Arts. 161 to 170). Then as regards the laws of succession, which have been partly re-established, they contain no special rights or saving clauses such as are found in other European countries (Art. 422, Note).

"The Code also embodies principles which formerly figured in ancient French Law, such as that 'credence is to be given to the unmarried mother when pregnant as to the paternity of her expected child' (Arts. 140 to 144). But in the Soviet Code such enactments have been re-edited with much more practical effect and in conditions to which they did not previously apply, so that the illegitimate seem to encroach upon the rights so far reserved for the legitimate offspring.

"Its list of the laws of affiliation and its consequent obligations starts off with a statement very extensive in scope and distinctly dictatorial in phrasing.

" 'Affiliation,' says Art. 133, 'is recognised as the basis of the family. There is to be no distinction between children born in wedlock and the offspring of unmarried parents. And the legislator carries this concept to its logical conclusion, both from the point of view of the impediment to marriage caused by consanguinity, and also as to the application of the rights which spring from relationship' (Art. 172).

"The family as laid down in the Code of 1918 is much more strictly limited than that recognised and regulated by our Codes of the last century. It comprises only 'the direct line of descent and brothers and sisters; and placed on the same plane as the descendants and ancestors are married couples, who are also included.' Such a family system is therefore far less stable than ours.

"This law is distinctly opposed to that of other countries both in its uncompromising phrasing and for the political objects which it has in view. Yet most of its provisions, when examined one by one, will be found to be the natural outcome of a free and exuberant interpretation in the minds of the masses of the functions of the law, which it will oblige our own traditional system and jurisprudence gradually to adopt. In the same way as the legislative work of the French Revolutionaries completely changed the outlook of German and English jurists and influenced the evolution of their legal systems during the nineteenth century, so the ideas embodied in the Soviet Code cause the laws in force in Capitalist countries to be viewed in an entirely new light" (Edward Lambert).

LEGAL POSITION OF WOMEN

Is the Soviet desire for woman's emancipation prompted by their principle of freedom of worship for all alike? It may well be so, for, from the beginning, the word of command has been—"no cultural revolution without emancipation of woman in law and in practice." "*Every cook,*" said Lenin, who had a fancy for impressive slogans, "*should learn how to govern the State.*" Soviet women have equal rights with men in the management of the economic side of life and at elections. A woman may attend the board meetings of factory workers, hold important positions on the workshop syndicates, be a director in business concerns, or a member of the Board of Trade, while in the political sphere she may frequently be promoted to positions of responsibility. Women ambassadors, barristers or judges are quite normal features in the Soviet Republic.

NEW FORMS OF SOCIAL LIFE

The Russian Revolution has not confined its activities to finance. The State control of daily life is one of its policies. Its objects are as follows:

1. Freedom for servants from their domestic labours by Socialising the normal requirements of living. (Communal kitchens, laundries and nurseries.)
2. Freedom for women from the care of children by common State-organised school teaching.
3. A collective life under the most agreeable conditions, both on working days and rest days.
4. Absolute equality of treatment for the manual labourer and brain worker.

In the State of the future no individual will be required to prepare his or her own meals. On 1 October, 1928, the number of meals served daily was 720,000. At the end of the Five-Year plan 4,800 huge cooking factories will have been created and popular restaurants will provide meals for 5,600,000 persons.

Laundries, equipped with the most up-to-date machinery, will wash, dry, disinfect and iron linen in a few minutes, and so dispense with the washing day at home.

Swimming pools, baths and douches, installed on the premises of every factory and open at all hours of the day, will take the place of the family tub. At home, sweeping or cleaning by machinery, the instalment of electricity and central heating will relieve the population of all domestic cares. The education of children will be conducted entirely on Socialist methods. The youngest children are placed in public nurseries, close to their parents' places of employment. Children from three to ten years of age will be brought up in the children's cities. They will be taught the rudiments of gardening. From the age of seven to sixteen, they will live in the students' cities, where they will be instructed in such tasks as they will later be required to perform in factory or on farm.

Children's and pupils' cities are to be built at a convenient distance from the towns inhabited by adults. The entire cost of educating the children is to be borne by the State. In the early stages of the Plan parents will contribute part of their wages towards school expenses. Later on, a portion of their earnings will be paid direct into the Exchequer and will be added to the funds specially allocated for children's education.

THE HOUSING QUESTION

In the days of the Empire the towns still bore the stamp of feudalism and bureaucracy. "The typical town of that age," writes Grinko in the *Five-Year Plan,* "is a central building, generally well built, the headquarters of local administration and trade, streets of luxuriously appointed mansions standing in spacious gardens, belonging to the feudal classes, officials, merchants or rich business men, and then squalid suburbs, grey and gloomy, and devoid of all amenities, which house the toilers in general and the poor employees in particular. In no single town throughout Imperial Russia, before the Revolution, had the workers efficient drainage, water systems, electric light, tramways, or even pavements."

The Five-Year plan proposes to increase the housing space allotted to every inhabitant from 60 to 70 square feet. To obtain even this very moderate increase in living room there will have to be an increase of town-building surface of (approximately) 35 per cent., viz. 180 square miles in 1927 to 243 square miles in 1933.

URBAN LIFE

The Soviet Government also proposes to group Socialist towns built on the lines of their latest system around the industrialised centres. These new Socialist cities will have from about 50,000 to 75,000 inhabitants. They will consist of 25 to 50 huge blocks of buildings, erected on the latest town-planning system and separated one from the other by broad roadways and grass-grown parks, so that all who live in them will be spared from smoke, dust, unpleasant smells and noise.

In these Socialist cities will be spacious houses, equipped with all modern amenities, in which each worker will have his or her own room. Since all domestic requirements will have been Socialised, they will not contain any private apartments, kitchens or wash-houses. When he leaves his own room, intended mainly for his hours of rest, the worker will find at his disposal in the very house which he occupies a reading-room, library, a room where he may take his meals, a fully-equipped gymnasium, swimming pool, baths, club, etc. In addition to the collective dwelling-houses the Socialist town will have a theatre, a central library, a hall for meetings, a building to house the local officials, scientific laboratories and a sports ground.

Such is the Socialist city destined to spring up around the industrial centre. But since many great urban industries often work in conjunction with agricultural concerns in the treatment of raw products, it is intended to build Socialist cities, partly agricultural, partly industrial, until the kolkhozy have sufficiently developed for Socialist cities exclusively rural to be constructed

THE NEW MAN

"Man must ever be changing." Such was Clemenceau's answer to Jaurès, an answer subtle yet challenging. The Bolsheviks profess to have accepted this challenge. "The Revolution has raised up a new man; the citizen of the Republic of Labour" (Henri Barbusse). "A new mode of existence, the building up of a new life itself, called for a new type of man," writes suavely the young economist Sabsovitch, one of the creators of the Gosplan. "It is for us to re-create such a man." "All the old rubbish was swept away in October," proclaims that star in the firmament, Ilya Ehrenburg, who has the knack of sweeping away old-fashioned scruples like dust before her broom.

This attempt to re-cast human mentality is the most enchanting adventure ever yet essayed by Red Civilisation, easy enough when their efforts have only to be directed to exorcising old respects and beliefs, but extremely difficult when mankind, torn between its old creed and its own passions, has to be dazzled with prospects of rewards of lasting value. In 1923 Trotsky set out to institute a type of Soviet Puritanism, doubtless as a kind of reaction to the orgies which always follow a revolution. The trial of the famous Bolshevik Krasnoshtchekov (1923), condemned to death for misconduct in his private life, showed the general desire under the NEP for the correction of morals. The charges of dissolute conduct brought before the courts in Astrakhan, Baku and Smolensk, as late as 1929, recall memories of the French Revolution at the time when it proclaimed the Reign of Virtue.

What is to be said of such an ambition? What will be the verdict of the future on the Five-Year plan? "Appalling failure," said M. Poincaré (November, 1930). "Yet, who knows?" writes M. Paul Marion. "By sacrificing hundreds of thousands of slaves, the Pharaohs raised up the pyramids of Egypt." "I have another reason for my doubts," said M. Caillaux (December, 1930). "Some thirty years ago Count Witte was explaining to me in my room at the Ministry of Finance the vast project of national organisation which he had in mind. His programme has been lost, buried in the sand."

The answer to our question depends entirely on whether, with Count Witte's rule replaced by the new Government, a new man has been raised up in the place of the Tsar's subject. "If Russia comes forth from the difficulties that beset her as a country better equipped and more fully organised, then indeed our laughter and scorn to-day will echo sadly in the ears of our children" (Lloyd George, December, 1930).

CHAPTER X

BY WAY OF CONCLUSION

The army—Aviation—Navy—Communications—The moral problem—Conclusion.

Homo homini lupus! The antagonisms existing between man of the old type and man of the new type, whose advent has been heralded by the rise of Bolshevism, are much too violent for the West to view with anything but scepticism and definite hostility the outrageous and wicked conduct of a State which has been raised up into an all-conquering society. Surprised by the War of August, 1914, and still more so by Russia's defection at Brest-Litovsk, France cannot rid herself of the fear that, when those States which were recently her enemies seek revenge and form a coalition against her, their fighting strength will be greatly augmented by the support given them by her former allies. This feeling of apprehension has become more and more marked in the course of time and has led a great many French people to look upon New Russia as the auxiliary of the *ancien régime* in Germany. There are Germans—Herr Arnold Rechberg among them—who are convinced that such is the case and who denounce the intrigues which are being carried on by Bolshevist agents with the Nationalists and members of the Hitler group. "The Kremlin is working feverishly to kindle a fresh conflagration in continental Europe. It matters nought to the Red leaders whether Italy and Germany or France and Poland are the victors. They are certain that the ultimate result of a new European war will be the triumph of Bolshevism in every belligerent country, first among the vanquished and later among the conquerors. They believe that particularly little risk attaches to their stratagem since Moscow is, in their opinion, impossible to attack owing to the vast distances which separate the capital from Western and Central Europe" (Herr Arnold Rechberg's letter to the *Dépêche de Toulouse*, 16 October, 1930).

And then there are the Soviet reports which, in commenting on the economic crisis, give even a clearer impression that the U.S.S.R. is on the look-out for war: that it is preparing a great conflict and making ready for it. And so, amidst the endeavours to secure peace and establish reason, M. Clemenceau's haughty words often pass through the minds of those who anxiously survey the situation: "Between your country and ours, it is a question of force."

We are therefore obliged to reconsider the question and to estimate the effect of Russia's entry into a European conflict—should such a catastrophe again occur.

For there is a Red army similar in its equipment to other armies, but imbued with a different spirit.

THE ARMY

In Soviet Russia, the risk of war is not invested with the same conditional, intermittent character as in our Western democracies: it is foretold in the *Communist Handbook* (the Party members' "missal," published annually by the *Muscovite Worker*), and described as the inevitable, logical uprising of the old world against the might of the new. The U.S.S.R., Revolution's sentry, must stand ready, always armed. In order to defend the Revolution itself, and later to hold fast to its conquests, the Bolshevist programme has always made provision for an army, for the leaders of the movement "believe in the bayonet thrust, not only as a means to break down tyrannies and free oppressed nations, but to deliver the proletariat from Capitalist exploitation" (Léon Blum).

The Red army was created on 23 February, 1918, a date which is always commemorated.

In 1913, the numerical strength of the Tsarist army was 1,400,000 men. During the period of Militant Communism, from 3,800,000 to 5,000,000 men served under the Red flag. This amazing feat of improvisation belonged to Trotsky. Between 1921 and 1924, when the general situation had improved after the introduction of the NEP and the restoration of internal peace, the armed forces were gradually reduced to 1,590,000 in 1922, 703,000 in 1923 and to 562,000 in 1924. This last figure gives the total number of Russian effectives in the U.S.S.R. since 1924.

The organisation of the Russian army is the outcome of the decree concerning compulsory military service issued on 18 September, 1925, and confirmed by the decree of 8 August, 1928, in virtue of which all citizens between the ages of nineteen and forty are obliged to serve in the armed forces. After two years of military service in regional training centres (this system is not yet fully developed) conscripts must, in theory, serve another three years.

"When called up, conscripts are posted by the recruiting board to the regular army, or to territorial units, or are placed in a special category forming reserves for the classes with the colours. For this reason, there are great variations in the length of service.

"Young men who are incorporated into regular units and the regular forces of territorial units are obliged to serve two years in the army and air force, and three years in the navy. Following this period of service, they are regarded as having been granted a period of long leave. During this time, they may be summoned to follow an instructional course for one month per annum. Men who are appointed to territorial units come up for training courses which vary in length from year to year, five months being the period for the first year, and two to three months in the following years. These training periods may not exceed ten months in all.

"Young men placed in the category forming reserves for the classes with the colours must attend training courses which last six months in all and which are distributed over the five-year period of their active service.

"All young men belonging to these various categories are placed in the reserve at the end of their fifth year's service. During the thirteen years that they remain reservists, they are liable to recall for training periods which last three months in all.

"Military law is not based on the principle of equality of burdens. Young soldiers may be posted to any unit, and on their appointment depends the nature and difficulty of the duties which they are called upon under law to perform. Russian conscription classes comprise, on an average, 1,200,000 men, of whom 900,000 are passed as fit for military service. A little less than one-third of this number are posted to the regular forces, one-quarter to territorial units, and the remainder, or approximately three-fifths, are placed in the category comprising reserves for the classes with colours. In the event of a call to arms, certain reservists belonging to cavalry groups are obliged to rejoin their corps with their horses; others belonging to the commissariat, with their teams. Extremely complicated in principle, this military law is all the more so in practice" (Colonel Reboul).

It is very difficult to estimate the numerical strength of the Russian standing army from outside owing to the arbitrary or complicated system of its organisation. According to some experts, it is 1,500,000 men when the territorial units are mobilised, but some estimates are as low as 700,000 or even 562,000.

The land forces are composed of twenty-eight infantry and seven cavalry divisions, also seven brigades of independent cavalry, all of which are regular units, and forty-two infantry and four cavalry divisions which are territorial units. Each infantry division is composed of three regiments of infantry, one of artillery, a squadron of divisional cavalry, a company of sappers and one signal company. Owing to the vastness of the sectors in which all these units may be called upon to operate independently, the infantry regiment in the Russian army has a greater developed autonomy than is found in Western armies.

"The infantry regiment is composed of the following units: A detachment of mounted scouts, a signal company, a chemical section, a sapper company, an artillery unit (two batteries of three 76 mm. guns each) which is part of its proper complement and three battalions. These last are numerically very strong, for they each include: three companies of light infantry, a machine-gun company and an artillery section composed of one 37 mm. (1·4 inch) gun and a 58 mm. (2·2 inch) trench mortar. The artillery regiment itself is composed of mixed groups. The first and second groups comprise two batteries of 76 mm. guns each and a battery of three 122 mm. (4·7 inch) guns: the third group is formed by two batteries of three 76 mm. guns and two batteries of 122 mm. (4·7 inch) guns" (Colonel Reboul).

The greatest difficulty met with in Soviet military organisation has been the recruitment of officers. In 1914, the Russian army was staffed by 50,300 officers, of whom 35,000 were mobilised. During the War, it was found necessary to train 214,000 officers, whereas France, with a nucleus of 30,000, had to aim at the training of 200,000 officers.

At the present time, 50 per cent. of the officers are of

working-class origin, 28 per cent. only belonging to the old bourgeoisie; and 48 per cent. are members of the Party, 4·8 per cent. are Consomols and 47 per cent. are non-party men. It is important to notice how great is the anxiety of the Soviet Government to keep this army, on which the fate of the regime depends, in closest contact with Communist theories.

Finally, the O.G.P.U. detachments must not be omitted: they represent a considerable force of mobile gendarmerie of which the Fascist army is the only parallel.

AVIATION

Always greatly attracted to science and carried away by scientific hopes and ambitions, Russia looks upon future wars from the viewpoint of discoveries in aviation and chemistry. With the object of ensuring her complete independence of foreign contractors, she has built factories for the manufacture of apparatus and engines. An immense company, the Ossoviakhim, has by means of collections, deductions from salaries and special taxes accumulated a special fund—entirely separate from State revenues—which is destined to finance the development of aviation, the purchase of aerodromes, the training of pilots, as well as to provide for chemical research in methods of gas warfare, both defensive and offensive. Measures are being taken for the individual instruction of the people in anti-gas protective methods and special organisation is being introduced to this effect: this is a movement to alter the present state of affairs in which the people are "unaccustomed to chemical processes." Some experts go even further, and are prepared to see the adaptation of the civil structure of society to military needs in the eventuality of war, which is considered inevitable.

In Russia, as elsewhere, perhaps more in that country

than anywhere else, profiting by the progress made in foreign countries and even more so by the discoveries of German experts—readily communicated by them to the Soviet—continual improvements are being conducted in the air force and the "chemical arm."

What is the composition of the air arm of the Red army? There are approximately 150 to 178 squadrons, comprising 1,400 to 1,900 aeroplanes, or 45 chaser squadrons, 21 bombing squadrons, 84 scouting squadrons, 120 fighting planes and 110 seaplanes. The machines in service are of the following types: Fokker, Nieuport, Blériot, Spad, Czechoslovak, Handley-Page, Potez, Ansaldo, Bréguet Savoia and Machini, representing the makes of European and American firms.

Garrisons are found throughout Soviet territory: ample provision for the air force has been made at Smolensk, Kiev, Tashkent, Kharkov and Moscow.

Training is given by a military Faculty and a technical Faculty. A school for pilots and the personnel of the technical branches possesses up-to-date laboratories. There are also schools for pilots at Katchka (Sebastopol), Borisoglebsk and Odessa; at Volsk there is a special school for pilots and mechanics, and at Orenburg a school of aerial combat, apart from the school for specialists of non-commissioned rank, attached to each aerial brigade. Finally, there are seaplane schools at Sebastopol and at Leningrad, where there is also an advanced school of aerostatics. This general system of training was established between 1927–1928.

THE NAVY

"Quite recently, a cruiser and two destroyers belonging to the Black Sea fleet passed through the Dardanelles and cruised about the Eastern Mediterranean, afterwards returning to their base. Of this the League of Nations was notified by the Straits Commission. This sortie, or rather this escapade, following close upon the passage through the Straits, some time previously, of a group of Russian men-of-war which was proceeding from the Baltic to reinforce the Sebastopol base, caused something of a sensation. The vessels from the Baltic included three cruisers and nine destroyers."

What is the importance and combative strength of the Russian fleet? "We must have 490,000 tons," Admiral Behrens declared at the Rome Conference in 1924.

According to official reports, the tonnage of the Baltic and Black Sea fleets would appear to be distributed as follows: four battleships of 23,000 tons and 23 knots, each armed with twelve 11·9-inch guns; a battle-cruiser of 17,200 tons and 21 knots, armed with four 9·9-inch and eight 7·9-inch guns; five cruisers of approximately 6,000 tons and 30 knots, armed with 5-inch guns; a seaplane carrier; eighty destroyers and twenty submarines. There are, besides, two destroyers and three submarines in process of construction.

The recruitment of the personnel gives every satisfaction, but ships' companies have a tendency to mutiny. Service traditions have been maintained.

But in the event of war the navy would find but little support forthcoming from the merchant fleet. Unlike England and even France, Russia cannot rely upon her merchant fleet as a reserve force for the strengthening, in an improvised form, of naval action.

Merchant shipping and the equipment of seaports have never been developed to any great extent in Russia. More than any other branch of national economy they suffered damage as a result of the Revolution.

In 1927–1928 the movement of merchandise in the sixteen chief Russian ports (Leningrad, Rostov-on-Don, Novorossisk, Odessa, Nikolaiev, Mariupol, Tuapsi, Murmansk, Kherson, Batoum, Baku, Archangel, Kertch, Enikale, Poli, Vladivostok) formed but 53 per cent. of the pre-war figure.

In 1928 the merchant fleet of the U.S.S.R. consisted of 1,377 vessels amounting to 227,443 tons gross, or 29 per cent. of the pre-war tonnage. It is important to note that the fleet of oil-tankers comprised as many as sixty-three vessels totalling 50,995 tons gross or 69·6 per cent. of the pre-war figure. This is explained by the importance of the transport of petroleum products.

In 1926 the U.S.S.R. was able to carry under its own flag only 5·7 per cent. of goods shipped to or from Soviet ports. The Government hopes to increase this proportion —but by only 20 per cent.—during the period embraced by the Five-Year plan.

The grand total of sea-borne merchandise is inferior to the pre-war figure. In 1927–1928 it only represented 20·4 million tons as against 36·8 in 1913. It is hoped that during the financial year 1931–1932, the figure will reach 33·9 million tons.

In consequence of this state of affairs, the Soviet Government is paying special attention to the building of merchant vessels and to the orders for ships placed abroad.

A considerable number has been constructed in different countries, France included. At the beginning of 1930 negotiations were opened with French ship-building firms, but nothing came of them. The order was then passed on to the Italians. Quite recently, the Press announced that a Soviet Commission had visited Italy and placed numerous orders. But these are plans which have still to be carried out and they need not, therefore, be discussed here: what has been actually accomplished is of a definitely mediocre character.

COMMUNICATIONS

The greatest need of the U.S.S.R. is an adequate system of railways. The system at present in operation in the Union owes its development to French capital in pre-war days. These railways, which were supposed to be strategic and indispensable on account of the inadequacy of the general railway system and water-communications, were paid for by French capital investments. But three years of civil war resulted in the destruction of 21,250 kilometres of permanent way, 3,672 bridges, 175,000 kilometres of telegraph and telephone lines and of more than 10,000 telegraph poles.

The length of railway lines in operation, which in 1913 was 58,000 kilometres, has (despite the wholesale destruction in the years 1918–1920) increased to 77,032 kilometres in 1928–1929 and should amount to 83,607 kilometres in 1932. This figure includes the 1,494 kilometres of railway line between Siberia and Central Asia. The Turksib, a strategic line which also serves economic interests, links the rich Siberian corn-fields with Turkestan where the land is irrigated and favourable to cotton-growing.

The other railway system of first-rate importance is the Moscow-Donbas line (1,067 km.). It is to be utilised for the transport of coal direct to the industrial districts of Central Russia.

In 1913 the Russian railways carried 132 million tons of merchandise. In 1928–1929 the corresponding figure was 176 million tons, which shows the remarkable progress made since 1913. The increase is particularly marked as regards the transport of cereals, coal, naphtha, wood-fuel, timber, iron and steel.

In 1913, the number of passengers carried by the railways was 25·2 milliards. In 1927–1928, the corresponding figure was only 22·7 milliards: but every year now sees an increase in passenger traffic.

Soviet reports emphasise the technical transformation of the railways. Bridges and embankments have been strengthened. The number of high-powered, up-to-date locomotives (steam and hydro-turbines) forms 45 per cent. of the total as against 27 per cent. in 1913. Consequently, the average composition of trains is 94·13 double-axle loads whereas in 1913 it was only 78·8. A truck-load, formerly 7·8 tons, is now 8·8.

The number of goods trucks in 1928–1929 was 475,000 and of passenger wagons 25,000. Railway receipts have exceeded two milliard roubles.

Finally, it should be noticed that the railways employed 1,149,000 persons in 1928–1929, the average monthly salary being 78 roubles (£8). Great difficulty has been experienced in increasing this number—or even in maintaining it—despite the intensive methods of recruitment employed.

Soviet reports emphasise the great efforts being made towards the construction of roads. The Press announces that negotiations have been opened with big American contracting firms which are to provide technical assistance and material.

Both road communications and means of conveyance are very indifferent. Even in 1926–1927 Russia, with a population of 150 millions, possessed only 18,000 motor-cars. The estimated figure for 1928–1929 was 28,000 and for 1920–1930, 30,000 motor vehicles. The figure fixed by the Five-Year plan for the end of 1933 is 893,000, which is to include 70,000 motor bicycles. At Nizhni-Novogorod, which is even now known in Moscow as the Soviet Detroit, factories are being built, and they should turn out 140,000 Ford cars per annum, twenty-four every hour or one every two-and-a-half minutes. The construction of these factories was begun in May, 1930, and completed in the autumn of 1931.

In the same way, the Soviets have begun to develop the water-ways. In 1927–1928, 90,000 km. of Russian rivers were navigable and 176,000 km. were utilisable for lumber purposes.

River transport in 1913 was estimated to be 47·6 milliard tons. In 1927–1928 it was only 45·2 millions.

The Soviet Press draws special attention to the efforts to be made under the Five-Year plan for the development of the canals and locks. The famous Mariinsk system, which connects Leningrad with the Volga, is to be completely transformed.

The projects which have been outlined above—together with any others that have not been mentioned—will depend for their realisation on the success of the Five-Year plan. Russia's destiny hangs on this econnomic victory, just as the fate of France hung in 1918 on the favourable issue of the War. In her struggle, which is of a different kind, Russia has reached that long drawn-out stage which is characterised by the application of rationing systems and coercive methods—that stage when the "morale behind the lines" forms one of the primary factors in national resistance.

THE MORAL PROBLEM

On this side of the Universe we are busy speculating on the failure of dictatorships. As regards Russia, a great many people have lost in gambling on her fall, or are now revising their positions as the years pass by. These gamblers invariably ask travellers back from Moscow: "Will it be this spring? Can they last long now?" "However crumbling their economic and moral foundations may be," replied M. Paul Marion in 1930, "dictatorships have at their command—particularly when there is the complication of a State system—unlimited possibilities and scope as regards their action which upset even the best founded prophecies." He had in mind, it is true, the possible evolution of Communism towards Socialism through the suppression of propaganda and as the result of a Socialist offensive of which there has been hitherto no trace in the manifestations of the Second Internationale. In fact, Red Russia has drawn back or concentrated her attention upon herself with the object of carrying out her great internal reforms. "*The theory of Socialism followed out in one country alone leads inevitably to the under-estimation of the difficulties which must be overcome and the exaggeration of what has been accomplished,*" wrote Trotsky, who looked upon this theory as "*the fountain-head of inevitable Social-patriotic follies.*" But because a State must live, and to live must make progress, and to make progress must equip itself, and in order to find the necessary equipment must suffer privation, the national aims of the Soviet Union are, despite Trotsky's warnings and criticisms, being gradually advanced by the stoicism of the revolutionaries. Certainly the Komintern is not idle, the international apparatus still exists, the Soviet State and the Communist Party remain linked together, if not unified. But the fierce flame of revolution has been turned so as to burn within. Other countries are not faced with the smallest danger; but there is another danger. It is not the faith of Soviet Russia that is different to others, it is the exercise of this faith.

Its exercise is not free from conduct which, measured by Western standards, is disconcertingly lacking in propriety. A recent trial of *saboteurs* which was staged, regulated and filmed as a means to rouse public enthusiasm, showed how the administration of justice might be utilised to stir up popular feeling: the noisy manifestations of penitence on the part of the accused men, their obvious mistake in introducing the names of foreign celebrities into the proceedings, and the sentences which are prematurely reduced by the grant of an amnesty or of special favours which make a mock of the trial—it is these happenings which lead us to believe that at Moscow there is a highly developed machine for the manufacture of enthusiasm.

This enthusiasm has been exported to a lesser extent since the Chinese Revolution ended in disaster, for the expense and the disappointments of that affair were certainly heavy and bitter enough to justify the return of all-conquering Communism to its native land. Every nation that lives on in expectation, readily making sacrifices, prefers on the whole to pass the time of waiting and of sacrifice in the trenches which are familiar to it. No Marxist spirit can prevail over this eternal, universal psychology whose offspring is patriotism.

Can it be described—to employ the Party jargon—as a *deviation from the official course*? Whether this is the case or no, it is no concern of ours to ascertain the truth. The only aspect of the situation that must be remarked is the synthesis of pride and Communist mysticism which now represents the spiritual endowment of the Five-Year plan. This synthesis has been effected deep down in the heart of the nation, but it finds contradiction in its affected attitude of suspicious internationalism. The Russian's love for Russia fills Communists' hearts, but according to these same Communists "the Soviet Union is but a place of refuge while the whole world is the field of action." One phrase is enough to convey this attitude of mind.

"On leaving the barracks after a visit to a regiment, I reflected that the army must certainly be called Russian since its administration lay entirely in the hands of the Moscow Government and the words of command were given in Russian. But when I made a remark to this effect much surprise was shown.

" 'No, Monsieur,' the colonel said to me, 'you have not seen a regiment of the Russian army but a regiment of the Red army. Our army is not national but international. If Russian is still the only language spoken in it, well, that is only an accident' " (Pierre Dominique).

CONCLUSION

Regarded with loathing by some and the greatest interest by others, a civilisation has been developing in Russia since the Revolution of October, 1917. Its ideals and methods—these may be denied: but not its dynamic force.

According to some, it is *a purgatory where men are cowed by relentless force.* To others who have suffered injury to themselves or damage to their property, it is an inferno, pure and simple. "We will never admit that the object of the movement is all that matters, that the end justifies and sanctifies the means," exclaimed Léon Blum. "The League of Nations alone," declared another great Socialist speaker, Charles Spinasse, "possesses sufficient authority to decide that only those States which come to an agreement concerning world peace and the limitation of armaments, and *who respect political liberty,* shall benefit from the international credit system." (Applause on the Extreme Left, the Left and several benches in the Centre. . . .) The Social-Democrats are waiting and hoping for the conversion of Communism to the creed of ritual democracy. This attitude of waiting and hope represents a policy or at least a political outlook.

Though holding to entirely different theories, Russian *émigrés* and French republicans all, more or less, attempt to judge the downfall of the Russian Empire and the regime that followed that upheaval by historical precedent. As for the great event of February, 1917, Montaigne's phrase is not inapplicable to it: "*Those who shake the foundations of the State are naturally the first to be swallowed up in its ruin. The fruit of the trouble does not remain with him who stirred it up; he beats and disturbs the water for other fishermen.*"

It seems an impossible task to bring on to the same plane for comparison with our own country's past history the frenzied yet constructive theories of a period which is so intense, so complicated, that it is beyond human power to portray. A Tocqueville out of his period, M. Henri Rollin has written three learned volumes of philosophy in an attempt to compare the spirit of the two revolutions; they do credit to his remarkable powers of analysis and also to the varied nature of our revolutionary origins. It remains none the less evident that the Russian Revolution is not a new edition of the old story with its glorious deeds and bloody incidents: it is a movement which has nothing in common with the past though its songs have been sung before and its march music and gallant airs are burnt into the memory of all peoples.

"*The French people,*" Robespierre declared, "*seem to have outstripped the rest of the human species by* 2,000 *years: there is even a temptation to look upon the French in the midst of other peoples as a species apart.*" There is a kinship of pride between the two Revolutions: the *Carmagnoles* which Barère sang at the tribune of the Convention thunder out, increased in volume by the artifices of propaganda, from all the loud-speakers of the Russian Revolution. The Committee of Public Safety defied Pitt and Coburg, the Politbureau defies *en masse* counter-revolutionary nations: the method is different, the inspiration is the same.

But it is not enough to discern the elective affinities of Lenin and Robespierre, to diagnose the nervous obsessions of Paris of 1793 in the development of the Moscow Reign of Terror, to estimate the heterogeneous influences of Bakunin and Clausewitz in a martial programme which is inspired by Brissot's age-distant words of counsel. The specific characteristics of the Russian Revolution must be recognised—that peculiar fervid enthusiasm with science as its basis, and that regulated dictatorship, mercilessly regulated, which, for the first time in history, rules over national economy.

"What can I, a Frenchman, learn from Bolshevism?" wrote Alfred Fabre-Luce. "Fear. It seizes me in its grip when I see this great country drifting away, breaking off from Europe like an island vast enough in itself to form a continent" (*Russie*, 1927). Fear—that may be an exaggeration or an under-estimation. I have endeavoured to awaken other sentiments by suggesting other points of view than those dictated by a fear that is born of hatred. It is my greatest hope that, as far as in me lay, I have written one of the rough drafts of peace which will be of service to future generations.

INDEX